7 Little White Lies:
The Conspiracy to Destroy the Black Self-Image

By

Jabari Osaze
Inspired by Dr. Edward Robinson

African Genesis Institute Press
Philadelphia, Pennsylvania

7 Little White Lies: The Conspiracy to Destroy the Black Self-Image

By Jabari Osaze
Inspired by Dr. Edward Robinson, Jr.

Published by
African Genesis Institute Press
P.O. Box 682
Glenside, Pennsylvania 19038
www.AfricanGenesis2.org

Cover Design: David Myers, Melanation Design Works
Interior Design: Jabari Osaze

Library of Congress Control Number: 2016903894

ISBN-13: 978-0692657676
ISBN-10: 0692657673

First Printing
March 2016

TABLE OF CONTENTS

About the Cover

Our cover photo comes from the David Hoffman/Boaz postcard collection which is part of the Smithsonian Institution's National Museum of American History. The 1898 photo features a white woman in fine Victorian clothing perched on a fancy chair while feeding a crying, naked, African American infant like an animal. How many collections of painfully racist photos are still sitting in attics throughout the United States?

This disturbing photo is an appropriate analogy for the thesis of this book. We continue to be fed by those who despise us and seek to prevent us from living into our full potential. They benefit from our stunted condition.

The author wishes to thank David Myers of Melanation Design Works for his wonderful cover design.

Dedication

Dr. Edward Robinson, Jr., J.D.
April 24, 1918 - June 13, 2012

Educator, historian, and author, Dr. Edward Robinson, Jr., was an advisor to the founders of the African Genesis Institute. He created the Institute's primary curriculum and served as the elder to its staff and participants. His life journey was set in motion when his maternal grandmother told him of the story of his family's ancestral origins in Benin City, Nigeria. He would spend his life uncovering the truth about African people. These efforts would result in the infusion of African and African American history into the curriculum of Philadelphia's public schools.

Dr. Robinson obtained his undergraduate degree from Virginia State College, his Juris Doctor degree from Temple University School of Law, and an honorary doctorate from Virginia State University. He managed two African American owned insurance companies, serving as the president of the Provident Home Life Insurance Company and the vice-president of the North Carolina

Mutual Insurance Company. He also served on the board of directors of the Federal Reserve Bank of Philadelphia.

Dr. Robinson's study led him to articulate the root cause of the problems that disproportionately affect people of African descent worldwide. Africans have been programmed by Europeans to hate everything African about ourselves. Dr. Robinson argued that four things needed to be done in order for African Americans to overcome the psychic trauma caused by this extensive misinformation campaign, our enslavement, and racial subjugation:

1. Raise race esteem by teaching ancient African history;
2. Increase financial and academic literacy (leaders read and readers lead);
3. Promote healthy lifestyles; and
4. Encourage entrepreneurship (make jobs don't take jobs).

One of the key mechanisms towards Dr. Robinson's goal was this book, which he inspired, *7 Little White Lies*. In authoring this book, we honor this illustrious ancestor. In his memory we seek to restore the rightful place of our African foremothers and forefathers.

Acknowledgements

Many thanks to Helen and Ali Salahuddin, founders of the African Genesis Institute, who have taken thousands of Diasporan Africans back to Africa. Over the years we have become much more than colleagues. We are family.

To Dr. John Henrik Clarke and Dr. A.A. Yosef Ben-Jochannan who educated and encouraged a young Cornell University student.

To my parents, Jeanette and Winfred Jacobs, for their endless love and support. I am because they made me who I am.

To my wife, Anika Daniels-Osaze, who has supported me in ways that I didn't even realize I needed. She has viewed every image and read virtually every word in this book. Her assistance was invaluable.

INTRODUCTION

lie (laɪ) *noun*:
   plural lies
   1. Something untrue that is said or written to deceive
   someone.[1]

little white lie (lɪtḷ waɪt laɪ) *idiom*:
   plural little white lies
   1. A small, usually harmless lie; a fib.[2] A lie about a
   small or unimportant matter that someone tells to
   avoid hurting another person.[3]

What is a lie? What are its effects? Can a lie be more dangerous
than a physical injury? Can it be more lasting and harmful than
broken bones? There have been many things that have been said
about people of African descent that number amongst the vilest of
human utterances. How are African Americans affected by these
mistruths?

A 2012 study by Indiana University published in *Communications
Research* aptly describes the harm done by the false, negative
representations of people of African descent.[4] The researchers
surveyed nearly 400 boys and girls between the ages of 7 and 12
from an array of racial and cultural backgrounds. They were
investigating whether there was a correlation between the time the
children spent watching television and their self-esteem. Their
findings were more stark and disturbing than virtually anyone
could have expected.

While nearly all of the subgroups of youth in the study saw
declines in self-esteem as the hours watching television increased,
one group seemed to benefit from *more time in front of the TV*.
Young boys of European descent who watch television feast on
depictions of themselves as powerful, wealthy, attractive, and in
control of their lives. They see themselves portrayed as
superheroes, secret agents, gods, cowboys, astronauts, soldiers,
scientists, kings, and lady-killers. While they aren't always
depicted as heroes, they are almost always the main character in

these representations. They have a choice. White boys were the *only group in the study to see their self-esteem increase as their TV watching hours increased.* By contrast, the self-esteem of African American boys was most damaged as they were inundated with depictions of themselves as criminals, victims, villains, and intellectual inferiors.

These findings are particularly troubling since African American and Latino youth watch an hour more of television per day than their European and Asian peers.[5] Youth of African descent are receiving a larger dose of the poisonous concoction which steals their confidence and their sense of themselves. While many wonder aloud why our youth continue to underperform in a wide array of educational areas, we must understand that their potential is being quietly stolen under the watchful eyes of their parents as they sit in front of the family TV. The painful lies that have been told about people of African descent have a tangible effect on its most important and cherished members. This book seeks to unravel some of the most prevalent and destructive lies about Africans.

The title of this book, *Seven Little White Lies: The Conspiracy to Destroy the Black Self-Image*, posits that these "untruths" have been intentionally crafted to harm the emotional and psychological well-being of people of African descent. However it is most interesting that in the "age of Obama", many still believe that the lies we will cover in this book are either completely true or at least relatively inconsequential. A 2011 Harvard University study found that while both African Americans and European Americans feel that racism against African Americans had diminished, whites actually believe that racism has been nearly eliminated.[6] In fact, the whites in the study actually believed that they were currently greater victims of racial bias than African Americans! In this text, we will prove that the fallacies that negatively affect the manner in which African Americans are viewed (and more dangerously, view themselves) are certainly not innocuous. They are not "little white lies". They are actually just as damaging as they are common. We will identify them, refute them, and even describe the effects of their continued prevalence. This book will be a manual for the restoration of the Black self-image.

On Terminology

The words we use are never unimportant. They are not apolitical. Words are the product of human interaction. They are inherently the result of attempting to describe things that we do not understand. They describe situations that make us uncomfortable. Words are the offspring of conflict. Conflict creates winners and losers. In this way, words tend to reflect the language of the oppressor, the language of the dominant. Words reflect the status quo. The status quo is dangerous to the oppressed.

As this book seeks to unravel some of the most dangerous misrepresentations of people of African descent, the terminology used in this effort was of critical importance. In some instances the terminology used may actually feel awkward to some readers. This is precisely because much of the language used to describe people of African descent is as common as it is noxious. Many believe that this language, which is clearly poisonous to African people, is unavoidable. Often when African Americans are challenged on their own use of the disempowering terminology which was crafted by their European oppressors, they will respond "You know what I mean ... I don't know how else I can say this."

Take for example the terms used in English for hair. Descriptive terms used for European hair are virtually all positive (or viewed as positive): silky, straight, wavy, flowing, fine, fair-haired, and easy-to-manage. Conversely, nearly all of the terminology used for African hair in the English language is negative: course, kinky, nappy, "peasy", and frizzy. If the terms you use to describe your very existence are negative, can you still believe that you are powerful enough to be an agent of change?

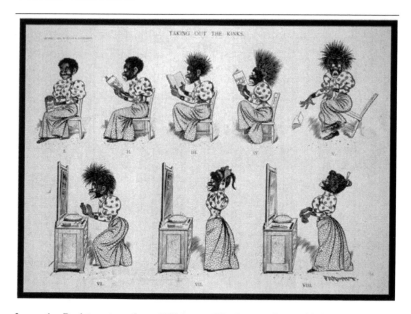

Image 1: Racist cartoon from 1895 issue of Puck magazine entitled *Taking out the Kinks*. A caricature of an African American woman reads a "hair-raising" ghost story. While she is terrified, she finds that her straightened hair is actually a good thing. The cartoon recalls the painful history of the lower status that was established during enslavement for African features.

Considerable time has been spent by oppressed people attempting to "reclaim" words which are clearly oppressive and damaging. How can you *re*claim words which you never owned? These words were fashioned for the expressed purpose of denigrating and harming. When will the "all-race" conference be held to inform the oppressed that the reclaimed terms are no longer tools for their continued oppression, but instead implements for their freedom? Can painful words ever lose their damaging intent while the oppressed are still oppressed? While this book is not technically a book on language, it certainly aims to confront its usage.

In order to address this imbalance, this book utilizes several corrective terms instead of the more common, disempowering terms. For example, those Africans who were kidnapped from Africa and forced to toil in the most inhumane conditions are often called "slaves". It is likely that the Europeans who were responsible for this heinous institution understood that the phrase could be used to further dehumanize their captives.

The term "slave" is a noun. It does not allude to the fact that these captives were forced into their condition. It disconnects the captives from the very thing that defines humans; their culture and homeland. This text uses the phrase "enslaved African" because it acknowledges the fact that these individuals have a culture, a homeland, and obviously a history. The term "enslaved" implies that someone forced these Africans into slavery. "Enslaved" asks for the reader to consider that the condition that the Africans are in need not be final; that those who enslaved them might be defeated. Similarly the common term, "Trans-Atlantic slave trade" is better described as the "Trans-Atlantic enslavement trade".

Many of the corrective phrases in this book are connected to the nation known as Egypt today. Interestingly, the ancient Africans who created one of the world's most influential early civilizations never used the word Egypt for their county. Scholars believe that the name is a mispronunciation of one of the nation's largest temples, Het-Ka-Ptah (House of the Soul of Ptah). When the Greeks conquered the nation, they were unable to properly speak the name of the city.

This book uses the name that ancient Africans actually used for their nation, Kemet (meaning the "black land"). Many other terms used in this book are also Ancient "Kemetic" words. When the Greeks arrived in Kemet they changed virtually all of the names they encountered. Modern European historians and Egyptologist are well aware of the original African names; many actually read the Kemetic language, the Medu Neter. It sometimes seems that by continuing to use Greek names when discussing Ancient Kemet, European historians have found an ingenious way to credit their ancestors for the magnificent accomplishments of ancient Africans. The Ancient Kemetic people argued that words have power; this is why they called their language the "Words of the Divine". They also believed that in order for those who have made their transition to the ancestral plane to continue to live, their names must continue to be spoken. As we continue to call these African giants by the names of foreign conquerors, we do great dishonor to our ancestors.

Table 1: Examples of Corrective *Kemetic* Terms Used in This Book	
Common Greek Term	**Corrective Kemetic Term**
Egypt	Kemet
Pyramid	Mrkhut
Obelisk	Tekhen
Step Pyramid	Khebu Neteru
Mastaba	Per djet

Readers will also notice that the author chooses to capitalize the word "Black" when describing people of African descent. For a very long time, people of African descent used "black" as their primary description for themselves. During this period, the hyphenated terms which allowed other groups to connect themselves to their land mass of origin (e.g., Irish-American) were rarely used for people of African descent. African Americans were clearly at a disadvantage. Utilizing a lower-cased "b" for the primary term for a people is the epitome of "linguistic racism". This book seeks to repair the subtle, yet damaging language inequalities regarding Black people. Leveling the linguistic, playing field is not justice. We must take into account long-standing inequities and their effect on self-image of a people. Subsequently, the term "white" has been left in lower case because it has always been accompanied in general discourse by terms which acknowledge the European heritage of whites. Therefore it can be used strictly as an adjective without denying humanity to the people it describes.

On the Selection of the Seven Lies

The lies covered in this book are as follows:
1. Caucasians are the Original People
2. Ancient Africa Contributed Nothing to Civilization
3. The Ancient Egyptians were 'Caucasian'
4. Hebrew Slaves Built the Pyramids
5. Africans Were Savages When the Europeans Enslaved Them
6. Columbus Discovered America
7. Abraham Lincoln Freed the Slaves

Each of these lies should sound quite familiar. They are often recited as mantras, included in rhyming poems taught to children in their most uncritical phase, the subject of major texts and/or films, and even the source of public holidays. These lies are sometimes considered material to what some believe is the very "historical fabric" of the nations they live in. Each was crafted by Europeans to misrepresent the history of African people. Without a history, a group becomes a "blank slate". They can be manipulated into virtually any purpose which those in power deem appropriate. This group can be turned into beasts of burden, savages to be blamed for the ills of society, sources of liberal charity, and consumers. They no longer have any social agency nor can they control their future. They cannot defend their interests; particularly because their interests are dictated to them. After these interests are "given to them", they will even fight to the death to protect those concepts that actually do them harm. Understanding one's history should, in some sense, be considered as similar to an inoculation. It protects you from those things that could make you quite ill or even kill you!

"A people without the knowledge of their past history, origin and culture is like a tree without roots."[7]
- Marcus Mosiah Garvey

After reading the comprehensive analysis of each of the mistruths, the reader will find that the seemingly simple statement serves almost as a "root concept". Many other dangerous, negative concepts branch off from them. It might seem that that the branch concepts are even more dangerous, but the author argues that the branch concepts remain prevalent precisely due to the fact that the root concept continues to exist—often unchallenged.

How to Read This Book

Each self-contained chapter of this book focuses on one of our seven lies. As we've explained, these are not listed in any hierarchical order.

Each chapter is divided into four sections: *Uncovering the Lie*; *The Real Deal*; *Reasons for and Effects of the LIE*; and *For Additional Research*. This structure provides the reader with a full understanding of the origins and pervasiveness of a lie before it is refuted. The author has gone to great lengths to unravel these lies in a scholarly fashion. The section regarding the reasons for and effects of the lie helps the reader understand the motivation and culprits behind the mistruth. These lies are not "zero sum games". One of the reasons that they persist is because a group receives tangible benefits from the continued belief in the lie. These benefits are obtained at the continued expense of the African.

The effects of the lie are often much more extensive than most recognize. Each of the lies may initially seem inconsequential to some, however in reality they are extremely damaging. In order for the condition of people of African descent to continue to improve, we must truly obtain a sense of our worth. Without an accurate sense of self, one can never truly achieve their goals. Scholars who are seeking to continue to study these issues in even greater detail will find the section entitled *For Additional Research* helpful. This section includes listings of other related texts and sometimes even videos.

The National Elder of the African Genesis Institute, Nana Kwa David Whittaker, Esq., often recites a proverb that appropriately describes the importance of unraveling the lies that we will cover in this book.

What you do for yourself depends on what you think of yourself. What you think of yourself depends on what you know of yourself. And what you know of yourself depends on what you have been told.[8]

The central task of this tome is to create dialogue within communities of African descent focused on a proper evaluation of our history. In order to bolster a truer sense of ourselves, we must dispense with the carefully crafted lies which continue to prevent us from once again becoming a global power. There is certainly no more important endeavor for the more than one billion Africans that have been among the most maligned people in history. Understanding that we are so much more than these lies is a revolutionary, motivational act.

CHAPTER 1:
"CAUCASIANS ARE THE ORIGINAL PEOPLE"

Image 1.1: Adam and Eve as the Caucasian Original Man and Woman? The Fall of Man (1616) by Hendrik Goltzius

Uncovering the Lie

While the idea of a European origin of humanity was quite popular until the early 1990s, this concept has been thoroughly dismissed. Many are now familiar with the fact that our earliest human ancestors were African. However, the European origin concept still influences the manner we view people of European descent and, by extension, all of the other peoples of the world in subtle but damaging ways. Let's explore exactly how and why the fallacy of the European origin of humanity became so popular en route to setting the record straight.

EARLY EUROPEAN CONCEPTIONS OF THE AFRICAN ROLE
If early humanity actually had its origin in Europe, one might

actually think that early European philosophers, historians, and intellectuals would have been the first champions of this argument. However, precisely the opposite was advanced by Europe's earliest sons and daughters. While Ancient Greece and Rome are often viewed as the foundation of Western (read European/"White") culture, both of these nations viewed Africa as their incubator.

Early Greek Mathematician and Philosopher, Plato, recounts a story in which the Greek statesman and poet, Solon ventures into Egypt in a period very near the end of its 3,000 year dominance. Solon attempts to engage one of the Ancient Kemetic (Egyptian) priests with stories of the "first man" who the Greeks called Phoroneus. The Kemetic priest reminds Solon that he was not equipped to discuss the ancient history.

> "O Solon, Solon, you Hellenes (Greeks) are never anything but children, and there is not an old man among you." Solon in return asked him what he meant. "I mean to say", he replied, "that in mind you are all young; there is no old opinion handed down among you by ancient tradition, nor any science which is hoary with age ... As for those genealogies of yours which you just now recounted to us ... they are no better than the tales of children." (Parenthesis added)[1]

Early Greek historians are also clear that they were, in essence, "created" by Africans. Their gods are no more than versions of the ancient deities of Africa. Diodorus Siculus (circa 90 - 21 BCE) tells us that Zeus, the very father of the Greek pantheon, dines regularly with the highly revered Africans.

> For Zeus had yesterday to Ocean's bounds. Set forth to feast with Ethiop's *faultless* men and he was followed there by all the gods. (Italics added)[2]

With an understanding of this early Greek history, it should not come as a surprise that the Greeks decided to etch the names of beautiful African women in the heavens for all time. The constellations Cassiopeia and Andromeda were named for an Ethiopian[3] queen and her daughter. Andromeda was so alluring that the Greek gods were jealous. The epic rescue of Andromeda by her demi-god hero, Perseus, was not only chronicled in popular Greek myth but in blockbuster Hollywood films in 1981 and 2010. Unfortunately, studio executives decided to cast European women in both versions of the film. Apparently African beauty in the eyes of early Europeans is so controversial that it must be expunged from popular history!

Image 1.2 - Andromeda Unleashed: (Top left) Judi Bowker (1981) and (Bottom left) Alexa Davalos (2010) contrast with the (Right) dark-skinned Andromeda in Picart's Perseus and Andromeda (1731)

The centrality of the African is also found in Roman history. While the founders of Rome are often portrayed as the wolf-suckled twins, Romulus and Remus, all of the mythological stories of the beginnings of this great "Western" nation actually revolve around a great number of African characters. Rome may have even begun as an outpost of the Africa nation of Carthage. Its founding is described by the poet Virgil in the epic tales of the Aeneid. The heroic story recounts the journeys of Aeneas, a Trojan solider who wanders the region, eventually falls in love with the

African/Carthaginian Queen Dido, and becomes the founder of Rome.

Trojan soldiers like Aeneas were often depicted as "swarthy" in both the ancient world and in Shakespearian productions. Perhaps the mythic origins of Rome describe how the "ancient" African world becomes infused in the "new" Western world. This heavy African presence in the Roman Empire explains how at least five North Africans would continue on to rule as Roman Emperors. If the Caucasians were the original people, why does it seem Western society is birthed out of more ancient African societies?

Image 1.3: Bust of North African Roman Emperor Septimus Severus and Portrait of His Family

AFRICAN ENSLAVEMENT, THE CREATION OF THE "CAUCASIAN", AND THE EUROPEAN ORIGIN STORY

So if early Europeans revered ancient Africans as the originators of humanity and civilization, when was the fictitious European origin concept conceived? How does it become so prevalent? These questions are only answered with a review of the drastically altered depiction of Africans during the Trans-Atlantic enslavement trade.

During the 1400s, large European nations (Spain, Italy, Portugal, etc.) sought to enrich themselves by searching for foreign nations to exploit. Even today the European land mass is relatively population, climate, and natural resource poor[4]. The opportunity to control resources outside of the region motivated European rulers to search for their riches elsewhere. These powerful monarchies decided to expend valuable currency to find new routes for acquiring spices. They also took advantage of the resources of distant peoples including gold, silver, and precious stones. In order to take permanent control of these lands out of the hands of other European powers, they created colonies which were considered the property of their expanding empires. Of course the native peoples of the "new world" were then seen as little more than additional resources for further exploitation. This painfully racist thinking led to frighteningly genocidal acts. For example, within 14 years of Christopher Columbus' presence on the island of Hispaniola alone, roughly *3 million people had been killed.*[5]

Soon after a failed attempt at establishing a colony at Roanoke Island, North Carolina, the English crown successfully established its first permanent settlement at Jamestown, Virginia in 1607. Other than the earlier experiment with the forced labor of Native Americans, the hard work on the colony's tobacco plantations was first handled by poor white indentured servants. These workers were mostly English and bonded to landowners for a period of 4-7 years. While this was no easy feat as they were treated very poorly, indentured servants who survived could then focus on their own lives. They were able to seek more equitable employment, purchase land, and even become the owners of their own servants[6].

By 1619, the first kidnapped Africans arrived at Jamestown. We know little about these Africans, other than the fact most had Spanish and Portuguese surnames and were quite skilled. These Africans would not be enslaved in the same sense that their descendants would be. They were initially utilized as indentured servants in much the same manner that poor whites were. In fact, these newly arrived Africans lived, worked, socialized, and even married their poor white counterparts. The level of camaraderie amongst these poor Black and white workers would seem counterintuitive today. This ethnically diverse but economically similar group even banded together to fight the colonial powers who exploited them.

Beginning in 1676, Nathaniel Bacon led one of the most famous uprisings of thousands of poor exploited workers against the powerful Virginia planters and the colonial governor.

> ... the rank and file were filled up partly with slaves and indentured workers, who had little interest in either the Indian war or in curbing the governor's despotism. The garrison at Colonel West's house, near West Point, consisted of about 400 men, of whom eighty were Negroes, and many others were servants. What they wanted was their freedom. But among them there must have been some of Bacon's veterans, for they continued to fight well.[7]

While Europeans may have had an innate prejudice toward Africans based on the stark differences in their physical appearance (i.e., facial features and dark skin), they didn't initially base their concepts of inferiority on the modern "racial" ideal.[8] During this period poor whites and poor Africans did not see their racial differences as their most important characteristic. They recognized their common economic status was a rallying cry which united them against the powerful white planters.

During this early colonial period, it seems the powerful planter class didn't view inferiority according to racial lines either. They were more likely to describe groups that they had a history of conflict with as "savage". The liberal author, Leonard Liggio, describes the planters' early conception of the different groups of laborers they exploited:

> Like the English village laborers, the Africans had been experienced agricultural laborers in the African villages. ... The Africans' tradition of the organic community of village society, of adaptability and learning and of agricultural experience made them the most likely substitute in the New World for the laborer of the feudal community of the old world ... Unlike the *savage* Irish and Indians whose uncivilized culture caused English racism to choose the extreme of extermination, the latter encounter with the civilized Africans led English racism to include them within the culture of the organic feudal community.[9]

One could imagine the difficulty the powerful colonial planter class had with maintaining control over their coerced work force. Poor white indentured servants were primarily Christian and restricted to forced labor for only a relatively short period of time (4-7 years). A number of European groups (in the colonies and at home) objected to the continued subjugation of their poor Christian brethren. Additionally, white indentured servants did not have extensive experience working the fields in a tropical environment. They could also flee the settlement and attempt to blend into the "freed" poor white populations in other areas.

Enslaved First Nations peoples (misnomered Indians) seemed particularly susceptible to European illnesses. They also knew the terrain better than their enslavers and could escape and return to their homes. The people of the First Nations were able to view the barbarism of indentured servitude first hand. They continued to struggle with the European planters to free their people. The African, however, seemed better equipped to deal with European illnesses, were skilled and even had experience working in tropical environments. Having been kidnapped from a distant land, these Africans could not easily escape and return to their homeland. While there were free Africans who had amassed wealth after the end of their indentured servant bondage, they could not be considered a group powerful enough to challenge the very existence of the cruel imposed labor of all Africans.

Large insurrections containing European and African indentured servants and freed poor workers threatened to overturn the entire hierarchy; particularly since the class of wealthy planters and colonial rulers was greatly dwarfed by these forced and poor freed workers. The powerful European rulers and the planter class needed to divide their workers in a manner which might prevent them from successfully coalescing around their shared economic deprivation. They resorted to powerful mass control and social stratification techniques. The concept of the "inferior race" was born.

By the end of the 1600s and the first quarter of the 1700s, colonial rulers had begun to both value Africans as cheap coerced labor while simultaneously searching for ways to limit the number of large rebellions. The authorities in each colony would gradually devise a number of laws, called the slave codes, which would racialize labor in the new world.

As Virginia was the first permanent colonial installation in what would become the United States, its attempts to permanently oppress Africans would lead the way for the rest of the colonies. In October of 1619, a Virginia statute distinguished between the labor of an African woman and an English woman. By September of the next year, a white man named Hugh Davis would be "soundly whipped, before an assembly of Negroes and others for abusing himself to the dishonor of God and shame of Christians, by defiling his body in lying with a negro".[10] Davis was then admonished to acknowledge his crime of "interracial fornication" at church the next Sunday.[11] By October 1640, the Commonwealth of Virginia seems to have devised a slightly different penalty for interracial fornication. For conceiving a child with an enslaved African woman owned by another man, Robert Sweat was forced to do penance at church while the African woman was whipped at the public whipping post.

These statues regulated far more than punishments for behavior. Statutes in February 1644 and December 1662 began to clarify the difference between Africans and their white counterparts who were indentured servants. These laws created racial enslavement by condemning the children of enslaved African mothers to the same condition.[12] By 1705, the Virginia General Assembly clarified this painful, permanent system of racial enslavement versus temporary indentured servitude.

> All servants imported and brought into the Country ... who were not Christians in their native Country ... shall be accounted and be slaves. All Negro, mulatto and Indian slaves within this dominion ... shall be held to be real estate. If any slave resist his master ... correcting such slave, and shall happen to be killed in such correction...the master shall be free of all punishment ... as if such accident never happened.[13]

While the slave codes had variations based on the colony that passed them, their effect in virtually every colony was clear. Africans were now permanently enslaved so much so that their children could not escape this wretched condition.

This powerfully effective strategy was both situationally intricate and psychologically simplistic at the same time. These laws targeted the group of workers who the rulers deemed extremely valuable (multi-skilled, resistant to disease, familiar with group labor, accustomed to tropical environments) and least able to escape (distance prevented both returning home and armed struggle by African nations). Describing the group of people whose physical features were the most different from your own as savages implies that Europeans were "super-humans" by a twisted form of the law of opposites. If Africans were by nature ignorant, Europeans must be endowed with intellect by nature. If Africans were primitive beasts, Europeans must be civilized by this twisted logic. Choosing to isolate African workers created a hierarchy that even poor, exploited whites could enforce through racist notions. While poor whites would focus on the subjugation of Africans as a form of self-esteem; wealthy, powerful whites could subjugate them both. This subjugation was relative as the position of poor whites was much better than enslaved Africans, but powerful whites relinquished a small portion of their control to these whites in order to maintain control of the entire system.

Image 1.4: The 1866 election poster from the Hiester Clymer campaign clearly depicts the manner in which racist notions served to both denigrate Africans and uplift whites by juxtaposition. While both Clymer and Geary were white, identifying Geary with a hideous caricature of an African and Clymer with a naturalistic drawing of a European was a powerful visual commentary.

It is in this highly racialized climate created by colonial rulers that arguments for the European origin of humanity begin to take seed. Clearly if Africans are savages without souls best suited to serve the Europeans, how could they be the original people? This thinking would become very prevalent during the late 1700s.

While the history of interest in the wide variety of human differences stems into our ancient past (for more see Chapter 3), it was not until the late 1600s that European intellectuals thought to introduce pseudo-scientific research into the endeavor. These "scholars" believed that race was a scientific fact not a social construct. As their extremely subjective research was conducted during the Trans-Atlantic enslavement trade, one should not be surprised with their racist findings.

French medical doctor and traveler, Francois Bernier provides one of the earliest "scientific" discourses in his book *Nouvelle Division de la Terre par les Différents Espèces ou Races qui l'habitent* ("New Division of Earth by the Different Species or Races which Inhabit it"), published in 1684. Bernier not only is the first to use the term "race", but creates four racial groups:

1. European, North African, Middle Eastern, South Asian and Native American Race
2. Sub-Saharan African Race
3. East Asian, Southeast Asian and Central Asian Race
4. Lapp Race (indigenous people of Scandinavian, Finland, Sweden, Norway, etc.).[14]

Bernier's research was a product of the racist concept of European superiority. Each of the races possessed different degrees of intellectual (rational) ability, and therefore some groups were better utilized as slaves.[15]

By the late 1700s discourse concerning the races and species of man reached a fever pitch. The work of Swedish botanist, zoologist, and doctor, Carl Linnaeus (1707 -1778) is still quite influential today. The universally accepted two-part naming structure according to the genus and species (such as in the classification of modern humans, Homo Sapiens) was in part established by Linnaeus. Unfortunately, he was also a major force in the advancement of "scientific racism". While describing his research into the origins of humans, Linnaeus created separate classifications for each of the four races of men based on continent, skin color, and racist characteristics (four temperaments):

Racial Classifications	Temperaments
"Europæus albus" (white European)	White, sanguine (optimistic in difficult situations), brawny; with abundant, long hair; blue eyes; gentle, acute, inventive; covered with close vestments; and regulated by customs
"Americanus rubescens" (red American)	Red, choleric, righteous; black, straight, thick hair; stubborn, zealous, free; painting himself with red lines, and regulated by customs

Asiaticus fuscus" (brown Asian); later changed to "Asiaticus luridus" (yellow Asian)	Yellow, melancholic, stiff; black hair, dark eyes; severe, haughty, greedy; covered with loose clothing; and regulated by opinions
"Africanus niger (black African)	Black, phlegmatic, relaxed; frizzled hair; silky skin, flat nose, tumid lips; *females without shame*; *mammary glands give milk abundantly*; *crafty, sly, careless*; anoints himself with grease; & regulated by **caprice (emotions)**

Table 1.1: Racial Classifications developed by Carl Linnaeus[16]

Think for a moment about how the work of Carl Linnaeus might have served to provide supposed scientific and intellectual license to those powerful individuals, groups, and institutions who sought to continue the violent subjugation and enslavement of African people.

Founding father, major author of the Declaration of Independence, and third president of the United States, Thomas Jefferson was an adherent of the concepts advanced by Linnaeus. In his *Notes on the State of Virginia*, Jefferson goes to great lengths to describe how the inferiority of Africans makes them best equipped to serve whites as the enslaved. It is often considered one of the most important books published in the United States before 1800.

The first difference which strikes us is that of colour. Is it not the foundation of a greater or less share of beauty in the two races? ... Are not the fine mixtures of red and white, the expressions of every passion by greater or less suffusions of colour in the one, preferable to that eternal monotony, which reigns in the countenances, that immoveable veil of black which covers all the emotions of the other race? (Africans are improved by interracial mixture). ... [Europeans have] flowing hair, a more elegant symmetry of form, their own judgment in favour of the whites, declared by their preference of them, as uniformly as is the preference of the Oran-ootan for the black women over those of his own species. The circumstance of superior beauty, is thought worthy attention in the propagation of our horses, dogs, and other domestic animals; why not in that of man? Besides those of colour, figure, and hair, there are other physical distinctions proving a difference of race. They have less hair on the face and body. They secrete less by the kidnies, and more by the glands of the skin, which gives them a very strong and disagreeable odour. They seem to require less sleep. A black, after hard labour through the day, will be induced by the slightest amusements to sit up till midnight, or later, though knowing he must be out with the first dawn of the morning. ... Comparing them by their faculties of memory, reason, and imagination, it appears to me, that in memory they are equal to whites; in reason much inferior, as I think one could scarcely be found capable of tracing and comprehending the investigations of Euclid; and that in imagination they are dull, tasteless, and anomalous (Parenthesis and brackets mine).[17]

With these perceptions of the lowliness of enslaved Africans, should we be surprised that Jefferson argues Africans are improved by interracial mixing? Perhaps this was his train of thought when at 44 years old he began a sexual relationship with Sally Hemings, a 14-year-old enslaved African. It is quite amazing that Jefferson is still revered as a founding father and architect of the United States rather than a pedophile and rapist.[18] Setting the record straight is critically important.

Another major discourse on the racial classification of humans during this period is advanced by the German physician, naturalist, physiologist, and anthropologist, Johann Friedrich Blumenbach. In Blumenbach's popular 1775 treatise, *The Natural Varieties of Mankind*, he argued that there were five major racial divisions: the Caucasoid, Mongoloid, Ethiopian (later termed the Negroid), American Indian, and Malayan. While Blumenbach is highly influenced by Linnaeus, he attempts to further advance his racist work. Blumenbach describes the races in a hierarchical sense; the Caucasian is the original human which then devolves into two distinct branches; one which includes the Native American and the Oriental and another which includes the Malay and the African.[19] Blumenbach also is the first to utilize the term

"Caucasian", which in itself separates Europeans from their African origin. He introduces the term simply because he believes the skull of a Georgian woman is the most attractive. Georgia is an Eastern Europe nation which was part of the former Soviet Union. Blumenbach argued that the world's most beautiful people live on the southern slope of the Caucus Mountain and that they must have been the original people. However, Europeans do not have their genetic, "racial", or cultural origin in the area of the Caucus Mountain, yet this erroneous term continues to be regularly used over 200 years later! Asians, Africans and other ethnicities, according to his twisted argument, developed different physical appearances due to environment and *poor diet.*[20]

Perhaps the most striking position advocating the concept of the European origin of humanity comes to us from the well-known French renaissance philosopher, Voltaire. Voltaire was engaged in the debate regarding the concepts of monogenism (first humans originated from one place) versus polygenism (first humans originated simultaneously or separately on different continents) which were popular in the 1700s. In his work, *Les Lettres d'Amabed*, Voltaire explains that the biblical position that humans were generated from one source (God created Adam and Eve), was ridiculous. How could all of humanity have one source when some of the races were so inferior to Europeans?

It is a serious question among them whether the Africans are descended from monkeys or whether the monkeys come from them. Our wise men have said that man was created in the image of God. Now here is a lovely image of the Divine Maker: a flat and black nose with little or hardly any intelligence. A time will doubtless come when these animals will know how to cultivate the land well, beautify their houses and gardens, and know the paths of the stars: one needs time for everything.[21]

Racist concepts were a hurdle to understanding the singular origin of humanity. Without recognition of the centrality of Africans in the origins of humankind, Europeans will never know themselves.

European authors for more than a century were so zealous in their belief that Europeans are humanity's original people that they attempted to ignore the mounting evidence in the abundant form of fossils and artifacts. This reality did not entirely stall the European attempt at placing themselves in a central place in the evolution of humanity. There were even those who sought to *create* artifacts to support their position!

Image 1.5: 1915 painting by John Cooke portraying the examination of the Piltdown Man skull. Charles Dawson and Arthur Smith Woodward are third and fourth in the back row.

In 1912, British archeologist Charles Dawson announced that workers found interesting skull fragments in a gravel pit in the town of Piltdown in East Essex, England. Dawson reportedly took these fragments to Arthur Smith Woodward, then the head of the geology department at the British Museum, one of the largest and most revered archeological institutions in the world. While Woodward took great interest in the find and returned with Dawson to the site on several occasions, all of the subsequent fragments were discovered by Dawson. Woodward did, however, work with the British Museum to reconstruct the skull. The noteworthy artifact was given the celebratory Latin name "Eoanthropus dawsoni", or

Dawson's Dawn-man. The artifact has been often called the Piltdown Man.

Almost immediately the reconstructed skull created shockwaves in communities of archeologists, anthropologists, historians, and scholars. Britain's Royal College of Surgeons found that the skull must have featured a brain which was similar to the size of modern man. This "discovery" came at a time when archeologists continued to feverishly search for the "missing link" between modern humans (Homo sapiens) and our common ancestor with modern chimpanzees. The find had another important result. It bolstered the argument that modern man had its beginnings outside of Africa. Imagine that the general argument was constructed in this manner: "lower" evolutionary ancestors, primitive man, had their origin in Africa, but modern "thinking" man had its origin in Europe. Perhaps this argument was appealing due to the common depiction of Africans as primitive and even ape-like.

While there were scholars who found the Piltdown skull troubling from its first announcement, it seems that the stature of the individuals and institutions involved buffered the skull from complete repudiation; even as other fossils seemed to make it highly questionable. The Piltdown skull was still cited as part of the paleontological story of the origins of modern man for over 40 years!

In November of 1953, *Time* magazine published the research of three scholars (Kenneth Page Oakley, Sir Wilfrid Edward Le Gros Clark, and Joseph Weiner) which proved that the artifact was falsified. The forged skull was actually the product of three distinct species: the skull of a human from the medieval age, the five century old jaw of an orangutan, and the teeth of a chimpanzee. The skeptical scholars who unraveled the hoax found microscopic tool marks from filing and discovered staining from iron solution and chlorine acid to create the "aged" look. Their chemical analysis of the fluorine which absorbed into bones from the soil around it provided definitive proof of the forgery. The inconsistent fluorine levels in the various sections of the reconstructed skull proved that the different portions of the skull could not have been buried in the pit at the same time.

Image 1.6 - Depictions of Africans as Savage: (Top left) Cover of book arguing Africans cannot be the "original man" by Charles Carol (1900); (Top right) Screen shot of Warner Brothers cartoon "Isle of Pingo Pongo" (1938); (Bottom left) Cover of Jumbo Comics' Sheena fighting "savage" African (1951); (Bottom right) Belgian Newspaper depicting Obamas as apes (March 2014).

Many of the details how this monumental fakery was created are still in debate today. Most scholars believe Charles Dawson was responsible for the debacle, but it remains unclear whether he did so single-handedly. Perhaps the entire picture will never be brought to light.

It should be stated that the Piltdown skull is far from the only archeological forgery to be identified. It is unique, however, in the length of time that it remained historical "fact" and the number of esteemed institutions involved in its progression. Why did the Piltdown Man remain part of the archeological narrative for so long? Influential American paleontologist, Stephen Jay Gould, described the racist ideas that allowed the Piltdown Man to remain relevant in the face of contradictory findings.

> Piltdown also buttressed some all to familiar racial views among white Europeans. In the 1930s and 1940s, following the discovery of Peking man in strata approximately equal in age with the Piltdown gravels, phyletic trees based on Piltdown and affirming the antiquity of white supremacy began to appear in the literature (although they were never adopted by Piltdown's chief champions, Smith Woodward, Smith, and Keith). Peking man (originally called Sinanthropus, but now placed in Homo erectus) lived in China with a brain two-thirds modern size, while Piltdown Man, with its fully developed brain, inhabited England. If Piltdown, as the earliest Englishman, was the progenitor of white races, while other hues must trace their ancestry to Homo erectus, then whites crossed the threshold to full humanity long before other people. As longer residents in this exalted state, whites must excel in the arts of civilization.[22]

Even after the dismissal of the Piltdown Man, the European origin argument did not disappear. Even its overtly racist versions continued to masquerade as scientific thought.

Carleton Coon's 1962 book, *The Origin of Races*, makes the ludicrous argument that the early human ancestor, Homo erectus, left Africa to develop into the Homo sapiens in five different places independently. It is hard not to hear echoes of the racist dogma which had its origins 200 years earlier in the Trans-Atlantic enslavement trade. Coon's argument is outlined in the book *Readings for a History in Anthropological Theory.*:

> ... the anthropologist Carleton Coon proposed that whites and blacks had evolved separately from Homo erectus into Homo sapiens, while having attained that goal two hundred thousand years before blacks. Thus, 'it is a fair inference,' Coon declared, that whites 'have evolved the most, and that the obvious correlation between the length of time a subspecies has been in the sapiens state and the levels of

civilization attained by some of its populations may be related phenomena.[23]

While Coon was a respected anthropologist, his argument defied basic logic and was clearly based on long-standing racist beliefs. If evolution is spurred on by adaptations to the environment, why should we believe that a species migrated to several distant regions and then evolved into virtually the same being in such different conditions? Unfortunately racist prejudice often trumps scientific thought.

So we have seen that the most esteemed early western civilizations held ancient Africans in the highest regard; considering them to be the founders of humanity. We have also followed the development of one of the most barbaric systems in human history, the Trans-Atlantic enslavement trade and its effect on the view of the centrality of Africans in the story of the rise of modern humans. We have even seen the large extents that European scholars have gone to misrepresent the African origins of humanity. What is the real story of how Africans became the fore-parents of all humans? How do we know that our early ancestors were African?

The Real Deal

THE AFRICAN ORIGIN OF HUMANITY
While paleontologists and anthropologists are still debating the nuances of the origins of modern man, the overwhelming majority now agree that humanity was born on the African continent. The picture has been clarified by both the fossil evidence and the ever increasing genetic data.

In November of 1974, American anthropologists Donald Johnson and Tom Gray happened upon the fossilized remains of an ancient female in Hadar, Ethiopia. The amazing find further bolstered the growing mountain of evidence that Africa was the original home of humanity. As the anthropologists continued to excavate the delicate remains, they decided to name the woman "Lucy" as their radio played the famous Beatles song, "Lucy in the Sky with Diamonds". Interestingly, Ethiopians gave her a more appropriate name, "Dinkinesh", meaning "you are wonderful" in the Amharic language. At 3.2 million years old, Dinkinesh was not only one of the oldest, early human ancestors unearthed at the time, her skeleton was also one of the most complete.[24]

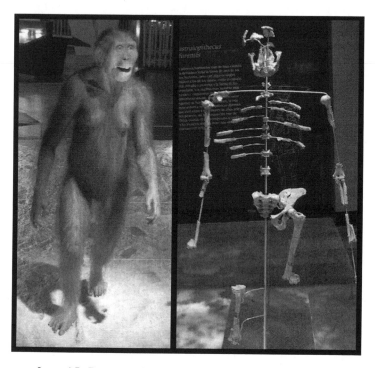

Image 1.7: Reconstruction of Dinkinesh and a Cast of Her Skeleton

The 3 1/2 foot tall Dinkinesh was a treasure-trove of information. Although her brain was still relatively small, scientists learned that her class of hominids had already begun to walk upright. Unfortunately the discovery did not immediately dismantle the European origin argument. While Dinkinesh is a close relative of the Homo genus, the major counter-argument is that evolution into Homo sapiens occurred after an earlier Homo species (Homo erectus) travelled to different sections of the globe.

Until recent advancements in the field of genetics, the argument concerning the African origin of humanity seemed to continually hover *near* accepted truth. Even with the accumulating numbers of fossils which pointed to Africa, some anthropologists continued to search for fossils on other continents which they believed could disprove the African origin of modern humans. Then, on January 11, 1988, *Newsweek* magazine featured a story on the front cover which described the culmination of years of genetic research into our African origins. The headlines would forever change our understanding of the birth of humanity.

Image 1.8: The cover of *Newsweek* Magazine (January 11, 1988) displayed an African Adam and Eve. Notice the subtitle acknowledges the impact of these "controversial" findings.

Often major scientific finds are shrouded from the public in scholarly journals. This time things were quite different. Only a year after the initial announcement to the scholarly community, *Newsweek* reported the results of years of painstaking research in full detail. Through studies of the genetic information which is transferred from mother to daughter indefinitely (mitochondrial DNA), researchers discovered that every single human on the planet is the descendant of one woman. While she was not the only woman alive in her time or even the first woman; her lineage is the only one that survived. The "Mitochondrial Eve", as she has been called, lived around 200,000 years ago and was probably an early member of Homo sapiens classification.[25]

Through the evaluation of *hundreds* of placentas of women from a wide range of racial, ethnic, and geographical backgrounds, the researchers announced another key finding. While it was clear that earlier ancestors of modern humans (perhaps Homo erectus) did leave their African homeland, the evolution to Homo sapiens took place in Africa. These African Homo sapiens eventually left Africa sometimes even living amongst these less evolved early humans. In some instances they mixed with these other groups (e.g., a small percentage of modern European DNA includes that of the Neanderthal[26]). Ultimately these "African" Homo sapiens migrated to all corners of the earth.

In the years since the controversial *Newsweek* cover, researchers have continued to find more evidence which cements Africa's place. In 2003, paleontologist Timothy White announced that the earliest Homo sapiens skulls were found in the Afar region of Ethiopia.[27] Additionally, forensic models of the earliest human fossils found in Europe (Romania, 2002) and the Americas (Brazil, 1975) revealed that their African features were still very dominant.

The concept of the European origin of humanity has been refuted. Africa was not only home to early ancestors of modern humans but also its most evolved form, Homo sapiens sapiens. Africa is the cradle of humanity.

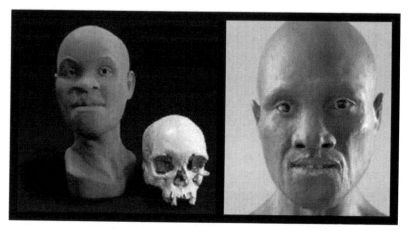

Image 1.9: Models of Luiza, an early woman in modern-day Brazil (11,500 years ago) and an early man in modern-day Romania (35,000 years ago)

Reasons for and the Effects of the LIE

The reasons for the continuing fallacy of the European origin of humanity are quite simple. One might think that having a "homeland" that is rich in natural resources or boasts a relatively large population would give them a claim to global dominance among the world's nations. Europeans cannot make ANY of these claims. Europe as a land mass is climate poor, deficient in natural resources, and has a relatively small number of people. Yet Europeans are the world's most powerful and affluent group. They had to leave their homeland to accomplish this. European "scholars" have created a number of fanciful arguments to justify their control of the resources of other peoples. How do they explain the conquest of areas that are abundant in these resources? The psychological, even popular, argument made is that Europeans are more intelligent, more able, more attractive, and more evolved. Therefore, they deserve to be in control of the globe's resources. This is why we will continue to contend with the fallacious arguments of their origin. Most of the arguments that were outlined in this chapter are primarily discussed in scholarly circles. This fallacious European origin argument has retreated primarily to popular culture. More people view a major summer blockbuster in their local theatre than will ever enter a college-level history course.

We now know that the early ancestors of modern humans had their origin in Africa. It is also true that these early human ancestors left Africa. Proponents of the European origin fallacy would have you believe that these early humans left Africa *and then evolved into the modern human*. This is incorrect. The early human ancestor, including Homo erectus, who remained in Africa evolved into Homo sapiens sapiens (the most modern human) and then left Africa. This is why the oldest human fossils in other regions still look distinctly African (see Image 1.9). Their physical features changed as they remained in these new environments.

This reality will not alter the discourse concerning the mothers and fathers of humanity until these concepts are fully understood by those who continue to be maligned. Africa is the origin of all humanity, but those who identify with it will gain the most in correcting this picture.

How could Europeans have subjugated their own "mothers and fathers"? We will see in a later section that Africa is not only the origin of humanity, but also human civilization.

For Additional Research

BOOKS
1. Finch III, Charles S. (1991). Echoes of the Old Darkland: Themes from the African Eden. Decatur, Georgia: Khenti, Inc.
2. Meredith, Martin. (2011). Born in Africa: The Quest for the Origins of Human Life. New York, NY: PublicAffairs.
3. Diop, Cheikh Anta. (1991). Civilization or Barbarism: An Authentic Anthropology. Chicago, IL: Chicago Review Press

VIDEO
1. Diop, Cheikh Anta. (1985). The African Origins of Humanity. For the People [Television Program] Retrieved from: https://www.youtube.com/watch?v=qi0IRivzlNM
2. Ashton, Paul (Producer) and Glover, Danny (Narrator). (2002).The Real Eve [Television Documentary]. Retrieved from: https://www.youtube.com/watch?v=yzAsXRq0XcQ

CHAPTER 2:
"ANCIENT AFRICA CONTRIBUTED NOTHING TO CIVILIZATION"

Image 2.1: (Top) Plaque from Germany's Gutenberg Square commemorating the creation of the printing press. (Bottom) Notice the depictions of the poor, kneeling Africans who are being unbound as they receive "civilization" from the West.[1]

Uncovering the Lie

The notion that the entire continent of Africa contributed nothing to human advancement is a very common falsehood. Even though scholars now agree that Africa is the birthplace of humanity, many people still question whether it assisted in the development of any of the major aspects of our modern society. Doesn't this seem contrary to basic common sense? If modern humans and their predecessors originated in Africa, wouldn't they have had a head start in creating "human culture"? This common sense argument is one that many have considered even before they were able to put all the facts together in order to prove it.

Consider how an intelligent young student of African descent grappled with these issues. As an adult he would play an unmatched role in proving the importance of Africa in the development of civilization. Let's hear a dramatic retelling of his story.

ARTURO SCHOMBURG: A DAY IN THE CHILDHOOD OF AN AFRICAN DIASPORAN HISTORIAN

The year is 1884. It's a warm spring day in the neighborhood of Santurce in San Juan, Puerto Rico. A young student approaches the blackboard. A bit small for his age, the boy's neatly pressed knickers are clean but somewhat frayed. They have been handed down a few too many times. His shoes are no different. The soles are worn, but they still sparkle due to the careful buffing they receive every other day. Jet-black, curly locks are neatly combed and styled, even though the longer strands tend to become unruly in the midday humidity.

The boy's tawny hands grasp the chalk. At the behest of his teacher, he carefully inscribes the names of the characters he can remember from the previous day's lesson on the Greek epic, *The Iliad*. "Fine job, Arturo." the teacher motions for the boy to return to his seat. The tall man's skin stands in stark contrast to his dark-colored blazer. His eyes momentarily scan the classroom searching the tiny raised hands for students who hadn't frequently participated. As he begins to call the name of the copper-colored girl in the first row, the teacher notices the girl's eyes are drawn behind him. The man shifts on his stool and notices that not only has the boy failed to return to his seat, but that he has actually walked a few paces toward him. His puzzled look demands a response. "What is wrong, Arturo?" the man now turns completely in the direction of the boy. It was quite unusual to see this expression on his prized student. The boy spent hours reading all of the books which graced the small wooden shelf in the back of the classroom. The teacher has already had to borrow books from the sixth grade classroom to satiate the boy's hunger for history. He was usually prepared for the day's lesson long before the teacher introduced it every morning.

The boy nervously shifts his weight from one leg to the other. "Where are the stories of people who look like me?" His little caramel brow furrowed as he demands an answer. The man takes a long uncomfortable breath as he searches for the right words. He didn't want to discourage the boy, but he needed to tell him the truth. The students would discover this issue on their own anyway. "I wish I could tell you something different, but you should know that the darker colored inhabitants of Africa produced no notable achievements, no great civilizations. They have not been on the world stage for very long". He watches the expression on the boy's face turn from surprise to disappointment and finally to sheer defiance. Arturo shoots back another question before the teacher could complete his next thought, "What were they doing during the time of *The Illiad*?" The man's voice is more authoritative than before. He continues, "There is no history to report."

Young Arturo sat quietly for the rest of the day. "How could they have done nothing?" he pondered. It didn't seem like all of the incidents in the stories they read were of major importance. Couldn't someone have at least recorded minor history from the Africans? How could there be *nothing*? In his soul, he knew that this response could not be right. His little hands roughly wiped anyway the tear which danced down his cheek. He would commit himself from that day forward to search for this history. He would begin to collect everything he could find that told his story. He devoted his life to filling in those pages of world history which were omitted. No child should ever experience what he felt on that spring day. He would be sure of it.[2]

While this narrative takes some license with the actual story of the early years of Afro-Latino Arturo Schomburg, the factual story is all too familiar to young students of African descent around the world.[3] Schomburg would eventually leave the island of Puerto Rico to continue his historic journey in the community sometimes known as the capital of Black America, Harlem, New York. He was a major cornerstone of the Harlem Renaissance period. His collection would become the nucleus of the holdings of the world-renown research library which would later bear his name, The Schomburg Center for Research in Black Culture.

Image 2.2 - Arthur Schomburg (1874 - 1938): An Afroborinqueno (Afro-Puerto Rican) historian, Schomburg's life-long quest to catalog African history led to the creation of one of the world's most important research centers, The Schomburg Center for Research in Black Culture.

The belief that Africans have no history worth noting prior to the advent of the Trans-Atlantic enslavement trade is quite common even during the first half of the 21st century. A large number of Western historians, influenced by the derogatory image of Africans during their enslavement, have spouted this false argument. We will outline some of these commentaries over the last 300 years and then dismantle them. Finally, we will then delineate some of the monumental contributions of Africans to human civilization. These contributions have been hidden in the missing pages of history for hundreds of years.

EUROPEAN "SCHOLARS" AND THE RACIST NOTION OF THE LACK OF AFRICAN CONTRIBUTIONS TO HUMAN CIVILIZATION

It should come as no surprise that Western authors after the 1700s viewed African nations as inferior and without notable contributions to civilization. As discussed in the previous chapter, European "scholars" considered Africans as savage as a result of the propaganda created to reinforce their exploitation during the Trans-Atlantic enslavement trade. They vociferously articulated their disdain for African nations. These authors believed that Africans were no more capable of creating great civilizations than animals were.

Few philosophers were more prominent during the 1700s than David Hume. Hume was central to the Scottish Enlightenment movement and influential to a number of fellow philosophers including Immanuel Kant, James Boswell, and Adam Smith.[4,5,6] While he is still revered by students of philosophy and Western history, few are familiar with his bigoted views on African civilization. His noxiously racist comments are present in full form only in an early version of his monumental work, *Essays and Treatises on Several Subjects:*

> I am apt to suspect the negroes, and in general all the other species of men (for there are four or five different kinds) to be naturally inferior to the whites. There never was a civilized nation of any other complexion than white, nor even any individual eminent either in action or speculation. No ingenious manufactures amongst them, no arts, no sciences. On the other hand, the most rude and barbarous of the whites, such as the ancient GERMANS, the present TARTARS, have still something eminent about them, in their valour, form of government, or some other particular. Such a uniform and constant difference could not happen, in so many countries and ages, if nature had not made an original distinction betwixt these breeds of men. Not to mention our colonies, there are NEGROE slaves dispersed all over EUROPE, of which none ever discovered any symptom of ingenuity; tho' low people, without education, will start up amongst us, and distinguish themselves in every profession. In JAMAICA, indeed, they talk of one negroe as a man of parts and learning; but 'tis likely he is admired for very slender accomplishments, like a parrot, who speaks a few words plainly.[7]

Hume plainly articulates how Western scholars' views on ancient nations and civilizations are filtered through the Europeans views concerning the intelligence and humanity of enslaved Africans. Hume recounts that he actually has been told of an African in

Jamaica (possibly enslaved) who is a man of great intellect; however, he cannot even fathom that his skills are genuine. After all, he believes that he has seen enough enslaved Africans in the colonies to believe that all are inferior. He concludes that the Jamaican example must actually be an African who is only talented at mimicking what he has been told "like a parrot".

Hume is certainly not alone amongst Western scholars in the virulence of his racist beliefs or his fundamental misunderstanding of the centrality of the contributions of African nations. These views didn't seem to abate during the 1800s either.

Georg Hegel is often considered "the summit of early 19th Century German thought" and even the "Aristotle of modern times".[8] Hegel is at least as revered in the field of philosophy during the 19th century as Hume was during the 18th century. Their stature is not the only thing they have in common.

> Africa ... is no historical part of the World; it has no movement or development to exhibit. Historical movements in it—that is in its northern part—belong to the Asiatic or European World. Carthage displayed there an important transitionary phase of civilization; but, as a Phoenician colony, it belongs to Asia. Egypt will be considered in reference to the passage of the human mind from its Eastern to its Western phase, but it does not belong to the African Spirit. What we properly understand by Africa, is the Unhistorical, Undeveloped Spirit, still involved in the conditions of mere nature, and which had to be presented here only as on the threshold of the World's History.[9]

Once again we find a Western philosopher who discounts the importance of African nations; however, Hegel seems to be more familiar with a number of the great civilizations in the region than Hume. He notes that Carthage (located in modern-day Tunisia, North Africa) and Egypt are of importance. Unfortunately, he also discounts whether these nations are African at all. As the influence that these African civilizations had on the development of early Western nations has become more familiar, this argument continues to be popular. British physician and ethnologist, Charles Gabriel

Seligman also advances the argument that every African civilization of renown could not possibly be ethnically or racially African. His 1930 book attempts to designate a number of different African races.

> Apart from relatively late Semitic influence ... the civilizations of Africa are the civilizations of the Hamites, its history the record of these peoples and of their interaction with the two other African stocks, the Negro and the Bushman, whether this influence was exerted by highly civilized Egyptians or by such wider pastoralists as are represented at the present day by the Beja and Somali ... The incoming Hamites were pastoral 'Europeans'--arriving wave after wave--better armed as well as quicker witted than the dark agricultural Negroes.[10]

Seligman attempts to describe the inferiority of Africans by placing it within Biblical folklore referencing the sons of Noah.[11] As Noah's ark saved humans and animals from the flood which destroyed all other living things, his sons are considered the ancestors of all modern humanity. According to the story, Noah becomes highly intoxicated one evening and falls asleep naked. One of his sons named "Ham" (Hamites) sees his father's nakedness and instead of addressing it, he tells his brothers. The brothers enter their father's tent to cover him. When Noah wakes, he curses Canaan, the son of Ham to be the servant of his brothers. In folkloric tradition of the Abrahamic religions, Ham is identified as the dark southern peoples of the world. In fact, Christian plantation owners during the Trans-Atlantic enslavement trade used Ham's punishment and the curse of his son, Canaan, to justify African bondage.

Seligman's argument is an attempt to "have one's cake and eat it too". According to the very religious folklore that he references, the Kemites and other Africans are Hamites. Seligman does not acknowledge that this folklore would attribute one of the world's greatest civilizations to Black folk. Abrahamic folklore also describes Semitic enslavement in Kemet, Seligman also knows that the Kemetic civilization long predates the Semitic people. Kemetic greatness is not a result of the late and relatively brief interaction with the Semites which occurs in the biblical myth. Seligman's use of this folklore would leave him in a tricky place if he wants to discount Africa's great civilizations. How does he address this contradiction? He simply attributes these civilizations to "white" Hamites.

The racist notion that Africans could not have created an advanced civilization has so thoroughly permeated modern society that this ludicrous argument is quite common. How could anyone possibly believe that *any* reputable nation on an entire continent over the course of several thousand years was the result of foreign influence? If one made this argument about any other continent, the general public would deem it laughable. However, many people believe this same argument when the continent of Africa is discussed. This argument must be dismantled by those who have the most to benefit, people of African descent.

While we have demonstrated that the racist notion that Africans contributed nothing to human civilization has been widely articulated for over 300 years, not every Western scholar during this period would agree. We will find that Europeans who are most familiar with ancient African societies acknowledged ancient African ingenuity. French philosopher and historian C.F. Volney[12] embarked on an amazing journey to Egypt and other countries in the region in 1782. What he discovers turns the racist argument that we have described on its head.

> Those piles of ruins which you see in that narrow valley watered by the Nile, are the remains of opulent cities, the pride of the ancient kingdom of Ethiopia (the term often used by author to reference ancient Black civilizations). ... There a people, now forgotten, discovered while others were yet barbarians, the elements of the arts and sciences. A race of men now rejected from society for their sable skin and frizzled hair, founded on the study of the laws of nature, those civil and religious systems which still govern the universe (Parentheses added).[13]

Not only does Volney note with palpable surprise that the originators of the most important elements of civilization are

Africans, but he also acknowledges the great travesty done to their descendants. In the cruelest irony, the sable skinned, frizzy haired mothers and father of civilization are now those who are rejected.

While his position is much more unusual, Volney is not the only Western scholar to recognize the central position of African nations in the development of civilization. Joseph McCabe, free thinker, writer, and former Roman Catholic priest, also contrasts the ancient position of the European.

> The accident of the predominance of white men in modern times should not give us supercilious ideas about color or persuade us to listen to superficial theories about the innate superiority of the white-skinned man. Four thousand years ago, when civilization was already one or two thousand years old, white men were just a bunch of semi-savages on the outskirts of the civilized world. If there had been anthropologists in Crete, Egypt, and Babylonia, they would have pronounced the white race obviously inferior, and might have discoursed learnedly on the superior germ-plasm or glands of colored folk.[14]

So if so many Western philosophers and historians described African nations as uncivilized, how can we prove this racist notion is wrong? How can we support the corrective arguments of Volney and McCabe? What are the contributions of African nations to civilization?

The Real Deal

In order to dismiss the racist notion that Africans contributed nothing to human civilization, we will outline several critical areas which advanced the progression of humanity. We will see that Africans were the ancient innovators who developed these fields and taught them to other racial/ethnic groups.

As Kemet stands at the forefront of early civilization and was the crown of ancient Africa, it will be a major focus of this section. We will also mention the accomplishments of other early African nations. Some might question the cultural and racial makeup of

Kemet. Establishing Kemet as culturally and ethnically African will be the focus of chapter three.

ANCIENT AFRICAN CONTRIBUTIONS TO SCIENCE AND MEDICINE

> The art of healing is [amongst the Kemites] divided up, so that each physician treats one ailment and no more. Egypt is full of physicians, some treating diseases of the eyes, others the head, others the teeth, others the stomach and others unspecified diseases (Brackets added).[15]
>
> Herodotus, Circa 5th Century, BCE

> In Egypt the men are more skilled in medicine than any of human kind.[16]
>
> Homer, *Odyssey*, Circa 850 BCE

Ancient Kemet's contributions to science and medicine are almost too numerous to number. At a time when writing was still a very new concept, Kemet had already recorded early doctors ... of both genders. There won't be historical records of doctors in other nations for over 1,000 years, but this nation's medical field already has specialists. Early physician, architect, prime minister and poet, Imhotep is the world's first recorded polymath (multi-genius).

Image 2.3: (Left) Bronze statue of Kemetic physician and multi-genius, Imhotep and (Right) wooden bas-relief of ancient dentist, Hesy-Ra

Imhotep, who lived around 2600 BCE, seems to have authored the world's earliest medical text, now erroneously called the Edwin Smith Papyrus.[17] The text focuses on traumatic injury, outlining 48 cases. It proves the Kemites recognized important organs such as the heart, blood vessels, liver, bladders, spleen, kidneys, and uterus. One section of the papyrus also deals with the importance of the pulse in diagnosing health. It is written in a manner similar to modern medical journals. It outlines a problem, describes previous approaches to resolving it and then applies a suggested treatment to a group which is split into the experimental section and a control section (which does not actually receive treatment). Scientists and scholars won't begin to arrive at this level of scientific study in the Western world for over 4,000 years![18]

While Imhotep's prominence occurred during one of Kemet's earliest eras, called the Old Kingdom by historians, he was not the only doctor of his time. Two important contemporaries are Hesy-Ra and Lady Peseshet.

Buried in a magnificent tomb in Saqqara, Kemet, Hesy-Ra was the chief of dentists and physicians and also the chief of scribes. Virtually all of the information available about Lady Peseshet comes to us from her son's tomb. It is clear, however, that she served as chief of female physicians and is one of the first female doctors in recorded history. Kemet had doctors in a wide range of specialties including ophthalmologists, proctologists, and even gastroenterologists.[19]

A well-spring of early important medical artifacts also displays the adeptness of Kemetic physicians: ancient dentures, the world's first prosthetics device and even the oldest surgical tools. While we find a number of items which are also used for spiritual healing, they are often intertwined with processes which a modern doctor could hardly discount. For example, a variety of amulets and wands protect pregnant mothers, but the Kemetic people also understood that a pregnant mother's body experienced significant chemical changes. They devised one of the first pregnancy tests as they used a woman's urine to measure the comparative growth of wheat and barley seeds. The procedure was quite effective at not only dictating pregnancy, but also the gender of the child.[20]

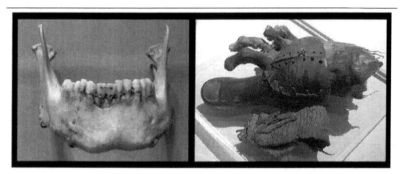

Image 2.4: Kemetic Dentures/Bridgework and the World's Oldest Prosthetic Device

While Kemet sits at the forefront of civilization, it is not the only African nation to bring excellence to the medical sciences. For example, the Akan people of West Africa created a procedure for small pox inoculation. The procedure was outlined by an enslaved African named Onesimus to the New England minister, Cotton Mather, who enslaved him.[21] This information was quite helpful as small pox outbreaks were common in the region.

There are also descriptions of advanced medical procedures in Uganda and Rwanda reported by European travelers in the 1800s. They witnessed African traditional doctors successfully conducting the surgical procedure often called the Caesarian section today.[22] These practitioners anesthetized the patients with banana wine and used the heads of biting ants to close the incision. The ants' heads were an effective means to suture wounds as they would naturally dry up and fall of.

ANCIENT AFRICAN CONTRIBUTIONS TO MATHEMATICS
As a result of the African enslavement trade, there are few who would believe that it was African nations who brought advanced mathematics into the world. It is actually possible that highly developed mathematical study spanned across several ancient African nations into the distant pre-historic past.

If most scholars familiar with the history of the world were asked about the origins of mathematics, they would probably begin with Greece and Rome, not a remote mountain region in Southern Africa. However, it appears that the story of mathematics begins in a region not too distant from where some of the oldest human fossils have also been discovered. Excavations in the 1970s in the Lebombo Mountains which stretch between Swaziland and South Africa unearthed one of the oldest mathematical artifacts in the world. The artifact is known as the Lebombo bone. A notched fibula bone of a baboon, the bone is dated to somewhere between 44,000 and 43,000 years old.[23] It is similar to the calendar bones which are still used by the San people of Namibia today. The artifact featured 29 distinct notches, which have led some to contend that it might have been a lunar counting devise used by a female mathematician.[24]

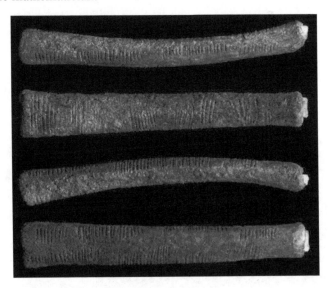

Image 2.5: The Ishango bone, pictured above from 4 sides, is permanently located at the Royal Belgian Institute of Natural Sciences in Brussels.

Roughly ten years earlier a very similar artifact was discovered by Belgian geologist Jean de Heinzelin de Braucourt near the Semliki River in the Congo. While much younger than the Lebombo bone, the Ishango bone is still one of the oldest mathematic artifacts in the world (approximately 20,000 years old).[25] Interestingly, the bone is also a notched fibula of a baboon. It has a sharp piece of quartz attached to one end. The notch system on the Ishango bone seems to be much more complex, than its predecessor. It features three columns of asymmetrically grouped tallies. Scholars differ on whether these tallies represent a numerical system or a lunar calendar which might have been used to track the female menstrual cycle. It is possible once again that the world's earliest mathematicians/astronomers were African women.[26]

Why would both of these African mathematical artifacts be created on the fibula of a baboon? The reason must be significant, especially when considering that 20,000 years and 1,200 miles separate them. What is the significance of the baboon in ancient African philosophy?

While a precise answer has not been determined, it is interesting to note that in Ancient Kemet, the deity of mathematics, lunar energy and esoteric wisdom is Tehuti (misnomered Thoth by the Greeks). Tehuti is usually depicted as an ibis bird, but the baboon is considered sacred to him. Is it possible that a unified mathematic school stretched thousands of miles and tens of thousands of years into African history? Additional research into this important history must be conducted.

Image 2.6: (Left) The Kemetic Deity, Tehuti (Greek: Thoth) in baboon form and (Right) Rameses III paying homage to Tehuti in ibis form. Take note of his headdress which seems to reference the phases of the moon as it seems to be both a crescent and full moon in one.

A land replete with stone structures in an almost unimaginable scale, it is obvious that Ancient Kemet featured an extremely advanced understanding of mathematics. Some authors who contest the extent that the Kemetic people utilized advanced mathematics usually do so with a peculiar argument. They attempt to compare Kemet to later civilizations that greatly benefited from extensive contact with them. In doing this they fail to give the important African nation credit for their level of mathematic comprehension thousands of years before so called Western nations (in this instance Greece and Rome) were even in existence.

At the very beginnings of Kemet, before virtually any other nation of note, we find that the new Kemetic kingdoms are using mathematics. Excavations of the Dynasty I and Dynasty II burials in the city of Abdju (Greek: Abydos) uncovered small ivory tags which were used to identify grave offerings. Some of these tags were etched with numbers. Just a few generations later this culture would build the world's first building in stone and even the massive pyramids which seems to attest to a comprehensive understanding of mathematics.

The Ancient Kemetic people also codified at least some of their mathematic studies in a number of papyri. These have come down to us in a rather haphazard fashion. Some were discovered at archeological sites; others found their way into the hands of Arab "antiquity dealers" who simply sold these important historical documents to Westerners. How many more of these historic documents would be found if they were treated with the respect they deserve? How many important documents, connections to ancient African genius and civilization, are deteriorating in dusty boxes in the homes of wealthy Europeans?[27] Perhaps we will never know.

Of the notable Ancient Kemetic mathematic texts which have been rediscovered and analyzed, two papyri are of major importance: the Moscow and Rhind Mathematical Papyri. Neither of these names are proper names for these texts. Most Kemetic papyri are currently known by the name of the modern city where they were found, the name of the European who purchased it, or for the location or institution where it currently resides. It is unfortunate that these monumental mathematical texts are not known for the types of problems they feature or the individuals who developed them.

The Moscow Mathematical Papyrus is permanently housed at the Pushkin State Museum of Fine Arts in Moscow (hence the modern name). It was previously named for Russian

Egyptologist Vladimir Golenishchev, who purchased the papyrus in the city of Luxor in 1892 or 1893. It is believed that the text was created in the Kemetic Middle Kingdom (around 1250 BCE). It includes 25 mathematic problems which are geometric or algebraic in nature. The problems include challenges to find the missing dimensions of a ship's parts, the strength of beer based on the quantities of ingredients, the amount of workers' output, and finally the proportions of 2 and 3 dimensional items.[28]

The Rhind Mathematical Papyrus is often considered the best existing example of Ancient Kemetic mathematics.[29] Its modern name comes from Alexander Henry Rhind, the Scottish antiquities collector who purchased it in 1858 in Luxor. It was rediscovered during illegal excavations in or near a temple built by King Ramesses the Great. The papyrus may have been written around 1650 BCE by a scribe named Ahmes for King Amenemhat III. The scribe Ahmes tells us that the text provides us with the "correct method of reckoning, for grasping the meaning of things and knowing everything that is, obscurities and all secrets".[30] Clearly a deeper, more esoteric meaning was placed on mathematics by the Ancient Kemites compared with our literal, mechanical applications today. The text is divided into three distinct books. Book one is comprised of tables outlining the Kemetic use of fractions with 20 arithmetic and 20 algebraic problems. These problems outline the Kemetic understanding of common denominators, linear equations, and arithmetic progressions. Book two focuses on geometric problems which find volumes and areas of objects. It concludes with devising the slope (or seked in the Kemetic language) of pyramids. Book three offers more problems on the multiplication of fractions, geometric progression, and even computes the fractions which correspond to the sections of the eye of Heru (Greek: Horus). The Rhind Mathematical Papyrus proves to us that our Kemetic ancestors invented algebra. Unfortunately, the scribe Ahmes receives no credit for this act. The next time a young student of African descent expresses frustration with mathematics and proclaims that he or she is not "good with math", we should ask the student one question: "How could you not be good at math when you created it?"

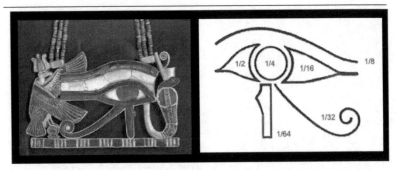

Image 2.7: The Eye of Heru (Greek: Horus) and corresponding fractional sections

ANCIENT AFRICAN CONTRIBUTIONS TO ARCHITECTURE
What is one of the most common misconceptions about contemporary Africa? Anyone who has traveled to Africa has probably been asked, "Do Africans live in huts?"[31] This question is not usually asked by folks who harbor racial animus for people of African descent. In that case it would be phrased as a statement ... not a question. The question often comes from people, from a wide range of ages, who are genuinely interested in Africa. It is even asked by people of African descent who have not visited the continent themselves. As innocent as the query might be, it is based on the racist depictions that have been advanced primarily by Europeans for over 300 years.

Image 2.8: (Top) In a scene from *Tarzan Finds a Son!* (1939), Tarzan towers over the "savage" Africans who live in huts (Top). (Bottom) *Jim Carrey in Ace Ventura: When Nature Calls* (1995). Note the huts in the background.

When asked whether Africans live in huts, how does a frequent traveler respond? They probably counter with, "Some Africans live in huts, but most live in large cities similar to the one you live in." Unfortunately, this response doesn't actually address the core of the issue. The specific discussion is probably not about "huts". People all over the world live in a variety of residential configurations. Is there anything objectively wrong with a hut in relation to other houses?[32] At a time in human development when our exploitation of natural resources puts us on the brink of global disaster, a locally-sourced home which withstands the elements well has a particular appeal. In reality the questioner might actually be trying to understand several deeper issues; issues that are scarcely discussed and are the remnant of hundreds of years of propaganda.

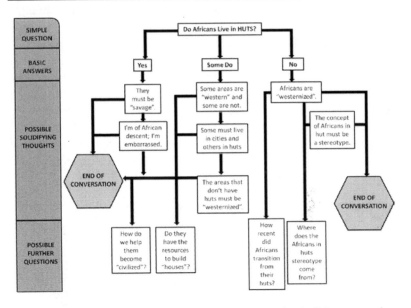

Table 2.1: Conversational Analysis - Possible deeper meaning in light conversations about "Africans in Huts"

In actuality, architecture is often used as a benchmark for judging a nation's degree of high culture and civilization. In roughly 140 BCE, the Greek poet Antipater of Sidon may have originated the list called the seven wonders of the ancient world.[33] These architectural accomplishments have captivated the world for nearly two thousand years. Over the last 130 years, countries around the world have been engaged in an ever increasing race to build the world's tallest building.[34] While taller, more complex structures may not necessarily be a corollary of civilization; nations have used it in this manner for quite some time. Where does Africa stand in this history? Jewish-American socialist thinker and publisher, E. Haldeman-Jullus had an interesting perspective on the matter.

> It is pretty well settled that the city is the Negro's great contribution to civilization, for it was in Africa where the first cities grew up.[35]

While many question African civilization and discount African architecture, it is in Africa that advanced architecture has its birth.

We will find that Africa has a history of architectural excellence which spanned nearly 4,000 years, boasting most of the world's architectural achievements as it virtually created the discipline.

Fairly early in the 3,000 year term of Ancient Kemetic history, the standard of excellence in architecture was set at a time before virtually any other European or Asian nation of note was in existence. At around 2667 BCE, the planning for the burial structure of Third Dynasty Kemetic ruler, Djoser Netjerikhet, led to a critically important development in architecture and engineering.[36]

Image 2.9: (Left) King Djoser Netjerikhet, (Center) the Khebu-Neteru or Step Pyramid, and (Right) the multi-genius, Imhotep

The standard burial development at the time of the planning of Djoser's burial tomb was called the "per djet" or the "house of eternity" (often called the Arabic term for mud bench, "mastaba"). The classic per djet during this period was a mud brick structure which tapered at its top and concealed a vertical shaft leading to an underground tomb. Djoser's second-in-command, the world's first recorded multi-genius, Imhotep created a radical plan for the development. He began by planning a large square per djet which would be built not out of mud brick, but out of stone. He then slowly built smaller stair-stepped square structures on top of each other. The magnificent Step Pyramid (Khebu-Neteru in the Kemetic language) was the final design; a gigantic, six stepped building which is widely regarded as the first large stone building in the world.

Image 2.10: Image of a typical per djet structure and diagram. [37]

A few short generations later another powerful ruler would once again seek to create a previously inconceivable monument. The Fourth Kemetic Dynasty ruler Khufu would base his eternal monument on his father's successful effort to build a flat-sided pyramid (mer or mrkhut). The Great Mrkhut is the only remaining structure of the seven wonders of the ancient world. Originally standing at 481 feet tall and covering an area of approximately 13 acres, the structure took around 20 years to build. Megalithic stone blocks varying in weight from 15 to 2.5 tons[38] were moved from their nearby quarry and placed so perfectly that a sheet of paper cannot be placed between them. These blocks were aligned to the cardinal points with only the smallest amount of deviation. In order to complete the positioning of the nearly 2,300,000 blocks within the projected time, 315 stones would have had to be moved per day (working 365 days and maximum construction time of 20 years). This magnificent structure should be considered an ancient African skyscraper, as it remained the tallest structure in the world for 3,800 years.[39] The Great Mrkhut has continued to captive people around the world for thousands of years, ironically, it is not entirely clear how it was built. Even with the use of modern tools, its construction is unfathomable.

Image 2.11: The Great Mrkhut (Pyramid) on the Giza Plateau

In 1978, archeologists from Waseda University in Japan attempted to build a model one-sixth the size of the Great Mrkhut at a spot overlooking the actual monument. They initially planned to utilize what scholars believed to be the types of ancient tools used to build the structure: wooden mallets and copper chisels. They also attempted to utilize manpower to move the blocks into place. They were actually unable to cut the stone with these tools or even transport the blocks successfully. They ended up using air hammers, flatbed trucks, cranes, and even helicopters. In the end, their structure was so badly built that the blocks had major fissures and scratches. The Egyptian government forced them to dismantle the structure and abandon the project. While many would likely discount African ingenuity and engineering skill, it seems that even modern societies have failed to equal it.

When compared to the mrkhut (pyramid) and the many other impressive architectural feats of the Kemetic people, it would seem that the obelisk would be a simple task. However, it still stands as a powerful example of an ancient high technology civilization. The sacred simplicity of the obelisk, originally called the tekhen by the Kemetic people, has been long sought after by European societies.

It is nearly impossible to visit an old cemetery in any nation in the world and not see modern replicas of the noble tekhen. From its ancient roots as a representation of the resurrection of Ausar (Greek: Osiris) and to the rebirth of the human soul, it has continued to be utilized as a signature of the afterlife. Additionally, there are probably thousands of significant modern monuments which are based on the tekhen (including the Washington Monument). It has become so common, that there are those who revere them that are not as familiar with its original meaning and Kemetic origin.

Many European countries once clamored for an original Kemetic tekhen. Of the roughly 50 known extant tekhenu (plural of tekhen), only nine of them remain in Kemet. The ancient Romans were truly focused on symbolically attaining the ancient spiritual power these monuments held. They removed more tekhenu from Kemet than any other group, while only 9 tekhenu remain in Kemet/Egypt, Italy boasts 11 today. Other modern Western cities coveted them as well. With the city of London boasting 2 tekhenu and Paris receiving a tekhen in 1833, it has been documented that New York's powerful elite also sought to receive one. They believed that obtaining one would cement the city as a cosmopolitan metropolis and a center of trade.

> A great way to open the harbor and the hearts of New York would be for Your Highness to present America with an Egyptian obelisk. After all, both London and Paris have been so honored.
> - William Henry Hurlburt, Editor of the *New York World* to Ismail Pasha, Khedive of Egypt (around 1869) [40]

It would probably be normal to ask what gave these individuals the right to negotiate over these ancient African monuments; one a powerful newspaperman and the other a representative of the Ottoman/Arabic regime which would later be in power in the country. The Khedive[41] (similar to a viceroy) was anxious to begin trading Egyptian cotton in the United States. The cotton industry in the U.S. had ground to a halt as a result of the Civil War and its aftermath. Africans were no longer forced to cultivate cotton as enslaved peoples. The conditions for the arrival of the tekhen in

New York City were created by the Civil War. The deal was consummated by an Arabic conqueror that was all too willing to give away a symbol of African high culture to benefit from the sale of Egyptian cotton in the United States. It is likely that all of the powerful men involved would have considered Africans as inferior and with little ability to offer much to human civilization.

Image 2.12: (Top) The tekhen of Tehutimes III was first moved from the Kemetic city of Iunu to Alexandria by Cleopatra to honor Marc Anthony or Julius Caesar. It was later taken to New York's Central Park. (Bottom) Close-up on base of the tekhen. Notice Bronze crabs which pin the structure and allow it to stand. [42]

As much as the tekhen has been pilfered and distributed around the globe, you might think that Western nations must have obtained an in-depth understanding of them. Compared to the mrkhuti (plural of mrkhut or pyramid) they would appear to be quite simple. There are usually just 2 large stones: one comprising the shaft of the tekhen and second serving as the base. Actually carving, moving, positioning and erecting the tekhen was an engineering marvel.

After three failed attempts, an American team of archeologists led by Mark Lerner, Rick Brown, Roger Hopkins and Gregg Mullen were successful in raising a 25-ton tekhen in Massachusetts using modern technology.[43] Imagine for a moment the challenge of erecting a tekhen the size of the one now residing in New York's Central Park. Originally consecrated by Tehutimes III (Greek: Tuthmose) for the Ancient Kemetic city of Iunu (Greek: Heliopolis) around 1450 BCE, the tekhen and its base weigh 225 and 49 tons respectively. It is still not clear how the 61 foot, solid red granite structure was carved. Some believe that heavy balls of an extremely hard rock, like diorite, were used to pound the rough figure out of bedrock. From there it would be moved over 420 miles from Aswan to Iunu in a specially made boat.

Scholars have also struggled with understanding how the Kemetic people erected such structures without the use of modern tools. These amazing structures would be placed so precisely on their bases that no mortar was be used to set the stone. It simply sat in divine balance for hundreds of years. Clearly the Romans did not have this knowledge. When the tekhen that eventually ended up in New York was moved to Alexandria by Cleopatra, it was damaged. They had to "pin" the tekhen up using 4 bronze crabs. Clearly Ancient Kemetic society featured advanced knowledge in the fields of architecture and engineering, a society so advanced, that it has continued to baffle both ancient and modern Western scholars.

Ancient Kemet is certainly not the only nation to feature awe-inspiring architectural achievements. There were probably others which have not had the benefit of extensive archeological study.

Approximately 900 miles south of Kemet's borders lay another nation which had achieved excellence in architecture and engineering. It is possible that the nation now called Ethiopia was known to the ancient Kemetic people as the land of Punt. If this is the case, it seems the Kemetic people viewed the land as their origin point, sending expeditions to the region on several occasions. This African nation boasts such an extensive history that it far out dates the history of any European nation of record.

Ethiopia, the only African nation which was not colonized by Western powers, also features 11 rock-cut churches which seem to defy architectural and geological laws. The churches were already 300 years old when the first Europeans set their eyes on them. When Portuguese priest Francisco Alvares visited them in 1520 CE, he struggled to find the words to describe them:

I weary of writing more about these buildings, because it seems to me that I shall not be believed if I write more, and because regarding what I have already written they may blame me for untruth, therefore I swear by God, in Whose power I am, that all that I have written is the truth to which nothing has been added, and [that] there is much more than what I have written, [but] I have left it that they may not tax me with its being falsehood [,] so great was my desire to make known this splendor to the world.[44]

It is believed that construction on the rock-cut churches of Ethiopia was initiated under the rule of Emperor Gebre Mesqel Lalibela, who was part of the Zagwe Dynasty. The churches are located in a city originally known as Roha, now known by the name of the powerful emperor, Lalibela. The city's layout and major landmarks are clearly references to Jerusalem. Emperor Lalibela sought to create a magnificent holy city.

Lalibela's rock-cut churches may have been carved during the 12th and 13th centuries. The intricate designs, which include multiple floors, vaulted ceilings, geometric interior and exterior embellishments, and magnificent pillars which support roofs, were all carved directly into bedrock.

Image 2.12: (Top Left and Right) Exterior of the world's largest rock-cut church, Biete Medhani Alem. (Bottom Left and Right) The beautiful ceiling design of Biete Maryam.

The largest of the churches, Biete Medhani Alem (House of the Savior of the World) is likely the largest rock-hewn church in the world at approximately 110 feet long, 77 feet wide and nearly 4 stories high.[45] Its gabled roof is supported by 34 large, rectangular external columns and 38 interior columns. The interior also features 4 large aisles and a barrel-vaulted nave.

While much smaller than Biete Medani Alem, the design features of two of the rock-cut churches are particularly important. The intricately carved and vibrantly painted ceiling of Biete Maryum is awe-inspiring. The exterior "cross" design of Biete Giyorgis makes it the most recognizable of all of the churches. It is often called the eighth wonder of the world. As with many of the churches, it features a baptismal pool which fills with ground water.

Image 2.13: (Left) The author standing at the best executed Ethiopian rock-cut church, Biete Giyorgis, which is in the shape of a cross. The church is carved several stories into the bedrock. (Right) Exterior of Biete Giyorgis at the elevation of its entrance.

Archeologists continue to be amazed by Lalibela's churches. The builders were masters of the most advanced architectural, engineering, and masonry skills. How were these Africans able to identify the depth of the bedrock necessary to support multi-story structures? Why have there not been discoveries of failed sites? Were they able to construct these without extensive experimentation? How could Ethiopian geological planning be so advanced that they could build complexes with churches and baptismal pools? They plotted the ground water table so accurately that they could use it to create the pools without eroding the foundation of the church structure. Africans have demonstrated these high-tech skills for thousands of years.

Certainly this discourse on African sites which demonstrate advanced skill in architecture and engineering could have included many more sites in other regions of the continent. These African architects were so sophisticated that one of their greatest skills was the ability to visualize a structure and remove unnecessary stone by carving deep into bedrock (e.g, Lalibela's churches) or even out of an entire mountain (e.g., Ancient Kemet's Abu Simbel). This creative technique could be called "negative architecture". An abridged list of important architectural sites follows:

Site	Country	Date/Period	Significant Feature
Abu Simbel (Rameses MeryAmun)	Kemet	c. 1260 BCE	• Massive temple by Rameses II • 4 sixty-foot tall seated statues of Rameses • Miracle of Light - shaft of sunlight illuminates holy of holies 2X per year
Karnak Temple (Ipet Isut)	Kemet	c. 1960 BCE	• Largest religious complex in world • Massive columns (some 80 ft high, 30 ft wide) in Great Hypostyle Hall; 134 in total • Massive Tekhen (2 still standing), tallest nearly 100 ft) • Sacred baptismal lake and tekhen seem to be source of Washington, DC's Lincoln Memorial Reflecting Pool
Western Deffufa	Nubia/ Kush	1,500 BCE?	• 3 Story mud-brick intricate religious structure (tilled walls, rooms, colorful paintings, gold inlay rooms, etc.)
Foundations of City of Kerma	Nubia/ Kush	3,500 BCE?	• Foundations of large buildings, smaller residential buildings, roads, etc.
Grand Mosque at Djenne	Mali (Timbuktu)	13 cent. (modern mosque completed in 1907)	• Massive intricate adobe walled building • Largest clay building in the world

Table 2.2: Additional sites which demonstrate excellence in African architecture

ANCIENT AFRICAN CONTRIBUTIONS TO LITERATURE

When most people around the world think of great philosophers, poets, and scholars, they probably don't think of Africans. This travesty is the result of the extensive racist propaganda which has been foisted against people of African descent. Simply review the literacy disparities which exist for students of African descent compared to students of European or Asian descent. What are the roots of these disparities? How did the most literate people of the world become its weakest performers?

When the South Carolina legislature passed the Negro Act of 1740, it sought to further restrict Africans who were enslaved in its borders in some familiar ways. The Act made it illegal for these Africans to travel on their own, assemble in groups, cultivate crops for their own benefit, and even earn money. These sections of the law were clearly structured to ensure the complete dependence of the enslaved African. If they could not travel on their own, any African found on a solitary journey would probably be considered a fugitive. If they had no way to earn money on their own, they would probably never be able to buy their freedom or the freedom of loved ones. While reprehensible, these sections of the law could be expected. If the State of South Carolina was attempting to strengthen the system of slavery and further subjugate the enslaved, these provisions are logical. Interestingly, two additional sections of the law also demonstrate just how wicked the law was.

One provision of the Negro Act of 1740 sought to ensure that children of enslaved people should have the same status of their mother.

> And be it enacted ... [t]hat all Negroes and Indians, (free Indians in amity with this government, and degrees, mulattoes, and mustizoes, who are now free, excepted,) mulattoes or mustizoes who now are, or shall hereafter be, in this Province, and all their issue and offspring, born or to be born, shall be, and they are hereby declared to be, and remain forever hereafter, *absolute slaves, and shall follow the condition of the mother*, and shall be deemed, held, taken, reputed and adjudged in law, to be chattels personal[.] (Italics and brackets added)[46]

Why was this provision deemed necessary? In Western cultures lineage is often traced along the paternal line. This is why married women and their children often take (or hyphenate) their husband's surname. Why was this different with regard to enslaved peoples? This provision actually acknowledged and adjusted for the prevalent rape of enslaved African women. If the status of enslaved

African women's children followed that of their father, an entirely new class of individuals would have been created. Perhaps this class would also threaten the entire system of enslavement. These biracial children would be wealthier than the same working class whites who were taught to harbor racist ideas. Early plantation owners were concerned that groups of Africans and working class whites would consolidate to overthrow the system that exploited them. South Carolina's elite could not allow this to happen.

Image 2.14: *The Three Young White Men and a Black Woman* (1632) by Dutch painter Christiaen van Couwenbergh addresses the issue of the sexual abuse of enslaved African women in vividly painful reality.

The other provision in the Negro Act of 1740 which best demonstrates the deviousness of slavery is the section which restricts the education of enslaved Africans.

> ... every person and persons whatsoever, who shall hereinafter teach or cause any slave or slaves to be taught, to write, or shall use or employ any slave as a scribe in any manner of writing whatsoever, hereafter taught to write, every such person and persons, shall, for every such

offense, forfeit the sum of one hundred pounds current money.[47]

This provision is quite interesting. South Carolina's law was written in light of a revolt of enslaved Africans, known as the Stono Rebellion, which occurred the previous year. Led by a literate African named Jemey, the Stono Rebellion was one of the largest revolts of enslaved Africans in the history of the colonies.[48] South Carolina's response to the rebellion clarifies that the most ruling class of the colony did not completely believe the propaganda about the inferior, animal nature of Africans. In order to control an animal, restricting movement is sufficient. In order to completely control a human, one must control the mind.

South Carolina was not alone in its approach. All of the colonies would soon pass "slave codes" which would vigorously restrict reading and writing among the enslaved Africans. They sought to create and maintain illiteracy among the world's first literate people, and ignorance among those who first nurtured the light of knowledge. This section of the codes was very effective in ensuring the subordinate position of the African.

So what was this thunderous drive that colonial masters and slaveholders were looking to subdue? What is the ancient literary history of the African?

Any discourse on the early contributions to the field of literature must begin with the African nation which seems to emerge nearly full-formed from the pre-historic era, Ancient Kemet. In fact, the artifact which describes the unification of the two separate regions into the nation we know as Kemet, is often described as the world's first historical document[49]; that is, the world's first artifact which includes writing that records an actual event.

Sometime around 3200 BCE, a ruler from Upper Kemet (located in what today would be called the south) moved into Lower Kemet (today's north) to conquer its rulers and consolidate the "two lands" into one nation. King Narmer's activities are recorded on the artifact known as the Narmer Palette. The palette was rediscovered in 1898 by the British Egyptologist James E. Quibell in the city of Nekhen (Greek: Hierakonpolis).

Image 2.15: The Palette of Narmer (front and reverse sides shown) records the successful movement north of the first Kemetic ruler, Narmer. The king unified the region creating the nation of Kemet.

On the front of the palette, the king is shown wearing the crown of the south "smiting" the people of the north, and then marching with his flags wearing the crown of the north on the reverse. Most importantly to our discussion, one can find the name of Narmer written above his head. The very event which creates the nation of Kemet also establishes it in history as a "literate" nation; the first of its kind.

With this auspicious beginning, it should be expected that this nation's body of literature would be significant. There are many documents of note in Kemetic literature. Perhaps none is more important than the Maxims of Ptahhotep, the world's oldest complete book.[50]

Comprised of 37 teachings on living a moral, productive life, the Maxims were written by Ptahhotep, the second-in-command of the

Fifth Dynasty ruler, Isesi. He tells us that he writes his teachings for his spiritual son, a young man who might be the successor to the throne. The author tells us that he only writes his wisdom down at the age of 110 after listening to his ancestors and to the divine. The teachings, which cover topics like domestic affairs, "vocational" success, and intimate relationships, are remarkably relevant today. While translations of the book are accessible and available for purchase in many venues, images of Ptahhotep are rarely printed. Perhaps this is due to the fact that his features are clearly African.

Image 2.16: Life-sized statue of Ptahhotep (left) and frieze from his tomb in Saqqara, Egypt.

The Maxims of Ptahhotep are one of the earliest texts in an important genre of Kemetic literature called sebayt or "wisdom" literature. Included in the genre is also the Instructions of Amenemope, which many scholars believe may be the actual origin of the biblical Book of Psalms.[51]

Just as Ancient Kemet influenced the books that would become the Bible, its influence is replete in Western society. While modern Western scholars are often careful to acknowledge it, Greek intellectuals learned much from the African nation.

Greek traveler and scholar, Diodorus Siculus explains:

> [Many scholars] celebrated among the Greeks for intelligence and learning, ventured to Egypt in olden times, that they might partake in the customs, and sample the

teaching there. For the priests of Egypt cite from their records in the holy books that in the former times they were visited by Orpheus and Musaeus, Melampos, Dsedales, besides the poet Homer, Lycurgus the Spartan, Solon the Athenian, and Plato the philosopher, Pythagoras of Samos and the mathematician Eudoxos, as well as Democritus of Abdera and Oenopides of Chios, also came from there.[52]

Ancient Africans gave birth to civilization. They stood at the cusp of a pre-historic world and through excellence in the fields of mathematics, literature, architecture, and medicine they selflessly provided the ancient world with the materials to enter the modern era. As we have demonstrated, numerous Western sources exist that have clearly attested to this role. Why have the fallacies depicting a primitive, uncultured people been offered? What is the reason for the lie?

Reasons for and the Effects of the LIE

The rationale for the "uncivilized" African depiction is two-fold. First, as we have already described in chapter 1, depicting Africans as without humanity and/or civilization affords their exploitation during enslavement. It allayed European consciences. After all, if Africans are essentially "beasts of burden", what's the harm in enslaving them? Hard work is what they were created to do. When poor and working class Europeans begin to believe this fallacy, the result is a wedge between all exploited people. This provides the powerful ruling class with easier social control over the entire structure of exploited people.

The second reason is not only much more common today, but it is also a bit more subtle in its racist perspective. The rationale is that since Africans are not capable of offering any contributions to civilization, the powerful Western ruling class can exploit more than just human resources. This class can also exploit the natural resources of the continent. Proponents of this view actually believe that Africans can't form their own governments, access their own natural resources, and establish the infrastructure to develop these resources on their own. Modern proponents feel that they simply need to establish more equitable terms of exchange and not be brutal to people in order to correct past injustices. "After all", the thinking continues, "there is nothing wrong with the West owning another region's natural wealth. They were not going to do anything with it anyway."

> Although Britain was not able to replicate its success in India everywhere across its vast colonial empire, it is still clear the empire gave its colonies real, tangible benefits. Wherever the British ruled, they erected a light, relatively inexpensive form of government that was not corrupt, was stable, and was favourable to outside investors.
> Its imperial civil servants may not always have been completely sympathetic to local peoples, but they were always motivated by humanitarian impulses and did their best in often difficult circumstances. Indeed, when we look at Africa, many of the benefits of imperial rule were squandered in the generations after independence with a succession of corrupt and brutal regimes.
> - Nick Lloyd, King's College London (2011)[53]

Arkansas Congressman Jon Hubbard harbored similar views in his book, *Letters to the Editor: Confessions of a Frustrated Conservative*:

> The institution of slavery that the black race has long believed to be an abomination upon its people may actually have been a blessing in disguise. The blacks who could endure those conditions and circumstances would someday be rewarded with citizenship in the greatest nation ever established upon the face of the Earth.[54]

Notice how these views never acknowledge the "underdevelopment" of Africa through de-peopling, colonization, and the manipulation of African governments. They describe Africa as the "dark continent"; undeveloped, dangerous, mysterious, and savage. There is no acknowledgement of Africa's amazing past and its trajectory which was greatly altered primarily by Europeans during the greatest human tragedy in history. This racist argument allows Western powers (and others) to continue to exploit the African continent undeterred. There need be no reparations or even fair trade with the continent, because, as the argument goes, Africans have never had the ability to effectively manage their own affairs.

This argument has not only been advanced by Europeans, but also by people of African descent who have been brainwashed to think that their people have no history and no civilization. Some of these pitiful Africans have even been thankful for their enslavement as it allowed them to escape the *savage* African continent.

> I'd like to take this time to thank you Caucasian people for inviting us here to America. That was real nice of y'all. You know y'all laughin' but I'm serious than a mother f*xxxxx ... 'cause I watch the Discovery Channel and Africa ain't a place a nigga want to be right now. Them mother f*xxxxxx over there starving, hungrier than a mother f*xxxxx. I'm staying right here in America where I can get a bucket of chicken for $3.95! You know what I'm saying? F*xxx the dumb s*xxx, man! Cause you always see them starving kid commercials of Africans look like they've been eatin' powdered donuts all around their mouth and s*xxx, flies all around their damn head. I'm watching last night ... one of 'em had a fly on his eyeball. On his goddamned eyeball! I'm sitting there yellin' at the TV set, 'Blink, mother f*xxxxx! Blink!' ... I ain't going back to no Africa. I mean America we got our own little problems with racism and s*xxx, but this the only country where you could start out with nothing and end up with a whole lotta s*xxx. Where the f*xxx I'ma do a comedy show in Africa? 'Live from hut number 3!' You know what I'm sayin? Monkeys throwing s*xxx at a nigga doing a show (throwing motion). 'Hey why don't you grab your monkey let me finish this show.'
>
> - Eddie Griffin, *Voodoo Child* (1997)[55]

African-American conservative news pundit, Rev. Jesse Lee Peterson has a similar view.

> I've often said that, 'Thank God for slavery,' because, you know, had not, then the blacks over here would have been stuck in Africa... Everybody and their Mama are trying to

get out of Africa and come to America and so God has a way of looking out for folks and He made it possible by way of slavery to get black folks into this country ... The ride over was pretty tough but you know, it's like riding on a crowded airplane when you're not in First Class. It's a tough ride. But you're happy when you get to your destination... I thank God that he got me here and to show my appreciation to the blacks who suffered as the result of coming here, and Arabs and blacks who sold us to the white man, the white man for going there and getting us and bringing us here, I want to say, 'Thanks'.[56]

It is one thing when your enemies question your humanity and your ability to contribute to civilization, it is quite another when you question yourself. The powerful European ruling class has no problem with Diasporan Africans shunning their motherland. If the continent of Africa is the birthright of its people, African-Americans are also heir to the most valuable land mass on the planet. When Africans state that they have no interest in a land they have been brainwashed to believe is "savage" and undeveloped, it simply means that powerful Europeans have less competition as they continue to rape the continent of its resources. Africans, continental and Diasporan, must reclaim the image of their African ancestors as the parents of civilization. This correction will also lead to ultimate African control of the continent. *There is no more important task.*

For Additional Research

BOOKS
1. Diop, Cheikh Anta. (1989). The African Origin of Civilization: Myth or Reality. Chicago, IL: Chicago Review Press.
2. Diop, Cheikh Anta. (1988). Precolonial Black Africa. Chicago, IL: Chicago Review Press.
3. Browder, Anthony T. (1992). Nile Valley Contributions to Civilization (Exploding the Myths). Washington, DC: Institute of Karmic Guidance.
4. Volney, C.F. (1890). The Ruins. New York, NY: Twentieth Century Pub. Co.

5. Hilliard III, Asa; Williams, Larry; and Dimali, Nia (Eds). (2012). The Teachings of Ptahhotep: The Oldest Book in the World Paperback. Grand Forks, ND: Blackwood Press.
6. Williams, Chancellor. (1992). Destruction of Black Civilization: Great Issues of a Race from 4500 B.C. to 2000 A.D. Chicago, IL: Third World Press.
7. Obenga, T. (1995). Readings in Precolonial Central Africa: Texts & Documents. Lawrenceville, NJ: Red Sea Press.
8. Saggs, H.W.F., (1991) Civilization Before Greece and Rome. Yale University Press.
9. Finch III, Charles S. (1998). The Star of Deep Beginnings. Decatur, Georgia: Khenti, Inc.
10. De Villiers, M. and Hirtle, S. (2007). Timbuktu: The Sahara's Fabled City of Gold. New York, NY: Walker Publishing Company.
11. Bauval, R and Brophy, T. (2013). Imhotep the African: Architect of the Cosmos. Newburyport, MA: Disinformation Books.

VIDEO
1. Wesley Snipes (Executive Producer) and St. Claire Bourne (Director). (1996). *Dr. John Henrik Clarke: A Great and Might Walk* [Motion Picture]. United States: Black Dot Production.

CHAPTER 3:
"THE ANCIENT EGYPTIANS WERE 'CAUCASIAN'"

Image 3.1: Screenshot from *Exodus: Gods and Kings* (2014) demonstrates how main characters are played by white actors. The film's black actors are guards, servants, or assassins.

Uncovering the Lie

The biblical epic, *Exodus: Gods and Kings,* was poised to be one of the biggest films of 2014. Acclaimed director Ridley Scott would create a colossal epic with sweeping vistas as large as the 1956 film, *The Ten Commandments.* This wasn't the only similarity. When the casting for the film was announced, critics immediately took to the internet to voice their concerns. Lynn Hamilton, a 56 year-old woman of Scottish descent, created an online petition to "tell Ridley Scott to stop racist casting". She adequately explains some of the film's problems with race.[1]

> The casting kind of looks like a throwback to the era of the Charlton Heston films and, as such, is playing into this very misguided idea that the origins of Judaism and

Christianity are in a community that looks like they're from Minnesota or Sweden ... If there was a Moses, then he would not have looked like Christian Bale. ... If you're going to create a story and tell a story that's set in ancient Egypt, then I guess I think that the characters should look like they belong to ancient Egypt ... I remember going to Sunday school class, and the teacher would pull these cardboard cutouts of Moses and Noah out of the box ... and they were invariably old, white men in robes. They looked like my next-door neighbor, but in robes. Imagine as a child to have that inculcated in me that all of the heroes of Christianity are white. I do think that's kind of wrong.[2]

Not all of the films actors were white, director Ridley Scott *did* cast actors of African descent, but their casting points to something even more disturbing. Nearly all of these actors played servants, guards, or even assassins. All of the film's major roles are played by white actors.

Confronted with this disturbing trend and dealing with threatened boycotts and protests, the film's creator and financer were forced to respond publicly. Director Ridley Scott argued that the project couldn't find funding if people of color were in major roles; racist "whitewashing" was the only solution.

I can't mount a film of this budget, where I have to rely on tax rebates in Spain, and say that *my lead actor is Mohammad so-and-so from such-and-such*. I'm just not going to get it financed. So the question doesn't even come up. (Italics added)[3]

Right-wing Chairman and CEO of 21 Century Fox studios, Rupert Murdock, was much more confrontational. He took to Twitter on more than one occasion to respond.

Moses film attacked on Twitter for all-white cast. Since when are Egyptians not white? All I know are. (11/28/14 8:07 AM)

Everybody attacks last tweet. Of course Egyptians are Middle Eastern, but far from black. They treated blacks as *slaves*. (11/28/14 8:22 AM) (Italics added)

Okay, there are many shades of color. Nothing racist about that, so calm down! (11/28/14 8:53 AM)[4]

While both men sound defensive about their casting decisions, they both seem to argue that the Ancient Kemetic people were not Africans. Scott implied that the historically accurate cast would be "Islamic" (Mohammad) while Murdock was much more abrasive. He relegates Blacks to "slaves". Perhaps this prospective would be more painful were it not for the fact that it is quite common.

Image 3.2: The racially and ethnically inaccurate cast of *Gods of Egypt* (2016) generated a "proactive" apology from its director, Alex Proyas, and Lionsgate Studios.

The film *Exodus: Gods and Kings* was not the only recent film to encounter public critique for its casting. The 2016 film *Gods of Egypt* featured Danish, Australian, and Scottish cast members as Ancient Kemetic people and its deities. The movie's producers were likely aware of the backlash faced by the creators of *Exodus*, both the director and studio actually apologized for their ethnically and racially inaccurate cast three months prior to the release of *Gods of Egypt*.[5]

The critically acclaimed actor Chadwick Boseman, was the only main character of African descent. While Boseman portrayed a "god" like his European counterparts, he also was the only "god" who referred to the European lead character as "my lord". This interaction seems to have subtlety alluded to the racial hierarchy depicted in the film. There were very few actors of African descent in the film. Nearly all of these actors were servants, peasants, or barely relevant extras.

Where does the "white Egyptian" argument originate? How does it become so prevalent? We will endeavor to describe the argument and its facets before defeating it.

ARGUMENT #1 - THE 'WHITE' EGYPTIAN: FOREIGN WHITES BUILT KEMET
When French linguist Jean-François Champollion announced in 1822 the translation of the ancient Kemetic writings on the artifact known as the Rosetta Stone, interest in Ancient Kemet reached a fever pitch.[6] Ancient Kemetic "hieroglyphs" had been widely recognized as the lost language of the most important early civilization. The process of deciphering the large granodiorite stone was far from simple. After its rediscovery by a French soldier, it took 20 years of diligent study before the writing would reveal its secrets.

The importance of the Rosetta Stone was recognized almost immediately. The artifact featured the same inscription in three different scripts: a formal "priestly" version of Ancient Kemetic Medu Neter (Greek: hieroglyphs) on the top, Ancient Kemetic Demotic (business/legal Medu Neter writing) in the middle, and Ancient Greek on the bottom. Champollion's announcement thrust Ancient Kemet into public consciousness. Who were these mysterious progenitors of civilization? How did they build these massive monuments and why did they entomb their kings and queens in wondrous vaults of gold? The answer that some of these early 'Egyptologist' would provide was stunning.

Champollion revealed little publicly on his thoughts concerning the racial and ethnic background of the Ancient Kemetic people during his life. However, one year after his death, his brother,

Champollion-Figeac, printed letters he received from his brother during his time in Egypt (1828 - 1829). In his letters, Champollion describes seeing a relief which is often called the "races of man" from the tomb of Senusret I.

Image 3.3: Picture based on a wall relief depicting the four groups of people the Ancient Kemetic nation had contact with (left to right): The Libyan, the Nubian, the Syrian, and themselves. Drawn by German Egyptologist Heinrich von Minutoli from the tomb of Seti I. This image is very similar to the relief which is found in the tomb of Senusret I

Champollion expressed embarrassment concerning the ancient depiction of the white European (called the "Tamhou" by the Kemetic people). He believes that they seem "savage". He continues to describe the similarities of the Kemetic and Nubian people.

Europeans who, in those remote epochs, frankly did not cut too fine a figure in the world. In this category we must include all blonds and white-skinned people living not only in Europe, but Asia as well, their starting point. This manner of viewing the tableau is all the more accurate because, on the other tombs, the same generic names reappear, always in the same order. We find there Egyptians and Africans represented in the same way, which could not be otherwise; but the Namou (the Asians) and the Tamhou (Europeans) present significant and curious variants.[7]

There are other Western scholars who agree with Champollion's position during this early era of the field of Egyptology including C.F. Volney (*Ruins of Empires*, 1791), Godfrey Higgins (*Anacalypsis*, 1838), Issac Cory (*Cory's Ancient Fragments of the Phoenician, Carthaginian, Babylonian, Egyptian and Other Writers,* 1878), and Gerald Massey (*Ancient Egypt Light of the World, Volumes 1 and 2*, 1907). Taking this position during the height of enslavement and immediately after its gradual dissolution in the Western world must have been quite challenging. As we have described in previous chapters, the very humanity of enslaved Africans was questioned during the Trans-Atlantic enslavement trade. However, this position is reversed as the field of Egyptology becomes more "institutionalized". The field will no longer explicitly acknowledge that Ancient Kemet was "racially" and ethnically African.

Image 3.4: Often considered the "father of American Egyptology", James Henry Breasted views were quite influential in the formative stages of the field.

Considered the "Father of American Egyptology"[8], James Henry Breasted is easily one of the most revered scholars in the field, even more than seventy years after his death. Breasted was the first American to earn a doctoral degree in Egyptology. In order to obtain the degree, as the field was virtually non-existent in the United States at the time, Breasted spent much of his adult life in Europe. He ultimately worked with legendary Egyptologist Adolf Erman in Germany.

As World War I commenced, the field of Egyptology was held captive by the machinations of the Nazi Party. With Egyptology still nascent in the United States and Europe ravaged by war, the field found itself on precarious footing.[9] At the close of the war, Breasted finds the environment primed to secure the field in the United States. One of the centers of the field, Germany, was now in shambles and the rest of Europe was either decimated or in considerable disarray. It is at this point that Breasted convinces the Standard Oil heir and philanthropist, John D. Rockefeller, to commit significant funding to his educational institution, the University of Chicago. Rockefeller's multi-year grant would establish the Oriental Institute at the University of Chicago with the expressed mission to expand the cultural and intellectual roots of Western civilization beyond Greece and Rome. This mission would also be wedded to Breasted's own racial and cultural biases. One would imagine his views would be greatly colored by the enslavement of Africans, which had only ended about 50 years earlier, and the continuing views of African inferiority. Breasted described his belief that the world's darker people played no role in the development of Kemetic society by dividing the world into artificial quadrants in his seminal work, *The Conquest of Civilization*.

> The population of the Great Northwest Quadrant, from the Stone Age onward, has been a race of white men of varying physical type. The evolution of civilization has been the achievement of this Great White Race .... On the *south* of the Northwest Quadrant lay the teeming black world of Africa, separated from the Great White Race by an impassable desert barrier and unfitted by ages of tropical life for any effective intrusion among the White Race, the

negro and negroid peoples remained without any influence on the development of early civilization.[10]

It would be unfair and overly simplistic to argue that it was Breasted's racist views which single-handedly generated the anti-African view of Ancient Kemet. As we have already described, painfully racist attitudes were created to ensure the success of the forced subjugation of Africans nearly 250 years earlier. There were certainly other Western scholars who argued that foreign Europeans from an unknown nation migrated to build Ancient Kemet. But one must ask if the powerful Rockefeller family would have assisted in the advancement of the field of Egyptology if it was believed that it was Africans who built this great ancient nation. Would these views become as prevalent if the major international centers of study were not weakened by war? With Western scholars in a variety of nations articulating the African racial and cultural heritage of Kemet during and immediately after African enslavement, could this concept have gotten stronger were it not for the growing role of the Institute and Breasted's racist ideas? We will see that the "white" Ancient Egyptian argument has also survived in other more subtle forms. We will explore both the overt and less obvious forms en route to refuting them.

DISMANTLING ARGUMENT #1 - FOREIGN WHITES AS BUILDERS OF KEMET

There are at least four basic counters to the argument that Ancient Kemet was built by foreign whites. First, we must begin with a simple logical counter. It is as simple as it is effective.

Ancient Kemet was an amazing high tech society which single-handedly brought humanity into civilization. As we've described in our previous chapter, Kemet provides the world its first body of literature, advanced mathematics, scientific and medical contributions, and massive feats of engineering and science. If we just look at the contributions in engineering and architecture, for example, we find the amazing pyramids (mrkuti) which continue to inspire awe thousands of years later. If James Henry Breasted is correct and a group of advanced Aryans ventured into North Africa to create one of the world's most advanced civilizations, where did they come from? Where in Europe (or elsewhere for that matter) did they create an earlier advanced society? Where are their earlier feats of architecture and engineering? For example, where are their pyramids? When Kemet was established by Narmer in 3200 BCE, there were no European nations of note in existence. Greece and Rome don't enter the world stage until 2,000 years later. There are those who would argue that these Aryans only created their advance civilization in Kemet, not prior. This nonsensical argument would be akin to a failing student becoming an honor student over the summer with absolutely no sign of preparation or additional work. This makes no sense.

The second counter to the argument that foreign whites were the builders of Ancient Kemet is a simple review of the manner in which the Kemetic people depicted themselves. The image from the book of gates which is found in tombs of Senusret I and Seti I (see image 3.2) is not the only depiction of the Kemetic people as African. We can also review the "personal portraits" of the rulers of this great nation. From coffin lids, tomb reliefs, drawings on papyri, and statues, there are millions of images across 3,000 years to review. In order to properly situate the African nature of Ancient Kemet, which of these images should we review?

A review of all of the available images of the Ancient Kemetic people would be quite interesting. However, with the sheer volume of them and the fact that they are distributed in museums and collections all over the world would make this a lengthy endeavor. Clearly there are many other rulers and important individuals who have demonstrative African features. However, not all of these individuals played an equally important role in Kemetic society. We will instead look at the rulers from the four "critical eras" of Ancient Kemetic history. These rulers established and maintained this great nation throughout its more than 3,000 year existence. This approach will allow us to gauge the African "nature" of this nation. Let's review the distinctive African features of these rulers.

Table 3.1: Faces of Kemetic Rulers Across the 4 Critical Eras

King Narmer Dynasty 1, c. 3100 BCE	King's Reuniter & Middle Kingdom Founder	King Ahmose Dynasty 18, c. 1570 - 1546 BCE	King Shabaka Dynasty 25, c. 716 - 702 BCE
Kemet's Founding Father	**Kemet's Reuniter & Middle Kingdom Founder**	**Indigenous Rebellion Leader & New Kingdom Founder**	**Kushitic (Nubian) Ruler who Reunites Kemet**
Originally the ruler of just the southern region, Narmer moves to conquer the northern kingdom creating Kemet. After this event, which is commemorated on the world's first historical document, the Palette of Narmer, Kemet will be known as the "two lands".	After the near total collapse of the Kemetic nation, a family of rulers from the important city Waset slowly work to re-unify it. This process spans 4 generations and culminates with Mentuhotep. He is highly regarded by his successors throughout the balance of Kemetic history.	After Kemet is ruled by foreign rulers often known as the Hyksos, a family from Waset (500 years after Mentuhotep) fights to remove the usurpers. The patriarch and eldest son are killed in separate battles. The matriarch, Queen Aahotep leads the war until her son Ahmose is of age. Together they conquer the Hyksos.	While often considered a foreign ruler, Shabaka assists his brother Piye to return Kemet to its former glory as it was controlled by weak regional 'kings'. Asked by the priests of Amun for help, Piye moves northward with Shabaka to conquer these petty rulers, renovate temples, secure important texts, restore stables, etc

Most Egyptologists virtually ignore the centrality of the rulers during these four critical eras. Prior to the advent of the internet and other media which allow curious individuals to view a large number of the depictions of the Ancient Kemetic people, Egyptologists did not need to justify the anti-African view. Today that position is clearly illogical, so it is normal for Egyptologists today to describe Kemet as '"multicultural". This allows them to acknowledge the overwhelming number of reliefs, statues, drawings, and coffins that display their owners as African, but to somehow imply that these items are insignificant in comparison to the entire body of artifacts. They will then reference the small group of images on artifacts which do not seem to display pronounced African features. This approach is extremely disingenuous. First of all, most of the artifacts display the images of African people. Furthermore, the Europeans that advance this argument are the descendants of those who found it advantageous to legally construct the "one drop of black blood" standard for blackness during the Trans-Atlantic Slave Trade. However, when it comes to the progenitors of civilization, they would have us believe that in order for these individuals to be considered African, they would need to have the darkest possible skin and the widest possible features. We must understand that even Africans on the continent today who have had little or no intermixing with foreign groups display a range of complexions and features that are still considered "African".

Was every single person who lived in Kemet during its more than 3,000 year history of African descent? Of course not, according to this ridiculous standard, none of the countries of Eastern Europe today should be considered European as long as they contain the smallest number of "ethnic" immigrants. We know that people from all over the Mediterranean traveled to Kemet as it was the most prosperous nation in the region. This does not alter the fact that it was a nation *primarily* inhabited, ruled, and populated by *indigenous Africans*.

The third counter to the "foreign whites were the builders of Ancient Kemet" argument is that the *Kemetic people actually described where they originated from.* Throughout Kemetic history they acknowledged their ancestral origins in the land of

Punt.[11]   The oldest existing reference to Punt in Kemetic texts seems to be on the artifact known as the Palermo Stone from the 5th Dynasty Kemetic ruler, King Sahure.[12]   Kemetic rulers in the sixth, eleventh, twelfth, and eighteenth dynasties sent expeditions to the nation of Punt, the nation that they also called "Ta-Neter", or the "Land of the Creator". The best record of these trips seems to be the expedition commissioned by Queen Hatshepsut of the Eighteenth Dynasty. Hatshepsut etched images of the Land of Punt on the walls of her magnificent mortuary temple, Djesser Djesseru. Among these scenes are images of full incense trees, animals, the homes of the people of Punt, and most importantly images of Punt's king and queen, Eti and Parehu.

Image 3.5: Wall relief from the mortuary temple of Queen Hatshepsut displaying Queen Eti and King Parehu of Punt during a Kemetic expedition to Punt. Note the steatopygic body shape of Queen Eti. Queen Eti's large buttocks is not only commonly found in African women nearest to the area where the earliest humans are found, but is a trait in virtually all early female deities around the world (e.g. the "Bird Lady" located in the Brooklyn Museum and the Venus of Willendorf, Austria)

For decades scholars debated whether Punt was located in Southern section of Northeast Africa or on the western coast of modern Saudi Arabia. It is likely that some of the reticence with locating Punt in Africa was due to racial bias. Also complicating the identification was the fact that ancient descriptions seemed to describe several different ways to reach Punt, including traveling by land, navigating the Nile River, or even navigating the Red Sea. However, the overwhelming majority of contemporary scholars have now solidified Punt as an ancient African nation. First they analyzed images of animals including fish, giraffes, hippopotami, and baboons. Many of these animals were strictly of an African origin.[13] Finally the location of Punt became even clearer in 2010 when a research team from the Egyptian Museum and the University of California performed oxygen isotope analyses on mummified baboons from Punt in the British museum. These studies showed significant similarities with modern baboons in the region around Eastern Ethiopia and Eretria.[14]

At long last, the African origin for the Kemetic people is described by the strongest source of all, the Kemetic people themselves. The Kemites always maintained that Punt was their source of origin.

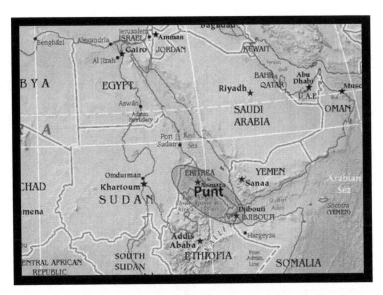

Image 3.6: Map of North Eastern Africa displaying likely location of the Land of Punt.

The fourth counter to the "foreign whites were the builders of Ancient Kemet" argument comes from the monumental work of one of the most esteemed African scholars of the last century, Dr. Cheikh Anta Diop.

Born in Caytou, Senegal in 1923 to a family of means, Diop demonstrated his intellectual prowess at an early age. In high school he created an alphabetic system to transcribe African languages and began writing a history of Senegal. He received the equivalent of his bachelor degree in Mathematics and Philosophy.

At the age of 23, Diop traveled to Paris to continue his studies. He soon enrolled in the Philosophy program at Faculté des Lettres de la Sorbonne. Diop was not just an extraordinary intellectual, but a broad thinker with the ability to master multiple complex subjects. He received his degree in Philosophy, and later two degrees in Chemistry.[15] Attempting to obtain his doctorate at the Sorbonne, Diop focused his controversial thesis on proving the Ancient Kemet rulers were of African descent. He wrote three separate theses on the topic without the acceptance of the university. Diop finally received the degree after supporting his work with a cadre of unassailable specialist in a wide variety of fields.[16] His extensive study in Paris allowed him to build expertise in fields including philosophy, anthropology, history, linguistics, physics, mathematics, and Egyptology.

Image 3.7: The Senegalese polymath known as "The Pharaoh", Cheikh Anta Diop, brought skills in an amazing number of fields to bear on the battle to recast Ancient Kemet in its proper African context.

Cheikh Anta Diop's life work was to reestablish Africa's role in the development of human civilization. He worked tirelessly to re-contextualize Ancient Kemet as culturally, linguistically, and racially African. He would bring together his disparate fields of expertise in a manner not previously seen.

One of Diop's most important contributions was his Melanin Dosage Test. Utilizing his advanced skills in anthropology and physics, Diop developed a test to measure the level of melanin in the boundary area between two layers of the skin, the epidermis and the dermis. Diop found that, contrary to the general position of other scientists, the melanocytes in this area were not damaged by the mummification process. By measuring the level of these melanocytes, one could accurately determine the amount of pigmentation. Diop conducted this process on mummies at the Mus'ee de l'Homme in Paris, proving the "blackness" of these royal mummies. He requested access to the mummies of several important rulers located in the Egyptian Museum in Cairo to no avail. It seems that this scientific approach to discovering the racial makeup of the Ancient Kemetic people was quite threatening.

While the argument supporting the migration of an ancient European group who supposedly built the civilization of Ancient Kemet has been dismissed, it is certainly not the only manner that the racial makeup of the Ancient Kemetic people has been misrepresented. Some of these arguments don't regularly appear in scholarly settings, but their effect is possibly even more wide-ranging and detrimental.

ARGUMENT #2 - KEMET'S GREEK RULERS ARE ETHNICALLY THE SAME AS INDIGENOUS KEMITES (FOCUS ON THE LAST STAGES OF KEMETIC HISTORY)
The global fascination with Ancient Kemet has certainly not been restricted to scholarly circles. From Roman emperors building Kemetic gardens in their palaces to Europeans using pulverized Kemetic mummies for medicinal purposes up until the early part of the 20th century, Kemet has resonated in the minds of people all over the globe for nearly all of human history.

Image 3.8: (Left) An apothecary vessel in Germany containing the pulverized bones of an Ancient Kemetic mummy[17] and (Right) an individual *selling the bodies of our Ancient Kemetic ancestors* (circa 1875). These mummies were available to the public for purchase.

Correspondingly, the "white Kemite" argument also has a similarly wide ranging reach. There are several common "pop culture" arguments which tend to be much less explict than scholarly arguments. Ultimately they don't need to withstand any sort of rigourous scrutiny to be effective. Afterall, more individuals will attend a major blockbuster film in one summer than will enroll in a college history course over a decade.

Perhaps the most prominent of the pop culture arguments advancing the concept of the European origin of Ancient Kemet is one that is nearly subliminal. It has been consistent over the course of the last hundred years. It is the implication that the Greco-Roman usurpers of Kemet in the latest period of Kemetic history are somehow ethnically representative of the nation's more than 3,000 year old tenure.

In order to effectively demonstrate this argument, virtually all of the feature and television films from the last 100 years were reviewed for this book. A very interesting pattern was noted. Forty-two film depictions could be placed in an identifiable period in Ancient Kemet history.

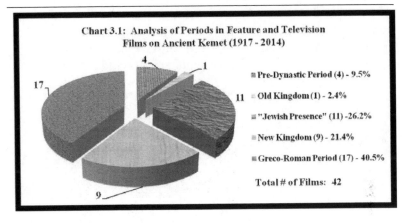

Chart 3.1: Analysis of Periods in Feature and Television Films on Ancient Kemet (1917 - 2014)

- Pre-Dynastic Period (4) - 9.5%
- Old Kingdom (1) - 2.4%
- "Jewish Presence" (11) - 26.2%
- New Kingdom (9) - 21.4%
- Greco-Roman Period (17) - 40.5%

Total # of Films: 42

Of the 42 film depictions, 17 (40.5%) depict the Greco-Roman period. The next largest portion of films, 11 (26.2%) depict the biblical story of the Jewish people in Kemet (Joseph and Moses).[18]

The prevelance of films which feature the Jewish people in Kemet seem to make logical sense. Seventy-three percent of Americans identify themselves as Christian[19]; biblical stories should appeal to a broad segment of the movie-going populace. However, when we discover that the largest segment of films depict the Greco-Roman period, we realize that another motivation may be at play. The Greco-Roman films, which mostly include Cleopatra VII as a major character, can credibly present people of European descent as the focus. Cleopatra was a Ptolemaic ruler; her lineage was Greek.

There are some who would argue that the reason that there are an inordinate amount of film depictions from this period is due to the story of Queen Cleopatra. Cleopatra is sometimes called a "woman of surpassing beauty"[20]. Her life was filled with political intrigue, brutal family squabbles, taboo inter-cultural liaisons, and romantic suicide. It would seem that she was primed for dramatic novelization. However, 3,000 years of older Kemetic history is certainly not without epic, sensational stories. Yet, we have not seen even one film on the founding of Kemet (King Narmer), the most powerful queen who comes to reign as king (Hatshepsut), or even of the family that wages a war to free Kemet of its cruel foreign rulers (The 17th Dynasty). The life of Cleopatra, and even the story of the Jews in Egypt to a lesser extent, has been so often depicted on the screen because the Europeans who create these films feel they can identify with her. The continued production of this story creates a formidable argument for a European Kemet not due to its historical accuracy, but simply by generational repetition.

Image 3.9: Cleopatra Throughout the Ages - (Left) Theda Bara starred in the 1917 silent film "Cleopatra". While only 20 seconds of the film have survived, it was one of the most successful and expensive films of its day. (Right) Laetitia Eido also played Cleopatra in the 2011 "docudrama", the Destiny of Rome. Why have there been so many depictions of Cleopatra VII?

DISMANTLING ARGUMENT #2 - KEMET'S GREEK RULERS ARE ETHNICALLY THE SAME AS INDIGENOUS KEMITES (FOCUS ON THE LAST STAGES OF KEMETIC HISTORY)

Dismantling the strategy of focusing on the Greco-Roman period in order to "whiten" Ancient Kemet is actually quite simple. The pop culture arguments are extremely effective because they reach a very large number of people and are almost undetectable, but they do not withstand basic scrutiny. The only thing truly necessary is a basic understanding of Kemetic history.

The Ptolemaic dynasty of rulers came into power in Kemet after it was taken out of the control of the Persians by Alexander the Macedonian in 332 BCE. This period initiates the control of Kemet by Greek rulers who remain in the country rather than returning home and controlling it remotely. Cleopatra VII, who comes to power after her family lived in Kemet for over 200 years, was the sixteenth Ptolemaic ruler. It is possible that she would be considered of "mixed race" background today, but clearly her line originated in Greece.[21] For the purposes of this discussion, we will continue to allow her to be of primarily European/Greek descent.

Attempting to equate the story of Cleopatra VII with the story of 3,000 years of Kemetic history is akin to casting Denzel Washington as the lead in a biographical film on American founding father, George Washington! She should probably not be considered ethnically representative of the Ancient Kemetic people.

At this point there are some who would ask the question: How can you prove the Greeks were ethnically/racially different than the Kemetic people? To answer this question we simply need to allow the ancient Greeks to speak for themselves. The highly-regarded, selectively-quoted, father of Western history, Herodotus explains that the Ancient Kemetic people who he visited around 454 BCE were "black" four hundred years before the reign of Cleopatra VII. When explaining why he believed another nation in the region was related to Kemet, he simply tells us that they look the same:

> For the people of Colchis are evidently Egyptian and this I perceived for myself before I heard it from others. So when I had come to consider the matter I asked them both; and the Colchians had remembrance of the Egyptians more than the Egyptians of the Colchians; but the Egyptians said they believed that the Colchians were a portion of the army of Sesostris. *That this was so I conjectured myself not only because they are dark-skinned and have curly hair.* (Italics added)[22]

Herodotus is not the only early Greek to describe the Kemetic people as African. As he opines in his treatise on understanding the relevance of physical traits and temperament, the philosopher Aristotle agrees.

> Too black a hue marks the coward, as witness Egyptians and Ethiopians ... and so does also too white a complexion, as you may see from women.[23]

While we can't agree with Aristotle's assessment that human bravery corresponds to complexion, this portion is irrelevant to our study. What is most important is that a much heralded Greek philosopher compares the Kemites with the "burnt face" Ethiopians and considers them both black! How could we possibly accept the subtle representation of Cleopatra as emblematic of the ancient African society that gave civilization to the world?

ARGUMENT #3 - THE ANCIENT KEMETIC PEOPLE ARE ETHNICALLY THE SAME AS MODERN 'ARABS' WHO CURRENTLY INHABIT THE COUNTRY

When the exhibit *Tutankhamun and the Golden Age of the Pharaohs* arrived at Philadelphia's Franklin Institute in February 2007, it did so with great fanfare. The roving international exhibit featured fifty objects from the tomb of the boy king; objects rarely seen outside of the Egyptian Museum in Cairo. The exhibit drew large crowds in Los Angeles, Fort Lauderdale, and Chicago. The Franklin Institute would mark the first time since the 1980's that an exhibition from the tomb of King Tutankhamun would arrive along the dense population corridor of the United States' Northeast.

The scores of African Americans who protested the exhibit seemed to catch organizers off guard. Unlike the international exhibition which visited the region during the 70s and 80s, this exhibit featured a silicon three dimensional model created by French forensic scientists from intricate scans of the skull of Tutankhamun. The model, which is still displayed today, seemed to support the concept that the king's features were quite similar to those of the people living in modern-day Egypt; people who many would call "Arabs". Protestors demanded that the model be removed from the exhibit.

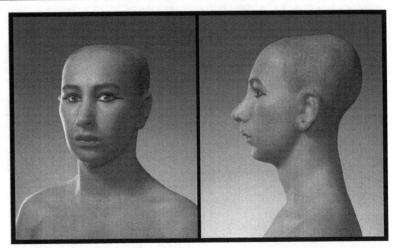

Image 3.10: The "Forensic" Three Dimensional Model of King Tutankhamun

On September 6, 2007, the Secretary of Egyptian Antiquities, Zahi Hawass came to deliver a lecture in tandem with the Franklin Institute exhibit. After facing protests aimed at the "Arabization" of the image of Tutankhamun, Hawass was visibly annoyed. He decided to directly respond to the protestors.

> Tutankhamun was not black, and the portrayal of ancient Egyptian civilisation as black has no element of truth to it ... Egyptians are not Arabs and are not Africans despite the fact that Egypt is in Africa.[24]

Hawass's puzzling comments are not unusual. Depictions of the Ancient Kemetic people in contemporary documentaries, museum exhibits, text books, and even popular images (like television commercials) are usually of "Arabic" ethnicity today. How can we debunk this representation and "re-Africanize" the Ancient Kemetic people?

Image 3.11: Arabs as the Kemetic people - (Upper Left) A recent Geico Insurance commercial, (Bottom Left) the History Channel documentary "Planet Egypt", and (Right) a documentary depiction of the African multi-genius Imhotep.

DISMANTLING ARGUMENT #3 - THE ANCIENT KEMETIC PEOPLE ARE ETHNICALLY THE SAME AS MODERN 'ARABS' WHO CURRENTLY INHABIT THE COUNTRY

Given the forensic model of King Tutankhamen, Zahi Hawass's quizzical comments seem to argue that the Ancient Kemetic people are "racially" and ethnically similar to the modern Egyptian people. It also appears that he would like to pretend that the modern Egyptian people are not Arabs. This position, which the author must admit he has personally heard from modern Egyptians, is quite interesting as the official name of the modern country is the "Arab Republic of Egypt".

Zahi Hawass might have expected that some of the discussion around the "African-ness" of the Ancient Kemetic people to be resolved with the creation of the three dimensional model. He sought to create the impression that the process of creating the forensic model was beyond racial bias or influence. Along with *National Geographic*, he led the effort to use modern forensic science to recreate images of the king. Computerized tomography (CT) scans and plastic models of the king's skull were given to three separate teams: French, Egyptian, and American. The

American team was not told who the subject was. It would later become clear just how biased the process actually was.

The public press release announced that the two teams that were told who the subject was at the outset decided that the traits they would use as a guide were "Caucasoid".[25] The American team used "North African" traits as their guide. This may seem like these decisions were made solely on the CT scans and skull models that the teams received, but we must ask ourselves an important question: If a forensic team received a request from the Egyptian government, wouldn't they automatically assume "North African" or even "Caucasoid references"? Furthermore, the press release does not acknowledge that this racial reference was not as clear cut as reported. New York University anthropologist, Susan Ashton describes this challenge in the Washington Post.

> Race, by contrast, was "the hardest call." The shape of the cranial cavity indicated an African, while the nose opening suggested narrow nostrils -- a European characteristic. The skull was a North African. With these guidelines, Anderson was able to build the shape of the face by attaching the muscles to ridges in the plastic skull and building the nose and ears from parameters developed by anatomists.[26]

Clearly Ashton's comments elucidate the fact that forensic science is still greatly influenced by "guidelines", a term which could also be described as "biases". In fact, racial and ethnic standards are routinely utilized in forensic reconstructions. Some of these standards may be less than reliable. For example, Ashton seems to have used the king's relatively narrow nostrils to categorize him as "Caucasoid". It should be noted, however, that relatively narrow nostrils are not unusual for peoples living in Northeast Africa. Considering many of the people of Ethiopia, Somalia, Kenya and several other countries have similar nostril structures and are never considered "Caucasoid", we must question the validity of these guidelines.

Image 3.12: Africans with "Caucasian" Noses? - (Left and Right) Pictures of Ethiopians priests and (Center) the Forensic Model of King Tutankhamen. Notice that the nasal structures are not too dissimilar with these men who are clearly African.

The problematic classification of "Caucasoid" seems to have led to even more egregious decisions on features which cannot be decided based on the CT scan of a skull: skin color, eye color, and even the thickness of lips. These traits tend to be even more associated with racial classifications than nostril widths. The French team's process of creating the now infamous three dimensional model was not described in the press release, but is clear in an article in National Geographic magazine.

> The National Geographic Society then chose and sponsored a French team to use the scans to create the first and most lifelike likeness. First a CT-scan-based skull model was made for forensic anthropologist Jean-Noël Vignal of the Centre Technique de la Gendarmerie Nationale.
>
> Vignal created a rough plastic skull, which was then passed along to a leading forensic sculptor, Paris-based Elisabeth Daynès. She applied an artistic touch and created a lifelike clay face meant to depict Tut on the day of his death.
>
> In addition to Vignal's scientific survey, Daynès referred to two wooden sculptures of Tutankhamun, which had been created during his lifetime. The combined sources allowed

her to flesh out details such as eyebrow thickness, nose and lip shape, and the approximate shape of Tut's ears.

From the finished clay model, Daynès created a plaster mold with a silicone "skin." *She then added a flesh color, based on an average shade for modern Egyptians. Glass eyes, hair,* and even historically accurate makeup completed the most lifelike portrayal ever of the long dead ruler. (Italics added)[27]

The creation of the forensic reconstructions of King Tutankhamen should be seen as at best flawed and at worst a piece of misleading propaganda. Dr. Zahi Hawass attempted to advance the forensic recreations as scientific. Hawass believed that the concept of Ancient Kemetic people as "Black Africans" had "no element of truth to it". Unfortunately the three dimensional model created by the French team continues to garner considerable amount of focus. Until he was recently removed from his role as head of Egyptian antiquities, Hawass has continued to utilize modern "scientific" processes on Kemetic royal mummies. Not all of the results of these processes have received public attention.

Dr. Hawass and a team of medical doctors and scientists worked to resolve one of the most controversial stories in Ancient Kemetic history, the possible assassination of arguably the last truly powerful ruler of Kemet, Ramses III.

At least one ancient text describes a series of protracted court cases which are known to modern historians as the Harem Conspiracy. The text implies that a group of individuals conspired to assassinate King Ramses III in order to take control of the throne. They seem to have been led by one of Ramses III's minor queens and their son, Pentawer. Hawass and his team utilized modern "forensic, radiological, and genetic" tools to finally reveal whether Ramses III was actually murdered and also to identify an unknown mummy as the king's son and possible murderer, Pentawer.[28]

While the team seems to have achieved their goals, a secondary, underreported result is quite important to this discussion. The team utilized genetic analysis to connect the unknown male mummy to

King Ramses III. This analysis yielded the genetic ethnic family, or haplogroup, of the powerful king. The Y chromosomal haplogroup E1b1a is the most common group found in sub-Saharan African men.[29] It would seem Dr. Hawass's argument that the Ancient Kemetic people "are not black" has been undone by his own research. It must be noted that this haplogroup occurs at a frequency of less than 10% in modern Egyptian males but is often found in rates over 70% in modern West African males.[30]

It should not be surprising that the racial/ethnic makeup of modern Egypt is different than that of Ancient Kemet. A basic understanding of history provides us with an explanation of the differences. Ancient Kemetic civilization lasted for more than 3,000 years with relatively little outside interference. However, around 800 BCE foreign incursions became much more frequent as several powers including the Persians, Assyrians, Greeks and Romans begin to contest for dominance in the Mediterranean region. When the Greeks finally take control of Kemet in 332 BCE, the intermittent periods of independent indigenous rule which mark the Late Period come to an end. Kemet would continue to be under the control of a variety of foreign powers including the Romans, the Persians, and the Byzantine Empire until 639 CE when the Arab Invasion of Egypt continues the transition toward the nation's current racial/ethnic makeup.

If we are able to understand that the current racial/ethnic makeup of the United States is radically different that it was prior to its conquest at the hands of European powers and the introduction of enslaved Africans, why are we not able to fathom the radical change in the population of Kemet/Egypt? It should be clear that large population shifts occur. Clearly a similar event occurred in Kemet. It is critical for us to understand that the Kemetic people were African and that their country was the culmination of African advancements which led to the seeds of civilization taking root in all sectors of the globe. This reality must become popular knowledge if African people will once again take their rightful place amongst the people of the world.

Reasons for and effects of the LIE

Without a deeper understanding of the role that Ancient Kemet plays in the collective human memory, it might actually seem that the debate concerning its "racial" and ethnic makeup is irrelevant. After all, what could the accomplishments of a society which flourished over two millennia ago have to do with our modern lives today? The reality is, however, that the "whitening" of Ancient Kemet is actually one of the most utilized intellectual themes of white supremacy.

Often individuals with little to no familiarity to ancient civilizations or the continent of Africa, or even history feverishly argue that it is absolutely impossible for the Kemetic people to be African. While seldom articulating it, they are actually saying, "How could the most influential ancient civilization possibly belong to the ignorant, cultureless, savage people of Africa". Of course the person voicing this sentiment would be branded a racist. This racist thinking has become so ingrained, that it does not need to be uttered. The concept of the "white"/European origin of Kemet is "popular shorthand" for white supremacy.

Image 3.13: Covers for the First Three Seasons of the Reality Show Survivor - While Survivor has aired for many seasons in "exotic" locations all over the world, these locations were never as ambiguously described as in the third season entitled, Survivor: Africa. The season's game was actually convened in Kenya's Shaba National Reserve. Wouldn't a season subtitled "North America" or "Europe" sound equally generic?

Accepting the concept of a European Kemet actually advances and supports many of the modern manifestations of white supremacy.

Let's explore this mindset. If Europeans single-handedly carried humanity from savagery to civilization, wouldn't it seem less egregious if they "took control" of foreign nations? After all, the world's darker-hued people weren't going to do anything productive with these lands anyway. Every time you hear someone articulately list European nations and then refer to a region of Africa as simply "Africa", we shouldn't actually feel offended, right? Many believe that nothing important has ever occurred in this large swarthy continent. It doesn't actually matter whether there are unique countries and cultures in Africa. Shouldn't Europeans take control of the world's vast quantity of natural resources? In fact, the enslavement of millions of people would be less nefarious. The enslaved were not productive members of advanced societies, right? They should've been honored to have had a hand in the advancement of human civilization. These people never contributed anything to the globe on their own. We must connect the fact that we have heard so little about the murder of ten million Congolese under the Belgians, or the trafficking of "conflict diamonds", or countless other African atrocities to the fact that these victims are not seen as equally significant human beings. This sort of thinking is born of the same type of bias which makes it incredulous that African people could have created one of the world's most important early civilizations; even though that nation is located on the African continent. This racist concept is also being refuted in the name of the movement which challenges police brutality in the United States, *Black Lives Matter*.

It should also be stated that this racist position is not only spouted by virulent white supremacists. "Well-intentioned" Europeans and even some people of African descent will advance this ideology unwittingly. Even liberal whites might reflexively advance this position because a corrective history challenges their very sense of themselves and their position in the world. Uninformed intellectuals of African descent will often discount the African origin of Ancient Kemet simply because the white Kemet argument is extremely familiar. They do not believe they are undermining themselves by spouting a white supremacist argument. They feel unreasonable or like "irrational Black radicals" who seem to state that Africans were the originators of everything. A recent statement of renowned African American intellectual, Dr. Henry Louis Gates, Jr. is emblematic of this.

Dr. Gates has spent his adult life advancing the work of African American intellectuals who have been nearly forgotten, searching for the African roots of African Americans, and embracing Africans across the Diaspora. However, his need to "be reasonable" has placed him on the wrong side of a number of important issues. In an article seeking to "protect academic integrity from politics", Gates derides a "vocal minority" within Black Studies who put forth "cultish, outlandish claims about the racial ancestry of Cleopatra".[31] His expertise does not lie in the area of ancient history, so it is clear that he has done little to explore the topic. Perhaps it is worse that he sums up the critical re-contextualizing of Kemet as an African nation by reducing it to a discussion about Cleopatra's racial makeup.

The tangible effects of the whitening of Ancient Kemet are disturbing. Imagine for a minute how little children of African descent would respond knowing that their ancestors gave the world virtually all of the elements of civilization. Students excelling in their classes would no longer be chided for "acting white". They might even expect themselves to rank at the top of the class in mathematics, reading, and the sciences. Instead, a recent national study found that popularity for white students increases with an increase in their grades. Paradoxically, higher grade point averages for African American and Latino students result in declining popularity. This anti-intellectual trend in communities of African descent in United States must be stemmed.[32]

"Go into any inner-city neighborhood and folks will tell you that government alone can't teach kids to learn. They know that parents have to parent, that children can't achieve unless we raise their expectations and turn off the television sets and eradicate the slander that says a black youth with a book is *acting white*"
    - Barack Obama, Keynote Address, 2004 Democratic National Convention[33]

The battle to re-contextualize Ancient Kemet as an African nation is of critical importance. The self-esteem and future success of our youth stand in the balance.

For Additional Research

BOOKS
1. Diop, Cheikh Anta. (1989). The African Origin of Civilization: Myth or Reality. Chicago, IL: Chicago Review Press.
2. Bauval, Robert and Brophy, Thomas. (2011). Black Genesis: The Prehistoric Origins of Ancient Egypt. Rochester, Vermont: Bear & Company.
3. Obenga, Théophile. (2004). African Philosophy: The Pharaonic Period: 2780-333 BC. Senegal: Per Ankh.
4. Poe, Richard. (1997). Black Spark, White Fire: Did African Explorers Civilize Ancient Europe? Rocklin, California: Prima Publishing.
5. Browder, Anthony T. (1992). Nile Valley Contributions to Civilization (Exploding the Myths). Washington, DC: Institute of Karmic Guidance.

CHAPTER 4:
"HEBREW SLAVES BUILT THE PYRAMIDS"

Image 4.1: A picture from a colorfully illustrated Haggadah which shows Jewish slaves building pyramids under the whip of a cruel Kemetic master. A Haggadah is a Jewish text which describes the order of the Passover Seder ritual, and tells the story of the Jewish Exodus from Egypt for Jewish children.

Uncovering the Lie

The year was 1977. Jewish Prime Minister Menachem Begin and Egyptian President Anwar Sadat were at the beginning of their historic negotiations to normalize relations between Israel and Egypt. If successful, their discussions would end decades of conflict and war between the two countries. In the first official visit of the Israeli delegation to Egypt, Prime Minister Begin made a routine stop at the Egyptian Museum in Cairo. The incident that followed was anything but standard.

While strolling amongst Kemet's vaunted artifacts, Begin uttered, "We built the pyramids".[1] These words caused great consternation amongst Egyptologists, historians, and even in the Egyptian press. Reasserting the Jewish role in Ancient Kemetic history through Judaic/biblical myth was not a popular way to ingratiate Israel to Egypt. Thankfully, aided by the United States, the negotiations continued. Sadat and Begin went on to share the Nobel Peace Prize in 1978.

Image 4.2: (Top) Egyptian President Anwar Sadat and Jewish Prime Minister Menachem Begin greet each other. (Bottom) Political cartoon by Palestinian political cartoonist Naji al-Ali showing Prime Minister Begin as builder of the pyramids. Notice the diminutive "Arabs" who look on as the aged Begin boasts the strength to build the massive pyramids. The smaller character on the right is the symbol of Palestinian defiance, Handala.

While some trace the story of enslaved Jews building the pyramids directly to Begin's utterance[2], its origins are actually much older. Let's explore the earliest sources of the story of enslaved Jewish pyramid laborers in Ancient Egypt prior to setting the record straight.

One of the earliest foreign descriptions of the Ancient Kemetic people and their accomplishments comes to us from the man who is often called the "Father of History", Herodotus. He is sometimes cited as the source of the epic of enslaved Jewish workers building the pyramids. While the veracity of his account is now entirely in doubt, Herodotus does describe what he was told about the construction of the Great Pyramid during his trip to Kemet in about 450 BCE.

> Cheops (Khufu) became king over them (the Ancient Kemetic people) and brought them to every kind of evil: for he shut up all the temples, and having first kept them from sacrifices there, he then bade all the Egyptians work for him. So some were appointed to draw stones from the stone-quarries in the Arabian mountains to the Nile, and others he ordered to receive the stones after they had been carried over the river in boats, and to draw them to those which are called the Libyan mountains; and they worked by a hundred thousand men at a time, for each three months continually ... Cheops moreover came, they said, to such a pitch of wickedness, that being in want of money he caused his own daughter to sit in the stews, and ordered her to obtain from those who came a certain amount of money (how much it was they did not tell me): and she not only obtained the sum appointed by her father, but also she formed a design for herself privately to leave behind her a memorial, and she requested each man who came in to give her one stone upon her building ... (Parenthesis added)[3]

Modern historians are now clear that nearly all of Herodotus's description of the building of the Great Pyramid is false. He depicts Khufu as a cruel ruler who brutally controls his people. He forces *one hundred thousand people* to work on the pyramid and even prostitutes his own daughter to pay for its construction. Perhaps this is the origin of the idea that "slaves" built the Great Pyramid. It must be noted however, that with all of the negative acts attributed to Khufu, Herodotus does not contend that he enslaved *foreign* people to build the pyramid. He does not even mention the Israelites, Hebrews, or Jews.

The earliest source of the story of the Jews building pyramids during their cruel treatment in Kemet seems to come to us from the first Jewish historian Titus Flavius Josephus. His *Antiquities of the Jews* seem to have been written around 100 CE.

> Now it happened that the Egyptians grew delicate and lazy, as to pains-taking; and gave themselves up to other pleasures, and in particular to the love of gain. They also became very ill affected towards the Hebrews, as touched with envy at their prosperity. For when they saw how the nation of the Israelites flourished, and were become eminent already in plenty of wealth, which they had acquired by their virtue, and natural love of labour, they thought their increase was to their own detriment. And having in length of time forgotten the benefits they had received from Joseph; particularly the crown being now come into another family; *they became very abusive to the Israelites; and contrived many ways of afflicting them: for they enjoined them* to cut a great number of channels for the river, and to build walls for their cities, and ramparts, that they might restrain the river, and hinder its waters from stagnating, upon its running over its own banks: *they set them also to build pyramids*: and by all this wore them out, and forced them to learn all sorts of mechanical arts, and to accustom themselves to hard labour. And four hundred years did they spend under these afflictions: for they strove one against the other which should get the mastery. The Egyptians desiring to destroy the Israelites by these labours; and the Israelites desiring to hold out to the end under them. (Italics added)[4]

While our discussion has been primarily restricted to sources that purport to be strictly "historical", it might be helpful to compare this description to a very familiar source, the Old Testament of the Christian Bible. Its description is much more comprehensive. Some scholars argue that the Book of Exodus may have been written around 600 BCE.

> And Joseph died, and all his brethren, and all that generation. And the children of Israel were fruitful, and

increased abundantly, and multiplied, and waxed exceeding
mighty; and the land was filled with them. Now there arose
up a new king over Egypt, which knew not Joseph. And he
said unto his people, Behold, the people of the children of
Israel are more and mightier than we: Come on, let us deal
wisely with them; lest they multiply, and it come to pass,
that, when there falleth out any war, they join also unto our
enemies, and fight against us, and so get them up out of the
land. Therefore they did set over them taskmasters to afflict
them with their burdens. And they built for Pharaoh treasure
cities, Pithom and Raamses. But the more they afflicted
them, the more they multiplied and grew. And they were
grieved because of the children of Israel. And the
Egyptians made the children of Israel to serve with rigour:
And they made their lives bitter with hard bondage, in
morter, and in brick, and in all manner of service in the
field: all their service, wherein they made them serve, was
with rigour.[5]

While our biblical source *does* seem to describe Jewish enslavement
in Kemet, it does not depict them toiling on pyramids like the
Josephus' account. It does seem, however, that the story of the
Jewish enslavement in Ancient Kemet might actually rest primarily
on these two early sources. Both sources could certainly be
considered biased, as they were probably written by Jewish authors.
There are no Kemetic sources which are similar to these depictions.
Additionally the Biblical source is at the very least conflated with
myth and symbolic parables. With only two sources, perhaps we
should ask how the story became so popular. Stories of Jewish
enslavement in Kemet and even of them specifically working on
pyramids have been well referenced all throughout Western popular
culture. In fact, the Jewish ordeal in Kemet has even been the very
subject of many popular dramatic productions.

Cecil B. DeMille's classic 1956 film, *The Ten Commandments*, not
only won an Academy Award but is the sixth-highest grossing film
of all time.[6] The film, which depicts Jewish enslavement in
Ancient Kemet using a number of sources (including the Bible,
Josephus, and Jewish Midrashic Texts, etc.), should be considered a
cornerstone of popular culture in the United States. The film has

been aired by the ABC network in its entirety every year since 1973 (with the exception of 2000), usually during both the Easter and Passover holidays. The broadcast can hardly be called religious charity, as it usually ranks first in the evening's time slot. In 2012, for example, *The Ten Commandments* scored the network its highest non-sports Saturday rating of the year.[7]

There have been scores of other depictions of Jewish slaves in Ancient Kemet in western popular culture. These representations span all the way into the silent film era of the early 1900s and continue into the current period. DeMille's *The Ten Commandments* should actually be considered a partial remake of his 1923 silent film, *Exodus*. In contrast, 2014's *Exodus: Gods and Kings* utilizes modern computer generated technology to retell the same story. It is interesting to note that this version implies Jewish labor on the pyramids as well, leading the Egyptian government to ban the film.[8]

The story of Jewish enslavement at the hands of the Kemetic people has also been rendered in animation. In 1998, DreamWorks Pictures released the biblical musical *The Prince of Egypt* to wide acclaim. The seventeenth highest-grossing, traditionally-animated film in history, the film also garnered an Academy Award for Best Original Song for "When You Believe".[9] The always controversial adult animated series, *Family Guy*, has also depicted Jewish slaves oppressed in Ancient Kemet in a 2005 episode. The enslaved followers of Joseph in this version are once again under the ever-present whip of Kemetic overseers as they are forced to labor on the pyramids.

Image 4.3: A screenshot from the Fox network animated show Family Guy. In a comedic interlude in the season four episode entitled, "The Courtship of Stewie's Father", enslaved Jews are seen toiling on Kemetic pyramids (see background).

It should be abundantly clear that the story of the Jewish people's cruel enslavement at the hands of the Ancient Kemetic people is thoroughly integrated within the ethos of western cultures. The "classic" depictions continue to captivate the attention of Americans at the same time new depictions are produced every year. Is this depiction accurate? Were the Jewish people enslaved in Ancient Kemet? Were they forced to toil on the pyramids? Let us re-establish the much damaged historical truth and even describe the continued effects of the story.

The Real Deal

SKILLED WORKERS VS. ENSLAVED PEOPLES
In order to understand what kind of workers built Kemet's pyramids, we must first attempt to understand the nature of their construction. Could low-skilled, unvalued, enslaved labor have constructed one of the world's most complex buildings?

Visitors standing at the base of the Great Pyramid have marveled at its enormity for thousands of years, but what is sometimes lost is just how intricate and precise it is. Upon its completion, it stood more than 481 feet and covered an area of approximately 13 acres. The gigantic stone blocks varied in weight from 2.5 to 15 tons[10] but were placed without the use of mortar so perfectly that a sheet of paper cannot be placed between them. The blocks were aligned so perfectly to the cardinal points that modern surveyors only calculate the error to one-tenth of a degree.[11] The structure remained the tallest building in the world for 3,800 years.[12]

With the nearly unimaginable precision of the placement of these immense blocks, one must ask a very basic question: Could this sort of labor have been done by a coerced labor force or by highly-skilled, well-compensated workers? Think of the most intricate, complex structures in our modern landscape. Could low-skilled enslaved people have built the Empire State Building, the Sydney Opera House, or the Burj Khalifa in Dubai (one of the world's tallest buildings)? Clearly unskilled labor is cheaper than highly-skilled labor. While we know enslaved people were not used to erect the buildings we've mentioned, why didn't the builders use scores of unskilled labors on these projects? Complex architectural and engineering projects have always required highly-skilled labor.

Is it possible that unskilled, enslaved people could have been used as brute force to transport blocks to the site and skilled labor used to complete the project? First we must recognize that the accurate placement of the monolithic stones must have required both intensive manpower and advanced surveying and engineering. Dividing these tasks would probably not have resulted in such a precise structure. Additionally we must imagine that simply adding massive amounts of unskilled labor to transport massive blocks would have probably had dire consequences.

It is believed that the construction of the Great Pyramid would have taken approximately 20 years. In order to position the nearly 2,300,000 blocks within the projected time, 315 stones would have had to be moved per day (working 365 days in each year)! This sort of labor would have either required highly-skilled workers experienced in the transportation of large objects or resulted in a massive number of casualties of lesser skilled workers. If enslaved workers were utilized on pyramid building projects like the Great Pyramid, one should expect to find tens of thousands of burials for enslaved workers who were virtually worked to death under the sheer weight of the task. What do the burials of workers tell us about the way they lived? Were they simply considered low-skilled "disposable" workers or were they highly-skilled and well-regarded? Prior to evaluating the excavations of the burial sites of Kemet's pyramid laborers, we will review the burials of enslaved peoples in the United States. What do the burials of enslaved peoples actually look like?

When workers began construction on the site that would become the Ted Weiss Federal Office Building in Lower Manhattan area of New York City in the early 1990s, they uncovered interments which were part of a site known as the "Negroes Burial Ground" in the late 1600s. The overwhelming majority of the 400 burials they unearthed contained Africans who were enslaved. The burial site was part of the largest colonial era cemetery of people of African descent.[13] Initially the federal government sought to keep the burials secret and pushed to continue their excavations and construction of the federal building, but pressure from the African American community forced the project to grind to a halt. The remains were taken to Howard University, a Historically Black College, for further study by anthropologist Michael Blakey. Blakey's study created a greater understanding of the lives of enslaved Africans. The *New York Daily News* described some of the preliminary findings in an article entitled *Slaves Worked to Death*.

A heartbreaking example of the stunted, horrific lives led by many of the slaves is the medical history of a 6-year-old boy known only as No. 39. The boy's teeth and bones tell his age and a medical history that includes malnutrition, anemia from birth, serious infections, indications of unusually developed muscles from heavy lifting and fractures of his neck bones indicating major trauma from carrying large loads on his head. Nevertheless, No. 39 was buried in the 1700s by someone who obviously loved him. He was interred among others stacked five deep in a cedar coffin, wrapped in white linen fastened with a copper shroud pin. His tale is one of 427 being sorted out by Howard University's African-American Burial Ground Project. The 427 sets of human remains were unearthed near City Hall six years ago during excavation for a new federal building. The site is believed to be the graveyard for as many as 20,000 slaves.[14]

Image 4.4: New York City's African Burial Ground Site - (Left) An aerial view of the African Burial Ground Memorial Site and (Right) Archeologists excavating the remains of an enslaved African interred at the site.

Skeletal studies of the interred remains displayed a wide array of extremely painful injuries and fractures. The very size and density of the bones of the females interred at the site were altered by the inhumane nature of the loads they were forced to carry. Researchers found the enslaved people who were buried had a very high mortality rate. Most of the adults suffered from lesions on their arms, shoulders, and legs. It was not unusual to find, multiple fractures, muscles literally torn away from the corresponding bones, and spines forced into cranial cavities. These enslaved Africans were forced to carry unimaginable loads. Pain, injury, and eventually death were routine even amongst enslaved children.[15]

The sort of misery visited upon enslaved Africans who were to single-handedly lift the Western world into the Industrial Era was nearly unimaginable. Their remains told the story of their benighted existence. At this point some simple question must be asked. How do these remains compare to those found in the burials of workers on the Great Pyramid and other pyramid sites? Would it not be logical to assume that the burials of the workers on the pyramids might be even more gruesome? If they were also coerced workers utilized to transport stones which weighed in anywhere from 2.5 to 15 tons, should we find similar if not worse injuries? Wouldn't we expect to find them extremely malnourished and with very high mortality rates? The studies of these archeological sites have yielded striking results.

When an American tourist on horseback accidently stumbled over a tomb wall in 1990, archeologists spent two decades excavating a controversial site. The results of the excavation, announced by The Egyptian government in January 2010, confirmed what some Egyptologists had argued for decades. The Great Pyramid was built by highly skilled *native* workers ... not slaves.

Excavations of the site revealed a number of vertical shafts approximately nine feet in depth with a dozen or so workers who seemed to have died during the building of the Great Pyramid. Examination of the workers' skeletons demonstrated that they had been utilized to perform the most challenging physical labor; as they showed signs of advanced arthritis and tended to have compacted lower vertebrae. Their bodies were not mummified, but they were buried in a fetal position with their heads pointing to the west. The burials also included jars which were probably filled with meals of bread and beer for the afterlife. Obviously they were held in high esteem as they were buried near the site of the Great Pyramid. Other studies of the site point to a large number of cattle and sheep which were butchered daily for their meals. Generally only the wealthy and the elite in Ancient Kemet were able to regularly consume meat.[16]

Archeologists now argue that as many as ten thousand workers may have labored in three month shifts. Construction of the Great Pyramid may have continued year round in order to complete it in time for the passing of the king. Clearly these workers were not coerced but highly valued and skilled. The discovery of the burial site provided an opportunity for scholars to express their understanding of the common misconception of enslaved Hebrew workers building pyramids in Ancient Kemet.

> Amihai Mazar, professor at the Institute of Archaeology at the Hebrew University of Jerusalem [proclaimed], "No Jews built the pyramids because Jews didn't exist at the period when the pyramids were built," ... Dorothy Resig, an editor of Biblical Archaeology Review in Washington D.C., said the idea probably arose from the Old Testament Book of Exodus, which says: "So the Egyptians enslaved the children of Israel with backbreaking labor" and the Pharaoh put them to work to build buildings ... Dieter Wildung, a former director of Berlin's Egyptian Museum, said it is "common knowledge in serious Egyptology" that the pyramid builders were not slaves and that the construction of the pyramids and the story of the Israelites in Egypt were separated by hundreds of years. "The myth of the slaves building pyramids is only the stuff of tabloids and Hollywood ... the world simply could not believe the pyramids were buil[t] without oppression and forced labor, but out of loyalty to the pharaohs (Brackets added)."[17]

The discovery of the Great Pyramid worker's burial also allowed questions about the historicity of the Hebrew slave story to emerge within the popular dialogue of modern Israel itself. Josh Mintz, writer for the online version of the oldest newspaper in Israel, raised some of these questions.

> Even if we take the earliest possible date for Jewish slavery that the Bible suggests, the Jews were enslaved in Egypt a good three hundred years after the 1750 B.C. completion date of the pyramids. That is, of course, if they were ever slaves in Egypt at all.

> It is hard to believe that 600,000 families (which would mean about two million people) crossed the entire Sinai without leaving one shard of pottery (the archeologist's best friend) with Hebrew writing on it. It is remarkable that Egyptian records make no mention of the sudden migration of what would have been nearly a quarter of their

population, nor has any evidence been found for any of the expected effects of such an exodus; such as economic downturn or labor shortages. Furthermore, there is no evidence in Israel that shows a sudden influx of people from another culture at that time. No rapid departure from traditional pottery has been seen, no record or story of a surge in population.

In fact, there's absolutely no more evidence to suggest that the story is true than there is in support of any of the Arab world's conspiracy theories and tall tales about Jews. So, as we come to Passover ... let us enjoy our Seder and read the story by all means, but also remind those at the table who may forget that it is just a metaphor, and that there is no ancient animosity between Israelites and Egyptians.[18]

The discovery of the burial of workers on the Great Pyramid is not entirely unique. Over one hundred years of excavations have been conducted at Hotep Senusret, a pyramid worker's village (known today as Kahun), which accompanies the pyramid of Twelfth Kemetic Dynasty Ruler Senusret II (circa 1897 - 1878 BCE). The village provides an intimate view into worker's skills, family organization, social institutions, and even food rations and compensation.[19, 20] A remarkable amount is known about the builders of Kemet's massive pyramids. It is absolutely clear that they were constructed by skilled workers, not enslaved Hebrews.

ENSLAVED HEBREWS AS BUILDERS OF KEMETIC CITIES AND PROBLEMS WITH THE HISTORICITY OF THE ENSLAVEMENT MYTH

Apologist of the myth of enslaved Hebrews in Ancient Kemet often relinquish the concept of Hebrew pyramid builders and point strictly to the biblical description as the source of their recomposed argument. The bible does not actually describe Hebrew exploitation as occurring during the building of the Kemetic pyramids. It mentions that the Hebrews "built for Pharaoh treasure cities, Pithom and Raamses."[21] This may explain why the cruel ruler in popular depictions of the exodus is usually Ramses the Great; even though the cruel pharaoh is never mentioned by name. Could it be that the popular depictions of Hebrews toiling forcibly on the pyramids are not entirely incorrect? Did a coerced Hebrew labor force build Kemetic cities and not pyramids?

Situating Hebrew enslavement at cities named Pithom and Raamses is burdened with the same problem that some scholars and historians encounter when they attempt to find literal historicity in many other sections of the bible. They begin their endeavor by *assuming that the biblical story is an historical event* and then they forcibly "shoe-horn" it into actual events while ignoring rampant inconsistencies and contradictions. This type of shoddy scholarship is regularly utilized in cable television documentaries. Unfortunately this approach has often been utilized in the search for these biblical cities.

> No Jews built the pyramids because Jews didn't exist at the period when the pyramids were built ... If the Hebrews built anything, then it was the city of Ramses as mentioned in Exodus.[22]
> - Amihai Mazar, professor at the Institute of Archaeology at the Hebrew University of Jerusalem

Published between 1901 and 1906, The Jewish Encyclopedia is subtitled a "descriptive record of the history, religion, literature, and customs of the Jewish people from the earliest times to the present day". It contains more than 15,000 articles and 12 volumes. While it is now more than one hundred years old, the American Jewish Archives still called the work the "most monumental Jewish scientific work of modern times."[23] The encyclopedia is reaching a new, broader audience as the unabridged series is now available online. The encyclopedia's entry on the biblical city Pithom is of great interest.

PITHOM

One of the cities which, according to Ex. i. 11, was built for the Pharaoh of the oppression by the forced labor of the Israelites. The other city was Raamses; and the Septuagint adds a third, "On, which is Heliopolis." The meaning of the term ערי מסכנות, rendered in the Authorized Version "treasure cities" and in the Revised Version "store cities," is not definitely known ... The location of Pithom was a subject of much conjecture and debate until its site was discovered by E. Naville in the spring of 1883 ... Here was formerly a group of granite statues representing Rameses II., standing between two gods; and from this it had been inferred that this was the city of Raamses mentioned in Ex. i. 11.

The Egyptian name, "Pithom" (Pi-Tum or Pa-Tum), means "house of Tum" [or "Atum,"], *i.e.*, the sun-god of Heliopolis; and the Greek word "Hero" is probably a translation of "Atum."

The discovery of the ruins of Pithom confirms the Biblical statement and points to Rameses II. as the Pharaoh that oppressed Israel. The name of the city Pi-Tum is first found on Egyptian monuments of the nineteenth dynasty. Important evidence is thus afforded of the date of the Exodus, which must have taken place toward the end of the nineteenth dynasty or in the beginning of the twentieth dynasty. (Italics added)[24]

After reading biblical passages, exclamations from professors of archaeology, coupled with pronouncements from legendary Egyptologists it would seem that there is substantive evidence of enslaved Hebrews in several Ancient Kemetic cities. None of these sources outline the significant, if not critical challenges with connecting the Hebrew people with an undiscovered Ancient Kemetic city.

First, we must understand that renowned Egyptologist Edouard Naville traveled to Egypt in the 1880s at the behest of the Egypt Exploration Fund (now known as the Egypt Exploration Society) for the explicit purpose of finding the "route of the exodus". Naville and the Egypt Exploration Fund worked to establish the historical accuracy of several biblical accounts.

Image 4.5: 19th century etching depicting enslaved Hebrews being brutally forced to erect Kemetic temples

Naville's excavations in the modern city of Tell-el-Maskhuta might have discovered the city which might have been called Pi-Atum or Per Atum (or House of Atum) in the Ancient Kemetic language. It is believed that Pithom is a Hebrew rendering of this name. Roughly eight miles away from the initial excavation site, two massive statues were discovered of the ruler Ramesses II with an inscription which also connects them to "Pi-Atum". In the vicinity of the statues were large storehouses for grain. These discoveries were enough for Naville to herald gleefully that he had discovered "The Store-City of Pithom and the Route of the Exodus".

> The founder of the city, the king who gave to Pithom the extent and the importance we recognize, is certainly Rameses II ... Very likely he found it necessary for his campaigns in Asia to have storehouses for provisioning his armies and also means of defence against invaders from the East. *We find here confirmation of the evidence derived from other monuments that he is the Pharaoh of the Oppression, as he built Pithom and Raamses, the site of which last is still uncertain* (Italics Added).[25]

While it is possible that a location known as Pi-Atum was discovered as a result of the excavations of Edouard Naville, the most important thesis of the find is simply assumed by "geographic association". Where is the archeological evidence of the presence and enslavement of the Hebrew people at this site? Finding a city dedicated to the most revered Kemetic deity of the period, established or maintained by the one of the most prolific builders of the period is an amazing find, however it does not automatically corroborate this story. Naville and many other archeologists believe that this portion of the ancient story is assumed factual simply because it is cited in the bible. We must understand that the bible is *not* a history but rather a book with *some* historical events in it.

The second major difficulty with the story of enslaved Hebrews building Kemetic cities seems to relate to the very description of the cities in the bible itself. Depending on which translated version of the bible is used, Pithom and Raames are described as "store-cites" or "treasure cities". Most historians argue that this refers to supply depots which would allow the Kemetic army to gather important provisions prior to foreign excursions. This is why Naville acknowledges the supposed importance of discovering buildings which might have been used as store houses (probably similar to silos). It is possible that these cities, including the site discovered by Naville, were utilized for this purpose. However, they might not have been used for this purpose until nearly *six hundred years later*![26] For example, Ramesses the Great moved the Kemetic capital from Men-Nefer (the city 'built in perfection' later called Memphis by the Greeks) to Pi-Ramesses. The capital city during the reign of Ramesses could certainly not be simply called a supply depot. As the capital was shifted back to Men-Nefer under later kings, the use of Pi-Ramesses changed. Historians and biblical scholars agree that the sources that were utilized to author the biblical passages were written much later. It would seem the author of the source material described these locations according to the usage during his time, not during the time period of any of the powerful New Kingdom rulers. The story seems quite anachronistic.

The biblical sources that make up the account of the sojourn in Egypt and the exodus in Exodus 1-15 were not contemporaneous with the events that they sought to portray. Even the earliest source, the so-called Yahwist (J), is variously dated from the tenth to the sixth centuries BCE (or even later), which by any reckoning of the date of the exodus is a long time afterwards. Furthermore, there is an increasing tendency towards the later dating of J, and it seems very likely that the geography of J's exodus account will reflect his familiarity with Egypt of his own day rather than preserve hoary traditions of place-names from the second millennium.[27]

Another major difficulty with the historicity of Hebrew enslavement in Kemet actually deals with the timeline established by the story in the biblical books Exodus and Joshua. After escaping Kemet, the Hebrew people wander in the desert for 40 years. Upon their emergence, they begin the conquest of Canaan by destroying the wall of the great city of Jericho. In a blow to the historical accuracy of the Jewish enslavement story, virtually all historians now acknowledge that this event could not have happened in a period contemporaneous to the rule of Ramesses the Great.

> ... the dating of the 'conquest' of Canaan by the Israelites to the period of the late 19th or early 20th [Kemetic] Dynasties with the exodus event preceding this by '40 years' of wilderness wanderings. In current discussion of the origins of Israel the conquest scenario may be ruled out as largely irrelevant to the discussion for the dating of the exodus. (Brackets mine)[28]

Image 4.6: Israel's Escape from Egypt portrayed by Moses' parting of the Red Sea. Illustration from a Bible card published in 1907 by the Providence Lithograph Company.

At this point we must ask whether there is any archeological evidence of the Hebrew enslavement in Kemet. The biblical story tells us that six hundred thousand Hebrew men (not counting women and children) left Kemet during the exodus. While modern Egyptologists disagree widely on the size of the population in Kemet during this period, the highest estimates are around five million. Counting only escaping Hebrew men, this would mean more than ten percent of Kemet's population would have left the country as a result of one incident. Imagine what percentage of working age laborers this group would have represented. This event would have been absolutely catastrophic to a modern economy. It might have been completely crippling to an economy which operated without the use of modern machines and computers to offset human labor.

> And the children of Israel did according to the word of Moses; and they borrowed of the Egyptians jewels of silver, and jewels of gold, and raiment ... And the children of Israel journeyed from Rameses to Succoth, about six hundred thousand on foot *that were* men, beside children. And a mixed multitude went up also with them; and flocks, and herds, even very much cattle.[29]

As we mentioned earlier, institutions like the Egypt Exploration Society, have been searching for the historicity of the biblical story in Kemet for over one hundred years. These groups have been unable to find any archeological evidence of over six hundred thousand people who live in a desert for forty years. Not one potsherd, one burial, or one campsite has been discovered.

> Most histories of ancient Israel no longer consider information about the Egyptian sojourn, the exodus, and the wilderness wanderings recoverable or even relevant to Israel's emergence ... Most important is the fact that no clear extrabiblical evidence exists for any aspect of the Egyptian sojourn, exodus, or wilderness wanderings. This lack of evidence, combined with the fact that most scholars believe the stories about these events to have been written centuries after the apparent setting of the stories, leads historians to ...

admit that, by normal, critical, historical means, these events cannot be placed in a specific time and correlated with other known history, or claim that the stories are believable historically on the basis of inference, potential connections, and general plausibility.[30]

Founded in 1880 with the expressed mission to "foster biblical scholarship"[31], The Society of Biblical Literature has come to a similar conclusion concerning the Hebrew exodus from Ancient Kemet.

The detail-laden account of the forty years of desert wandering is also fraught with historical and archaeological inconsistencies and does not appear to reflect one historical context but rather a layering of numerous historical events over time.[32]

Some of the readers of this book will probably be uncomfortable with the fact that the enslavement of the Hebrew people is a myth. Unfortunately, the term 'myth' has been poorly defined. Many believe that a myth is a story that is not 'true'. The term 'myth' in the modern western world has obtained a negative connotation. In actuality, myth is a story or parable which provides a profound telling of basic 'truths'. They are constructed to provide a deeper understanding of 'how to live'. As long as we continue to assign value to our spiritual myths according to their historical factuality, we are reducing our religious texts to newspapers. History tells us what happened and myth explains what should continue to happen. In order to benefit from the story of the exodus, we need to re-mythologize it; not seek to situate it in history.

It should now be clear that the story of the Hebrew people's enslavement and exodus from Kemet was not a historical event. This reality is extremely controversial as it is a central tenet of Judaism, Christianity, Islam, and the Baha'i faiths. These Abrahamic traditions comprise more than half of the world's population. In some circles, describing the Hebrew enslavement story as an *ahistorical* event would likely provoke a violent response. Even the descendants of those depicted most negatively, people of African heritage, would argue forcefully for the story's historicity. It must be reiterated that this book is not based on religious concepts, but cemented by a corrective historical analysis.

If taken as a historical event, the construction of the pyramids by enslaved Hebrews undermines the role of African people in the development of civilization. Furthermore, as Diasporan Africans are primarily Christian, belief in the historical enslavement of the Hebrew people also retards their very interest in the history of their ancestral home. Perhaps this is the most insidious reality of this misrepresentation. Those people who were *actually* cruelly enslaved recoil from the true history of their ancestors, even long after the physical chains have been removed. A corrected history may not earn Africans any friends among those who practice the Abrahamic religious traditions in a literal sense. However, we must find bravery in the uncovering of our truths. We will be unable to return to greatness without it.

THE ACTUAL PRESENCE OF HEBREWS IN ANCIENT KEMET

While most historians and scholars now doubt the historicity of the story of the Hebrew people's enslavement and exodus from Ancient Kemet, it does seem that there are some historical sources which seem to identify small groups of Hebrew people in Kemet at a later ancient date. For the most part, these sources describe relatively minor events. As Kemet remained a powerful nation for over three thousand years, foreign people continued to enter the nation through several means for a variety of reasons. During the period when Kemet was under the control of the Persian Empire (circa 650 BCE), a community of soldiers settled in the Southern Kemetic region known today as Elephantine Island. Aspects of the lives of these soldiers are extensively captured in a series of Aramaic papyri.[33]

It is also possible that the Hebrew people were involved in at least one major event in the history of Ancient Kemet. While modern historians are not in agreement on whether the foreign rulers often known as the Hyksos (Kemetic: Heka Khaesehet or Rulers from Foreign Countries) were early or "proto" Hebrew group, early Jewish historian Titus Flavius Josephus does argue that the Hyksos are the Hebrew people. Josephus describes some of the actions of the Hebrew ruler who would control Kemet.

> They burnt down our cities, and destroyed the temples of the gods, and treated the inhabitants most cruelly; killing some and enslaving their wives and their children.[34]

It is possible that the Hyksos are initially welcomed into Kemet, as depicted in a Twelfth Kemetic Dynasty noble's tomb. They would establish the capital in the northern delta city Avaris and rule Kemet for over two hundred years. A letter from the Hyksos King Apophis to the patriarch of a powerful indigenous family in the southern Kemetic city of Waset seems to have led to an epic rebellion.

Often called the Quarrel of Apophis and Seknenre (Seqenenre Tao), the Kemetic text explains that King Apophis complains to the Kemetic patriarch Seqenenre Tao that his "hippopotami were keeping him awake at night". Perhaps this unusual statement is a warning for Seqenenre Tao not to become too convinced that he was actually a king in the southern region of Kemet. The hippopotamus is symbolically related the Kemetic deity Set (or Sutekh) who was sacred to the Hyksos. The letter convinced Seqenenre Tao to mount a rebellion to expel the Hyksos from Kemet. After the indigenous rebellion leader is brutally killed, his eldest son leads the revolution quite successfully before his untimely death. As the youngest son, Ahmose, is still too young to be seen as the leader, the family matriarch, Aahotep leads the rebellion herself. When her son Ahmose comes of age, he and his mother fight the Hyksos to finally remove the cruel usurpers from Kemet. In order to ensure the Hyksos would be unable to return, King Ahmose follows them all the way to Canaan to thoroughly defeat them.

Image 4.7: Recreation of tomb scene which may depict the Hyksos entering Kemet with the permission of its people circa 1900 BCE. The original image is from the tomb of a 12th Dynasty official Khnumhotep II who lived under King Senusret II.

While historians are divided on whether the foreign "Asiatic" rulers known as the Hyksos are the proto-Hebrews, it should be clear that this story places the Hebrews in a radically different position. Unlike the biblical exodus, this story has corresponding archeological evidence.

The story of the cruel enslavement of the Hebrew people at the hands of the Ancient Kemetic people is not a historical narrative. There is no reliable archeological evidence or textual support for coerced Hebrew labor during the building of the pyramids or Kemetic cities. This well-known myth continues to ruminate in the collective psyche of people in the United States and around the world. Why does this myth continue to have so much appeal? What are the effects of the myth on Africans today? Let us examine these critical issues.

Reasons for and effects of the LIE

Many scholars believe that the stories of the Hebrew enslavement and exodus were crafted much later than when they were situated. The Nineteenth Dynasty reign of Ramesses the Great is usually dated to somewhere around 1279 - 1212 BCE while the earliest period for the authorship of the stories of the Hebrews in Kemet seems to be the Twenty-Sixth Dynasty (circa 664 - 525 BCE).[35, 36] Many historians now believe that these well-known stories were not only invented, but written more than six hundred years after they were purported to have occurred! The early motives for crafting the story of Hebrew enslavement were to foster nationalistic and religious unity among the Jewish people. The story provides the Jewish people with an ancient origin within the crucible of the most powerful nation in the region. It is the most uplifting story of the entire Jewish mythos. God favors the tiny, exploited people while he rescues them from the all-powerful potentate for the simple price of their faithfulness. The Jewish people are the chosen people; regardless of the trials and tribulations, they are destined to prevail. The myth would become a cogent, inspirational touchstone not only for the Jewish people, but later for many others.

As a segment of Judaism becomes Christianity, these powerful themes of salvation through faithfulness and sacred victories over overwhelming power are slowly subsumed into a larger, more diverse populace.

Today, no demographic group today utilizes the story of the Hebrew condition in Kemet more than people of African descent in the United States. After roughly four hundred years of oppression in the US, the mythic story of four hundred years of Hebrew enslavement resonates with Black folk. Both obvious and subtle references can be found throughout African American political, spiritual, and social thought.

Perhaps no person was held in higher regard by enslaved Africans than the irrepressible, larger-than-life heroine, Harriet Tubman. Tubman would not only escape from her enslavement in Maryland on September 17, 1849,[37] but she would return at least nineteen times, freeing around seventy other Africans. She later became a nurse and spy for the Union Army during the Civil War and even advise Jim Brown with his rebellion of enslaved Africans. Connecting her brave acts to the mythical enslavement of the Hebrews, the famed abolitionist William Lloyd Garrison, would dub Tubman "Moses".[38] The name would remain with her.

In the first mass migration of formerly enslaved African Americans during the late 1800s, the movement from the states along the Mississippi River to states like Kansas, Oklahoma, and Colorado was dubbed the "Exoduster Movement"[39].   African American preachers from the wide array of religious denominations have also utilized the Jewish exodus to ensure their followers that faithfulness and determination will secure their eventual freedom.

Dr. Martin Luther King, Jr. and El-Hajj Malik El-Shabazz (better known as Malcolm X) are often described as diametrically opposed leaders of the African American civil/human rights era. Dr. King, a Baptist preacher, was the movement's greatest adherent to non-violent action while Brother Malcolm, the national spokesman for the Nation of Islam, was an articulate advocate for self-defense. Contemporary historians often argue that their views were actually more in sync than previously understood.   Regardless of their differences and similarities, both leaders drew on the mythic imagery of Hebrew enslavement in Ancient Kemet.

> Now, what does all of this mean in this great period of history? It means that we've got to stay together. We've got to stay together and maintain unity. You know, whenever Pharaoh wanted to prolong the period of slavery in Egypt, he had a favorite, favorite formula for doing it. What was that? He kept the slaves fighting among themselves. But whenever the slaves get together, something happens in Pharaoh's court, and he cannot hold the slaves in slavery. When the slaves get together, that's the beginning of getting out of slavery. Now let us maintain unity.[40]
>
> - Martin Luther King, Jr.
> "I've been to the Mountaintop" Speech, April 3, 1968

[The Honorable Elijah] Muhammad isn't saying, "Give us part of this country." His solution is, as I think I've said, is the complete exodus of our people from this country back to our own homeland where we can live among our own people, and that this government should supply us with all of the machinery and tools necessary for us to till the soil back home and develop our own agricultural system, feed, clothe and shelter ourselves, and thereby make our own people an independent people standing on our own feet. (Brackets added)[41]

- Minister "Malcolm X" El Hajj Malik El Shabazz
Speech at Columbia University, November 20, 1963

So what is the difficulty with African Americans and other Diasporic Africans connecting themselves to the victorious myth of enslaved Hebrews? Biblical parallels have inspired countless African Americans to persevere under the face of perhaps the most inhumane conditions. How could this be an issue?

This orientation also biases African Americans *against* Kemet. Kemet is not just the "flower of African civilization", it could easily be considered the most influential nation in human history. Africans are amongst the world's most exploited people on the planet. As we continue to shake off the shackles of enslavement and colonialism, we have begun seeking our own historical contributions. Unfortunately, forsaking Ancient Kemet as the oppressors of the Hebrew people prevents us from finding our monumental greatness. This historical travesty must be overcome. Once again the words of Dr. Martin Luther King, Jr. highlight this point very well.

You will remember that at a very early stage in her history the children of Israel were reduced to the bondage of physical slavery under the gripping yoke of Egyptian rule. Egypt was the symbol of evil in the form of humiliating oppression, ungodly exploitation and crushing domination. The Israelites symbolized goodness, in the form of devotion and dedication to the God of Abraham, Isaac and Jacob. These two forces were in a continual struggle against each other-Egypt struggling to maintain her oppressive yoke and Israel struggling to gain freedom from this yoke. ... The Egyptians, in a desperate attempt to prevent the Israelites from escaping, had their armies to go in the Red Sea behind them. But as soon as the Egyptians got into the Red Sea the parted waves swept back upon them, and the rushing waters of the sea soon drowned all of them. As the Israelites looked back all they could see was here and there a poor drowned body beaten upon the seashore ... This story, at bottom, symbolizes the death of evil. It was the death of inhuman oppression and ungodly exploitation. The death of the Egyptians upon the seashore is a glaring symbol of the ultimate doom of evil in its struggle with good. There is something in the very nature of the universe which is on the side of Israel in its struggle with every Egypt. There is something in the very nature of the universe which ultimately comes to the aid of goodness in its perennial struggle with evil.[42]

-Dr. Martin Luther King, Jr.
The Death of Evil upon the Seashore, May 17, 1956

As long as Africans continue to equate their greatest civilization with the very symbol of oppression and "evil", we will never truly find our collective genius. We will never be able to set the historical record straight.

For Additional Research

BOOKS
1. Moore, M. and Kelle, B. (2011). Biblical history and Israel's past: the changing study of the bible and history. Grand Rapids: Wm. B. Eerdmans Publishing Co.
2. Killebrew, A. (2005). Biblical peoples and ethnicity: an archaeological study of Egyptians, Canaanites, Philistines, and early Israel 1300-1100 B.C.E. Atlanta: Society of Biblical Literature.
3. Greenberg, G. (1996). The bible myth: the African origins of the Jewish people. New York: Citadel Press.
4. ben-Jochannan, Y. (1991). African origins of the major "western religions". Baltimore: Black Classic Press.
5. Lehner, M. (1991). The complete pyramids: solving the ancient mysteries. London: Thames and Hudson.
6. Verner, M. (1997). The pyramids: the mystery, culture, and science of Egypt's great monuments. New York: Grove Press.
7. Tompkins, P. (1971). Secrets of the great pyramid. New York: Harper Row.

CHAPTER 5:
"AFRICANS WERE SAVAGES WHEN THE EUROPEANS ENSLAVED THEM"

Image 5.1: "Savage Africans" - (Top Left) English-Canadian singer and comedian Anna Russell poses with South Africans and recalls the "savage" imagery on the cover of her comedy album "In Darkest Africa". (Top Right) Ringling Bros., Barnum, and Bailey Circus exhibition of "Ubangi Savages". (Bottom) Safari filmmakers Martin and Osa Johnson photographed with "savages". Notice their relative placement in the picture.

Uncovering the Lie

The notion that Africans inhabited a "savage", "dark continent" is very common and as old as the United States itself. As described in

Chapter 3, powerful European interests created the concept of African inferiority in order to exploit the entire working populace. Poor whites would fight to maintain their birthright—their racial superiority—while not understanding or acknowledging their own exploited condition. The "savage" caricature also served as justification for the most inhumane treatment of kidnapped, enslaved Africans. This chapter will outline the establishment of the African savage stereotype during their enslavement.

In the age of Obama, there are many who recognize that the concept of pre-colonial Africa being savage is ridiculous. These individuals would be amazed at how the lie has metastasized and flourished into modern cultural understandings. This chapter will also elucidate how notions of African savagery have led to alarming but routine actions. While the fallacy can be easily refuted, it is certainly more important to identify how it continues to inform how the continent of Africa, and people of African descent are viewed, sometimes with deadly consequences.

AFRICAN "SAVAGERY" AND THE GLOBAL TRANS-ATLANTIC ENSLAVEMENT TRADE
In the public debate which eventually led to the abolition of the enslavement of Africans in Great Britain, advocates of the inhumane institution testified in the British Parliament from July 1789 to July 1790. These pro-slavery testimonials routinely stated that the forced transportation of kidnapped Africans which led to the death of millions was actually an improvement over the alternative of continued life in backward Africa. The testimony of Mr. Norris, a slave ship captain, has been paraphrased in the lengthy document describing the proceedings.

> [The Africans] had sufficient room, sufficient air, and sufficient provisions. When upon deck, they made merry and amused themselves with dancing. As to the mortality, or the loss of them by death in the course of their passage, it was trifling. In short, the voyage from Africa to the West Indies "was one of the happiest periods of a Negro's life." ... the African, unhappy in his own country, found in the middle passage, under the care of the merchants, little less than an Elysian retreat [Brackets added].[1]

The concept that the middle passage was both humane and comfortable was later refuted by further testimony before the Parliament. Africans kidnapped by British slavers experienced previously unknown horrors along the ocean journey.

The kidnapped Africans were forced to lie on shelves which filled nearly all of the ship's space beneath the main deck. Each prisoner was only given a space of approximately 5'6" in length, and 16" in width. The hold's ceilings were not usually higher than 5'8" but were sometimes only 4' high.

The extremely cramped space was not the only cause of discomfort. Every two male prisoners had their wrists and ankles shackled together and locked to ring-bolts which were affixed to the floor. They were only unbolted from the floor for a few hours each day when they were forced to jump around in their shackles (dancing) on the main deck after eating. Refusing their daily exercise prompted severe beatings. They were only allowed to drink approximately a pint of water a day and were fed a gruel-like meal (sometimes yams and horse beans) twice a day. As this nightmare voyage could take anywhere between 6 weeks to 6 months, large numbers perished or even found ways to commit suicide.[2]

In a simplistic manner it would seem that the individuals who accurately described the barbaric enslavement voyage were setting the entire record straight. However, these testimonies to the British Parliament did not describe the West African nations which the Africans were taken from. The testimony may have prompted sympathy for the kidnapped African, but it did little to undo the savage African fallacy. As a result, the movement to end the Trans-Atlantic trade of African people may have seemed quite similar to today's movement to end animal cruelty to many of the Europeans who supported it. It probably did little to establish the fundamental humanity of Africans or to situate Africa's primary place in world history.

Image 5.2: Statue of Frederick Douglass in Harlem, NY - Formerly enslaved African, author, and powerful rhetorician, Frederick Douglass had a long partnership with the most popular abolitionist of European descent, William Lloyd Garrison. Douglass and Garrison were often known to share the stage at public events. In these engagements Douglass would recount the horrors of his personal experiences with enslavement while Garrison and other members of the American Anti-Slavery Society would provide the philosophy behind abolitionism. This relationship began to unravel when Douglass decided to play a larger role. He wanted to also provide his own analysis, as any fierce, sharp-minded intellectual would do. Douglass in a primary role seems to have been difficult for Garrison and other abolitionist of European descent.[3]

People of European descent who had a vested interest in the system of slavery continued to describe Africans as fortunate to be forcibly removed from their savage homeland. Many of the comments about African lives on plantations were quite similar to those delivered to the British Parliament on the middle passage.

> ... we ought to consider whether the negroes in a well regulated plantation, under the protection of a kind Master, do not enjoy as great, nay even greater advantages than when under their own despotic governments, or even than the greater part of our common labourers, our tradesmen, and our manufacturers; but even in these examples, it will be said, they have a free agency, a liberty of their own, nor can I deny it, though I may with confidence say that this liberty is rather a detriment, than an advantage to them; it is their common practice on the Saturday Night, when they receive their wages, to sit down to drinking, and not to return, in general, to their work, until nearly half of the week is expired, from which period they are obliged to

labour harder than any slave, under even the most cruel Master ...[4]

Wealthy English politician and 1st Earl of Sheffield[5], John Baker Holroyd argued that immediate termination of the Trans-Atlantic trade of enslaved Africans might create an economic hardship. He was a proponent of "slave breeding", as it could eventually make the kidnapping of Africans obsolete. With an acknowledgement of the brutality of the journey by "slave ship", Holroyd's view might have been considered more humane. Clearly this view was not based on recognition of the humanity of Africans.

Holroyd not only argues that the Africans were better off under western enslavement than they were in their African homeland, but he adds another oft-mentioned aspect to the argument. Africans were already enslaved by their countrymen in Africa. Western enslavement is more humane.

> Although we have no right to determine or choose for the Negroes, in respect to their removal from Africa to the West Indies, yet there seems little doubt that their situation is in general changed much for the better. They are slaves in Africa and their lives as much at the mercy of their uncivilised owners as those of their cattle. They are slaves still, but to civilised masters. They are protected, and their servitude protected by law.[6]

Holroyd argues that Africans are better off as cattle, enslaved in western countries because of the sheer savagery of their homeland. After all, they were already enslaved, but in Africa their masters were "uncivilized" and not controlled by law. In this chapter we will describe African nations prior to and during the Trans-Atlantic enslavement trade.

Why is identifying and refuting the African savage fallacy so important? It is not unusual for people from a variety of different ethnic and racial backgrounds to explain that the enslavement of African people took place "a long time ago". They argue that in order to move forward we must move on from this painful past. People of European descent who hold the belief often exclaim that they "did not own slaves". People of African descent who believe similarly will state that the past is far "too painful", that "our people sold us too", or even that we need to move beyond blame and take responsibility for our present. The major problem with this thinking is that it fails to understand how many of our contemporary beliefs, interactions, and even our language is a product of this history. Our modern world is a result of our past. In this chapter, we will also shed light on how the African savagery fallacy impacts the manner that people of African descent are viewed and even how we view ourselves. Dismantling this powerful erroneous belief is of critical importance.

The Real Deal

PRE-COLONIAL AFRICAN SOCIETIES: CIVILIZED OR SAVAGE?
The myth of African savagery in the United States, which originated during African enslavement, is nearly two hundred and fifty years old. It has been well ingrained into the racist narrative which the United States was founded upon. Therefore, one would think that the general esteem that the Ancient Kemetic people (and several other ancient civilizations founded by Africans) are held in would be quite contradictory. The key is that while Ancient Kemet is located on the African continent, many don't consider the society African (this myth was unraveled in Chapter 3). This book has established that an anti-African Kemet is a farce; however there are other issues with using Kemet as a primary counter to the African savage falsehood. Kemet is the nation that gives civilization to the world, but its prominence occurs nearly a thousand years prior to the start of the Trans-Atlantic enslavement trade. Additionally most enslaved Africans who are forced to come to the Western world were captured in West Africa[7], thousands of miles from Northeast Africa. For these reasons, the most direct way to counter the argument that Africans were savages when Europeans came to enslave us is to review the African nations that were prominent in West Africa in the period immediately prior and during the cruel enslavement trade. This section will review the three major West African empires which existed from 300 CE to 1591 CE. European nations first began legally trading with West Africa, but by the mid 1400s began exploiting the continent illegally.

By describing these impressive African civilizations we will prove that Africans in West Africa were far from savage but rather created powerful societies which competently wielded the mechanisms of state.

GHANA EMPIRE: 300 CE? - 1235 CE

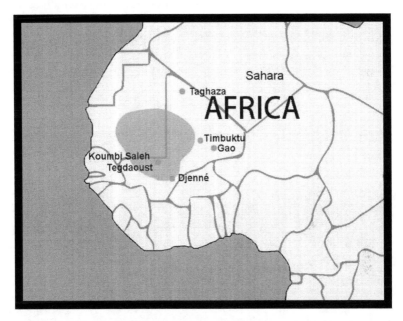

Image 5.3: Approximate Location of the Ghana Empire - This early West African nation straddles modern day southwestern Mauritania and western Mali.[8]

Scholars now agree that organized groups existed in the area considered to include Ancient Ghana since at least 1700 BCE[9]. Little is known about the grouping of people in the region at this time. These people were part of the groups of people who became prominent in the southern boundary of the Sahara (Arabic: desert) which transforms into a grassy savanna known as the Sahel (Arabic: shore). Sometime around 300 CE, the dominant people in the region known as the Soninke founded an influential nation which was actually known as Wagadu. "Ghana" was actually the title of the ruler effectively meaning "war chief". One of the other monikers of the ruler, "kaya maghan" or "lord of gold", tells quite a bit about how the nation comes to prominence.[10] The industrious citizens of Wagadu seem to have engaged in trade for a very long time. They probably utilized small pack animals to haul salt, copper, and dates across the region. However, because of the short supply of viable water sources to the immediate north of the Sahel; this trade was primarily restricted to local partners. With the domestication of the camel, the Ghana Empire would become a very powerful nation. Traders could utilize the camel, which could travel for several days without water, to corner the trans-Saharan trade of gold and salt. While Ghana was replete with gold, salt was a commodity they sought in their semi-arid climate in order to preserve food. The Soninke, who controlled the caravans which travelled all over the Western Sahara, northeast Africa, and the Mediterranean, would create an empire by 800 CE.

Image 5.4: A modern day trans-Saharan caravan travels from Agadez to Bilma in Niger. Similar to their ancient predecessors, these traders are hauling salt. The bi-annual round trip caravan takes approximately three weeks. [11]

Nearly all of the existing historic descriptions of the Ghana Empire come to us from Arab scholars. A scholar from Cordoba, Spain, Abu Ubaydallah al-Bakri, wrote a detailed description of the nations of ancient West Africa in 1068. al-Bakri outlines the capital city of the Ghana Empire, Koumbi Saleh:

> The city of Ghana consists of two towns situated on a plain. One of these towns, which is inhabited by Muslims, is large and possesses twelve mosques, in one of which they assemble for the Friday prayer ... In the environs are wells

with sweet water, from which they drink and with which they grow vegetables. The houses of the inhabitants are of stone and acacia wood. The king has a palace and a number of domed dwellings all surrounded with an enclosure like a city wall ... On every donkey-load of salt when it is brought into the country their king levies one golden dinar, and two dinars when it is sent out ... The nuggets found in all the mines of his country are reserved for the king, only this gold dust being left for the people. But for this the people would accumulate gold until it lost its value ... It is related that the king owns a nugget as large as a big stone ... The king of Ghana, when he calls up his army, can put 200,000 men into the field, more than 40,000 of them archers. [12]

As West Africa's first recorded ancient empire, the Kingdom of Wagadu was one of the most influential nations in history. As can be expected, at some point in history the ethnicity of the originators of the powerful nation becomes contested. A similar denial occurs with virtually all prominent ancient civilizations which were founded by Africans. In this instance the founders of ancient Ghana are not just misrepresented as European in origin, but also as Islam-influenced Arabs.

Historians of the colonial period were inclined to attribute the creation of the kingdoms of Sahel to nomad invaders from the north, of white origin and of a higher civilization. [One prominent European scholar of the 19th century argued that the founding of Wagadu was due to a] migration of so-called 'Judeo-Syriens', who wandered from Libia to Bornu or Air and then westward across the savannah. To these white migrants [he] ascribed the creation of ... Ghana. This and other hypotheses are based on ... the (now obsolete) assumption that the peoples of the Sudan could not develop organized states themselves. [13]

Additionally, as least 2 prominent Arab scholars, Ta'rikh al-Sudan and Ta'rikh al-Fattash, recounted older reports that the first kings of Wagadu were European while the citizens were the African people known as the Soninke. [14] It should be noted however, that none of the historical Arabic sources prior to the twelfth century describe the founders of Ghana (or Songhai) as having a different "race" or ethnicity than the people of the nation, the Soninke. In fact, the authors who wrote their descriptions during the same period of the Ghana Empire explicitly referred to the founders as African. These Arab scholars include Yakoubi (872 CE), Macoudi (944 CE), Hawqal (977 CE), Al Birouni (1036 CE), and Al-Bakri (1068)[15].

Image 5.5: Nineteenth Century Soninke Soldiers memorialized in a French manuscript by Colonel Frey (1890)[16]

It is quite interesting that the term which was coined by the Arabs for the region beneath the immense Sahara was "Bilad al-Sudan" or the "land of the Blacks".[17,18] As we begin to acknowledge the true importance of Wagadu, we must ensure that it remains African and that it is not further victimized by revisionist history.

The causes of the eventual decline of the Ghana Empire are somewhat unclear. Some scholars attribute the decline to the country's near complete transition to Islam. Others cite the possible sacking of the empire by an outside power. Possible suspects in this sacking are the West African ethnic group, the Sosso or the Almoravid Berbers who resided mostly in northwestern Africa and

Spain. However, archeologists have not identified the rapid cultural upheaval which usually occurs in foreign conquests. It is more likely that the Ghana Empire was simply absorbed into the next major ancient West African empire of antiquity, Mali.

MALI EMPIRE: 1230 CE - 1600 CE

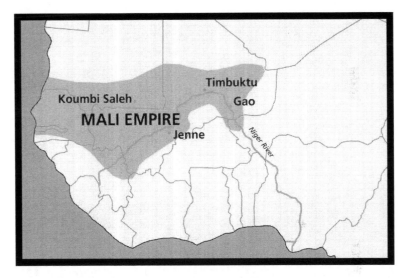

Image 5.6: Approximate Location of the Mali Empire - The West African empire straddles eight modern day countries including, The Gambia, Guinea, Guinea-Bissau, Ivory Coast, Mali, Mauritania, Niger, and Senegal.

During the thirteenth century, the Mali Empire, one of Africa's most powerful nations would come into prominence out of the ashes of the Wagadu Empire. While most who are familiar with the history of the empire call it "Mali", the name seems to have been first mentioned by the Arab Scholar, Ibn Battuta.[19] The Mali Empire was also known by the name of its capital city, Niani, and its native name, Manden Kurufaba (meaning the assembly of the Manden).[20] The architects of the great Manden Empire were known as the Manden-Ka or the "people of Manden". Today Manden-Ka is often rendered as Mandinka, Mandinko, or Mandingo.

In the void created by the decline of the Wagadu Empire, one family sought to unify the fragmented groups which comprised the former the empire. Known by the surname Kante, the members of the family were skilled blacksmiths who were part of the Sosso people. The patriarch of the Kante family, Sumanguru, would eventually succeed in combining these nations. He controlled the former capital of Wagadu, Koumbi Saleh, and also the caravan routes which helped to enrich the former empire. However, the oral tradition maintained by the griots of the Mandinka people describes Sumanguru Kante as a cruel ruler.[21]

> But Soumaoro (an alternate rendering of Sumanguru) was an evil demon and his reign had produced nothing but bloodshed. Nothing was taboo for him. His greatest pleasure was publicly to flog venerable old men. He had defiled every family and everywhere in his vast empire there were villages populated by girls whom he had forcibly abducted from their families without marrying them. The tree that the tempest will throw down does not see the storm building up on the horizon. Its proud head braves the winds even when it is near its end. Soumaoro had come to despise everyone. Oh! How power can pervert a man. (Parenthesis added)[22]

As these storytellers relay the story, the Mandinka awaited an influential ruler to free them from the emperor's grasp. They chronicle the rise of the first king of Mali/Manden in their most important story, the *Epic of Sundiata*. While there are certainly questions as to how much of the story has been altered by hundreds of years of griot interpretation, some scholars argue that the major aspects are relatively accurate descriptions of historic events.[23]

According to some versions of the Epic, the Manden were led by an attractive and able king named, Maghan Kon Fatta. The king was married, but received a prophecy that he would also wed an "ugly woman" who would bear him a powerful heir to succeed him. Accordingly he married a hunchbacked woman named Sogolon who would bear him a child named Sundiata. King Maghan Kon Fatta's first wife, Sassouma, was quite jealous of Sogolon and her son and ridiculed them. To make matters worse, Sundiata was a sickly boy who was unable to walk. However, the boy's determination was unparalleled. He would use the ridicule of his older brother (the son of the king's first wife) to motivate him. Eventually he willed himself to walk.

Image 5.7: Majestic West African Griots at the Service of their King - Griots or Jeli have been responsible for chronicling the oral history for their people since time immemorial. This 1890 illustration was by a French military officer, Colonel Frey.

After the death of King Mahgan Kon Fatta, Sassouma would have her son, Dankaran Touman assume the throne against the wishes of her deceased husband who sought to honor the prophecy. Fearing for her family, Queen Sogolon would flee to the neighboring Mema Kingdom. While in Mema, Sundiata would become as "strong as a lion". A renown hunter, Sundiata would find himself as the heir to the throne in his adopted land. Meanwhile, his brother, Dankaran Tourman, was confronted with a major challenge as the King of Manden. The cruel King of the Sosso, Sumanguru, sought to defeat the Manden who were becoming rebellious due to their ill-treatment at the hand of the king. As King Dankaran Tourman fled Manden, Queen Sogolon convinced her son, Sundiata, to galvanize the neighboring factors and return to Manden. Sundiata would eventually defeat King Sumanguru and the Sosso in battle. The weakling prince, who was born to a hunchback mother, would become the first king of the Manden Empire.

To solidify his new kingdom, King Sundiata Keita would take the title "mansa" or "king of kings". Additionally, he established a peaceful reign with the "Kouroukan Founga" as the nation's constitution in 1236 CE. One of the earliest constitutions in the world, the name Kouroukan Founga describes the location which Mansa Sundiata Keita met with his wise men to establish the charter. The location was essentially a cleared area in the forest near the village of Kangaba where the participants met on granite bedrock. The document would allow the Manden and other aligned peoples to create an empire larger and more powerful than the Ghana Empire. [24] It "contains a preamble of seven chapters advocating social peace in diversity, the inviolability of the human being, education, the integrity of the motherland, food security, the abolition of slavery by razzia (or raid), and freedom of expression and trade."[25]

Sundiata Keita would continue to rule the Manden Empire for approximately 20 years and with the assistance of his generals the empire would continue to expand. After his death in around 1255 CE, each of his three sons (Mansas Wali, Wati, and Khalifa Keita) would come to power.

Perhaps the most interesting fact is that while the *Epic of Sundiata* is considered the national epic of several contemporary West African nations (including Mali, the Gambia, Senegal, and Guinea), Sundiata Keita is not the most renown king of the Mali Empire. The reign of Sundiata's grandnephew, Mansa Kankan Musa, would become most heralded. Mansa Musa would expand the Empire of Manden to a size larger than any other nation in the world during its time.

Musa Keita came to power in an unusual manner. Many of the rulers of the Manden Empire were Muslim even though the majority of their citizens practiced other traditions. It was normal for the Mansa to appoint a regent to serve on his behalf as he made his Hajj, or pilgrimage to Mecca. Often the regent would be later named the sole head of the empire. Musa Keita was chosen to serve as regent to Abubakari Keita II. Abubakari II would later completely relinquish the throne as he sought to explore the furthest reaches of the world. In 1311 CE, nearly two centuries before

Christopher Columbus, Abubakari II would attempt to cross the Atlantic Ocean. The Arab scholar Al-Umari quoted Mansa Musa directly as he recalled the terms of his ascent to power.

> The ruler who preceded me did not believe that it was impossible to reach the extremity of the ocean that encircles the earth (meaning Atlantic), and wanted to reach to that (end) and obstinately persisted in the design. So he equipped two hundred boats full of men, as many others full of gold, water and victuals sufficient enough for several years. He ordered the chief (admiral) not to return until they had reached the extremity of the ocean, or if they had exhausted the provisions and the water. They set out. Their absence extended over a long period, and, at last, only one boat returned. On our questioning, the captain said: 'Prince, we have navigated for a long time, until we saw in the midst of the ocean as if a big river was flowing violently. My boat was the last one; others were ahead of me. As soon as any of them reached this place, it drowned in the whirlpool and never came out. I sailed backwards to escape this current.' But the Sultan would not believe him. He ordered two thousand boats to be equipped for him and for his men, and one thousand more for water and victuals. Then he conferred on me the regency during his absence, and departed with his men on the ocean trip, never to return nor to give a sign of life.[26]

The quest for a better understanding of the world that we inhabit was not simply a gift of European explorers. Africans long explored the "unknown" world. In fact, some scholars argue that Abubakari II might have actually succeeded in arriving in the "new world" of North America.[27] While the successful and unsuccessful exploits of European explorers are routinely heralded, the explorations of Africans continue to go unreported although it is now an accepted scientific fact that Africans populated the globe. How else would they have gotten there? Clearly the work of Mansa Abubakari II deserves much more focus.

Image 5.8: The Hajj of Mansa Musa was so impressive to the Europeans who heard of the travels of the Malian King, that he was immortalized in the Catalan Atlas (1375 CE). The Spanish map makers who created it attempted to define the boundaries of the Manden (Mali) Empire. Mansa Musa himself is depicted sitting on a throne with a European style crown on his head and a large gold nugget in his hand.

Similar to Mansa Abubakari II, Mansa Kankan Musa was also a devout Muslim. In fact, every ruler in the Keita dynasty would trace their lineage to Bilal, the companion of the Prophet Muhammad who served as the Muezzin; the individual who would call the devout to prayer.[28] Mansa Musa's description of his predecessor was taken during an interview with the Arab scholar Al-Umari in Egypt. Musa traveled there during his trip to Mecca. His Hajj is possibly one of the most noted pilgrimages ever taken.

In 1324 CE, Mansa Musa began his historic journey to Mecca with more than 60,000 companions and 500 servants[29] carrying more than 10 pounds of gold each. This caravan also included 80 camels, each weighted with nearly 250 pounds of gold dust.[30] The emperor would travel across the Sahara and remain in Egypt for 3 months prior to crossing Arabia and ending in Mecca. Musa camped near the mrkhuti (Greek: pyramids). It is reported that he gifted the sultan of Egypt with 40,000 gold coins and even presented the sultan's deputy with 10,000 coins.[31]   As a sign of his charity he constructed a mosque in every town he visited.[32]   He gave gold to so many of the regular people who showed kindness to him throughout Egypt that the global gold market took 12 years to recover.[33]   How was Emperor Musa able to wield so much gold? The wealth of the Manden/Mali Empire was not only based on the control of the trade routes which crossed the Western Sahara but also the secret gold mines of the city of Wangara. So opulent was the Manden Empire and its most powerful ruler, Mansa Musa that he is still considered the most wealthy person in history nearly 700 years later.[34]

The balance of the reign of Mansa Musa was quite eventful. Upon his return he celebrated the recapture of the strategically important trading city of Gao. Making a detour to the city during his return trip, Musa captured the two young sons of the King of Gao, Ali Kolon and Suleiman Nar. Both children returned to the Manden capital city, Niani, and were educated in the court of Musa to ensure the compliance of Gao. The Gao prince Ali Kolon would be important in later events of dominant nations in the region.

Mansa Musa was a man of culture and education and also an extensive builder. He returned from his pilgrimage with at least four direct descendants (shurafa) of the prophet Muhammad and their families. Musa also brought scholars and architects back to Mali. One influential architect was an Arab named Abu Ishaq As-Saheli from Andalusia, Spain.[35]   As-Saheli would build Mansa Musa a large domed, rectangular palace and mosques in Gao and the city of Timbuktu.   In Timbuktu, As-Saheli would build Djinguereber Mosque, a monumental structure made primarily of organic materials such as fiber, wood, and straw. The mosque's unique pyramidal minarets recall the mrkhuti (pyramids) of Ancient Kemet while the grand prayer space can hold over 2,000 worshipers.

Djinguereber is one of the three magnificent institutions (the other two being Sidi Yahya and Sankore) which comprised the University of Timbuktu; one of the most influential early universities in the world.   The university boasted an enrollment of approximately 25,000 students whose studies were religious but also featured majors in a wide variety of fields including medicine, mathematics, science, chemistry, and geometry.[36]

Image 5.9: The Magnificent Djinguereber Mosque - Notice the conical and pyramidal minarets which are reminiscent of the mrkhuti (pyramids) of Ancient Kemet. Mansa Kankan Musa brought his architect, Abu Ishaq As-Saheli, back from his pilgrimage to design the structure. It was one of three major institutions which made up the University of Timbuktu, a major institution of higher learning in its time.

Along with the City of Djenne, the Empire of Manden featured world-renown centers of learning. Unfortunately this little-known fact is still being undermined. The manuscripts of the University of Timbuktu are in danger of destruction. Nearly 700,000 documents[37], including large numbers of the manuscripts, have not been cataloged, preserved, or translated (while many of the texts are in Arabic, some are written in regional dialects). Some of these documents were burned by the radical Islamist group, Ansar Dine, in 2013.[38]

Image 5.10: The Historic Manuscripts of Timbuktu -

(Top): The fragile manuscripts are finally being catalogued. Possibly numbering more than 700,000 documents, the manuscripts are the spiritual and intellectual legacy of the powerful West African empires.

(Bottom): Two of the pages of a Timbuktu manuscript which focus on advanced mathematics and astronomy.

After twenty-five years of prosperous rule, Mansa Musa would leave his empire to his son sometime between 1330 and 1340 CE. The death of the great mansa would see the beginning of a slow decline in the Manden Empire. The cultivation of other gold mining sites to the east of Mali certainly had an effect, but it is likely that the inability of Musa's successors to manage a far-flung empire with a large number of less powerful vassals and kings would be even more troubling. The families of the city of Gao would once again use their strategic placement along key trade routes to wrest power away from the Manden Empire around 1400 CE. Gao would become the capital city of the Songhai Empire.

SONGHAI EMPIRE: 1464 CE - 1591 CE

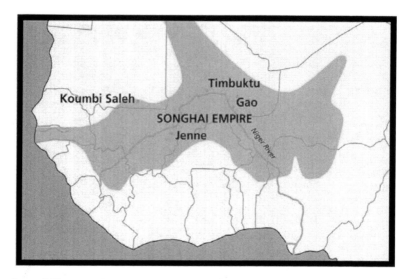

Image 5.11: Approximate Location of the Songhai Empire - The final of the three great pre-colonial West African empires; the Songhai Empire straddles ten modern day countries including, The Gambia, Guinea, Guinea-Bissau, Benin, Nigeria, Mali, Mauritania, Niger, Burkina Faso, and Senegal.

The powerful Songhai Empire, the last of the three great empires in pre-colonial West Africa, was carved out of the ashes of the Manden Empire. In fact, an event during the powerful rule of Mansa Kankan Musa served as epic foreshadowing for its rise.

As Mansa Musa made his return trip from his pilgrimage, he detoured to witness the aftermath of the recapture of the rebellious city of Gao. After receiving the surrender of the king, Musa took the king's two young boys captive to ensure the people's compliance. The princes, Ali Kolon and Suleiman Nar, were taken back to the capital city of the Manden Empire, Niani. They were educated in the court of Mansa Musa. The princes would be forced to serve as soldiers in Mansa Musa's army and even called on to subdue their own people. The wealthy inhabitants of Gao continued to rebel. They had a long history of their own and resented the taxation of the Mali Empire. The people of the city of Gao were actually made up of several groups who developed skills which capitalized on particular complementary aspects of life on the banks of the Niger River.

The Sorko seem to have established the first small settlement on the banks of the river, and therefore became expert boatmen. They built their boats with dense wood from the tall cailcedrat tree and established brisk commerce as they ferried both goods and passengers along the river. The Gao (also spelled Gow) seem to have been the second group to arrive in the area. They developed expertise contending with the dangerous animals of the river, including hippopotami and crocodiles. These two groups began at some point to speak the same language and allied to create a small, but powerful kingdom. Additionally the Do People (pronounced Doh), Mossi, and Tuareg Berber would later become part of the kingdom.[39,40] The rise of the Ghana Empire increased the lucrative trans-Sahara trade and allowed Gao to become an important terminus. As a self-sufficient mid-level kingdom, conflict with the Mali Empire was inevitable.

When the Gao princes, Ali Kolon and Suleiman Nar, were forcibly taken to Niani by Mansa Musa, they were treated like valued members of the court. They were educated and groomed. However they were forced to subdue their own people in the city of Gao as soldiers. Ali Kolon was enraged by their treatment. He vowed to return to Gao with his brother to liberate his people from the Manden Empire. The princes carefully planned the escape route during periods when the king was on expedition; strategically depositing weapons and supplies along their course. They eventually fled to Gao with the palace guards pursuing them. Prince Ali Kolon would continue to fight the Manden Empire from Gao. Kolon would continue to weaken the Manden Empire and would take the name Sunni Ali. Sunni Ali would work with his brother to unify the region's groups, and also establish the Sunni Dynasty. These rulers would eventually magnify the power of Gao and shift the relatively powerful Songhai Nation into the Songhai Empire.

After Mansa Kankan Musa's death in 1337, The Manden Empire struggled to find rulers as successful in keeping the far flung nation intact. In 1360 CE, Musa's grandson, Mari Djata II, comes to power after the final influential ruler of Manden, Mansa Suleyman, by leading a struggle to wrest control of the empire for himself. The Arab Muslim historian, Ibn Khaldun, describes Mari Djata II as a "bad ruler who oppressed the people, depleted the treasury and nearly pulled down the structure of the government."[41] The next few mansas of the Manden Empire might have been honest rulers. However, they seem to just have been administering the dissolution of the empire.

The Manden Empire remained powerful enough to control the majority of the region until around 1400 CE. In this period, they were unable to deal with insurrections on multiple fronts. In the extreme north sections of the empire, the Tuareg People fought for control of the salt and copper trade by taking control of the city of Takkeda.[42] The people of Djenne also revolted[43], and of course the Songhai people of the city of Gao also pressed for their autonomy[44]. It is also possible that Gao pillaged the capital city of Mali during this period. While Manden/Mali could no longer be considered an empire, the region's people still gave the nation recognition and respect, even though large sections would come under increasing control of other powers. The kings of Manden continued to be called mansas and even during the time of Songhai's most powerful ruler, the traditional boundary of Mali was still recognized.[45]

The city of Gao had established a powerful nation long before becoming the region's major power. The first king, Dia Assibia, established a monarchy which lasted sixteen generations. The power of Songhai began with the united families of the Sorko and the Gao, who eventually became dominant based on the overwhelming power of their military. It appears the name Songhai originated not as an ethnic or linguistic designation, but as name of the elite class of rulers who led the empire. Songhai was ruled by warrior kings with the names Sunni and Askia. Their warrior rulers utilized highly skilled horsemen and war canoes. Their ability to utilize any terrain to their advantage was unparalleled.

After the fall of the Mali Empire, several regional powers clustered around their traditional seats of control. However in 1464 CE, the fifteenth ruler of Songhai, Sunni Ali Ber came to power. A skilled military mastermind, Sunni Ali is often confused with the prince who fled Mansa Musa of Manden. Some historic sources seem to conflate the two men, but the accepted timeline of events would cover a span of nearly 125 years.

One of the reasons Sunni Ali Ber ("Ber" meaning "The Great") was successful in forging Songhai as a far-flung empire was probably due to his tolerance of the various spiritual forms of the region. Many of the historic descriptions of the period which come to us from Arabic Muslim scholars are not favorable to the king.[46] He took a Muslim name, but allowed traditional African religious to co-exist. In his *History of the Sudan*, Abdurrahman Es-Sadi explains:

> He surpassed all the previous kings in his bravery. His conquests were many, and his fame extended from the rising to the setting of the sun. If it is the will of God, he will be spoken for a long time.[47]

Image 5.12: Mounted Central West African Cavalryman in an 1820 engraving by British visitor, Edward Francis Finden

Religious tolerance aside, Sunni Ali was a legendary general. His military conquests began with securing his boundaries from the Mossi raiders from the south. He then pushed the Fulani and Dogon, who were long term rivals, back into their territories. Having defended the heart of the Songhai Empire, Ali then captured the legendary city of Timbuktu in 1468 CE from the Tuareg who controlled it since the dissolution of the Manden Empire. With the addition of Timbuktu came control of an intellectual center of the region and an important trade route for gold and salt.

Image 5.13: Constructed from organic materials including wood and mud, the Great Mosque of the City of Djenne is still in use today. The original mosque on the site might date to as early as 1200 CE. The renovation and reconstruction began in 1906.[48]

Next Ali turned his attention to the city of Djenne, located 250 miles southwest of Timbuktu. Djenne was virtually a well-protected island during the period of the year that the Niger River flooded. Ali could utilize his specialized war canoes during the flood. However the battle for the city shifted into the dry months when the canoes were useless. In order to take the city and its access to the southern gold routes, kola nuts, and ivory, he blockaded the city for seven years. As the city of Djenne neared famine, the young chief of the town eventually rode out to surrender in 1475 CE. When Ali learned the chief leading the opposition had perished in the blockade leaving his young son in charge, he decided to marry the queen mother. She was sent to the Gao, capital city of Songhai, as an honored member of the court. Sunni Ali took control of the ancient city. His exploits in the siege of Djenne would be recounted for hundreds of years.

Sunni Ali Ber would continue to expand the Songhai Empire finally engulfing virtually all the land held by both the Ghana and Mali Empires. The powerful king would eventual become a vaunted ancestor somewhere around 1493 CE. His son, Sunni Baru would succeed him briefly as the sixteenth and final king of the Sunni dynasty. One of Sunni Ali's generals would challenge Sunni Baru for the throne arguing that Baru was not a Muslim and therefore should not lead. The young king would eventually go into exile, leaving the general, Muhammad Ture to ascend to the throne of the empire.

As General Muhammad Ture took the throne in 1493 CE, he assumed the throne with the name Askia Muhammad (often known as Askia the Great), establishing the Askia Dynasty. Muhammad would begin his reign by shoring up the furthest boundaries of the kingdom. A devout Muslim, he made his Hajj in 1495. This was an impressive affair, but paled greatly in comparison to the pilgrimage taken by Mansa Musa.

> An army of one thousand infantrymen and five hundred men on horseback and camels accompanied Askia Muhammad on his journey. He took three thousand pieces of gold, of which a third was used to pay expenses, a third was given as alms and used to support an inn in Mecca for Sudanese (meaning sub-Saharan Africans from the area sometimes called the Sahel) pilgrims, and a final third was used to purchase merchandise. (Parenthesis added)[49]

Perhaps Askia Muhammad's religion made him much more comfortable with the Arabs and Tuareg who were encroaching from the north. Sunni Ali had battled with Tuareg to capture several important areas (Timbuktu, Takkada, etc.). Concerned that the scholars and Muslims living and operating in the learning centers of the empire would align with the Tuareg on the basis of religion against him, Ali was quite restrictive to the Muslim scholars in those cities. Ture allowed these intellectual/religious centers to flourish unchecked once more. This enhanced regional trade and provided a considerable economic boost. He was also able to attack the Mossi on the basis of religion and called for a jihad against them.

Ture fostered international trade as well, maintaining relationships with Spain and the rest of the Mediterranean world. It might have been expected for him to bolster the empire by aligning it with Islamic law, but Ture actually engendered significant secular administrative reforms for the empire, such as establishing rules for travel along trade routes, taxes, and uniform trade measures. During this period of expansion, the empire flourished. The Moroccan historian Leo Africanus was quite impressed with the empire. He described his visit to the city of Timbuktu during this timeframe.

> The houses of Timbuktu are huts made of clay-covered wattles with thatched roofs. In the center of the city is a temple built of stone and mortar, built by an architect named Granata, and in addition there is a large palace, constructed by the same architect, where the king lives. The shops of the artisans, the merchants, and especially weavers of cotton cloth are very numerous. Fabrics are also imported from Europe to Timbuktu, borne by Berber merchants ... The royal court is magnificent and very well organized. When the king goes from one city to another with the people of his court, he rides a camel and the horses are led by hand by servants ... There are in Timbuktu numerous judges, teachers and priests, all properly appointed by the king. He greatly honors learning. Many hand-written books imported from Barbary are also sold. There is more profit made from this commerce than from all other merchandise ... The people of Timbuktu are of a peaceful nature. They have a custom of almost continuously walking about the city in the evening (except for those that sell gold), between 10 PM and 1 AM, playing musical instruments and dancing.[50]

Askia Muhammad also focused on education and study. During this period Songhai produced a large number of scholars in the field of religious study, mathematics, and science. Several Islamic texts created during the reign of Muhammad are still in use today.

After a long reign of nearly 37 years, the now feeble Askia Muhammad was deposed by his son, Askia Musa, in 1528 CE. He died ten years later. The Askias would continue to wield the lofty Songhai Empire for decades after the conclusion of the reign of Askia the Great, though not at the heights of the great king. Infighting and the failure to continue to modernize the military would eventually lead to the fall of Songhai at the hands of the Moroccan sultan Ahmad al-Mansur. Initially al-Mansur would take advantage of the weakened central authority by demanding taxes for the trans-Saharan trade routes long controlled by West African nations. Askia Daoud (reigned 1549 - 1583 CE) would oblige the sultan sending a large payment in gold. This would only stave off the complete collapse of the empire momentarily. A civil war would embolden al-Mansur to dispatch an army to defeat Songhai at the Battle of Tondibi in 1591 CE.

With the curtain closing on the Songhai Empire, over one thousand years of powerful West African empires came to an end. During this period we find intellectual prowess, unparalleled wealth, excellence in science and mathematics, humanistic social contracts, brave rebellion leaders, ingenious military generals, well-designed metropolitan districts, and expansive cosmopolitan territories. Of particular note is that these nations have always held the griot in high regard. Historical events in West Africa are often chronicled in writing by outsiders who reveled in the civilized sovereignties they encountered. When the Portuguese begin their forays into Africa in the 1430's, they interact with nations which had been long established. They did not find disorganized, uncultured savages. The savage stereotype was craftily engineered for two evil purposes. First, the stereotype was created to absolve European consciences for commission of some of the most inhumane, barbaric, evil actions against millions of human beings. Second, the stereotype was created to prevent people of different ethnicities/races from realizing that they are all exploited by a wealthy ownership class.

Perhaps even more important than understanding the danger of the African savage stereotype, is acknowledging how the stereotype has metastasized. The stereotype might not always look exactly as it was initially introduced, but the modern versions are just as painful and hazardous. We will next explore harmful effects of the stereotype in our contemporary society.

Reasons for and the Effects of the LIE

Throughout the entire history of the United States, the public depiction of the African savage has morphed to justify the crudest exploitation of people of African descent. These justifications have been used to resolve any European ("white") guilt. During enslavement the savage myth was transformed in popular stereotypes that painted Africans as childlike, happy, and sometimes over-sexed. These characters justified the enslavement of African people. They were happy to be enslaved. If they were freed they would be unable to care for themselves or even put the valuable lands that they were taken from to good use.

As these racist stereotypes became more prevalent amongst whites, some actually argued that the Africans' desire to escape enslavement was a mental illness. In 1851, American physician Samuel A. Cartwright, actually coined the term "drapetomania" as the mental illness which caused Africans to attempt to flee their enslavement. Cartwright argued that as the Bible called for the slave to be obedient to his master, their desire to escape could not have been coherent.

Table 5.1: Popular Versions of the African "Savage"

Stereotype	Description	Purpose of Creation
Sambo	• An African boy or man • Easily amused • Overly spiritual and superstitious • Lazy, always looking for ways to escape responsibilities	African men are incapable of honest and diligent work. Therefore, they should be owned and directed by whites. Enslavement is good for them.
Uncle	• Older African man who is intensely loyal and happy to serve • Does not harbor resentment for decades of enslavement • Very attached and loyal to the children of the enslaver • Not sexual in any way	Africans are grateful for their enslavement. Pleased to have "served" (slaved) for white owner.
Mammy/ Auntie	• Counterpart to the uncle stereotype but rarely in a genuine relationship	Same as uncle.

	with him • Heavy set, large breasted, older enslaved African woman • Very pleased to serve the white enslaver • Extremely loyal; loves children of enslaver as if they were her own (although she often neglects own children); often breast feeds slaver's children • Overly spiritual; vessel of folk wisdom • Not sexual in any way	
Buck/ Mandingo	• Muscular enslaved African man • Superhuman strength but extremely childlike and unintelligent • Overly sexualized character • Dangerous if not controlled by intelligent whites • Mesmerized by and desirous of white women (he is dangerous to them)	If not controlled, the buck would destroy themselves and the societies around him. The stereotype counters the position of liberal whites and abolitionists who believe the enslaved should be freed.
Pickaninny	• Enslaved African child • Often depicted alone, nude, or without proper adult supervision • Impervious to pain • Often depicted with animals • Harm to these children (usually by wild animals) is amusing	Africans are not rational, productive adults when enslaver is not in control. In their natural state, they are animals.
Jezebel	• Usually light-skinned attractive enslaved African (product of sex with enslaver) • Over-sexed; Is able to seduce enslaver	Justifies the rape of enslaved women (she is attractive unlike "unmixed" Africans). Unlike buck who is violently sexual and dangerous, she convinces enslaver to have sex with her even though she is his property and unable to consent.

These racist stereotypes were extremely popular. Virtually every man, woman, and child would have been familiar with them. The characters could be found in almost all children's stories, live theater productions, and early films. In the period immediately prior to and after the Civil War, we still find the uncle, sambo, mammy, jezebel, auntie, and pickaninny in popular depictions, but the buck/Mandingo becomes more prevalent. This brutish character mirrored white concerns about newly-liberated Africans. They are not depicted as happy slaves, but now as dangerous animals with a penchant for violence and raping white women. The stereotype of the brutish buck was constructed to leave Europeans blameless for the violence perpetrated on Africans. During enslavement when Africans were considered nothing more than property, slaveholders had an incentive not to wantonly murder them. Their value was based on their ability to work (or breed). Killing Africans during this period was not financially viable. After the Civil War, this financial incentive no longer existed. The radical reporter and activist, Ida B. Wells-Barnett, chronicled the prevalence of lynching of African Americans after the Civil War in her popular pamphlet, *The Red Record*. As Wells-Barnett describes, white lynch mobs often argued that the African American victim had raped or defiled a white woman.

> Dr. Hass, editor of the leading organ of the Methodist Church South, published in its columns that it was his belief that more than three hundred women had been assaulted by Negro men within three months. When asked to prove his charges, or give a single case upon which his "belief" was founded, he said that he could do so, but the details were unfit for publication. No other evidence but his "belief" could be adduced to substantiate this grave charge, yet Bishop Haygood, in the *Forum* of October, 1893, quotes this "belief" in apology for lynching, and voluntarily adds: "It is my opinion that this is an underestimate." The "opinion" of this man, based upon a "belief," had greater weight coming from a man who has posed as a friend to "Our Brother in Black," and was accepted as authority.[51]

In a March 1900 speech on the floor of the United States Senate, South Carolina governor and senator Benjamin Tillman seemed proud to confirm that whites lynched African Americans with regularity. The racist senator connects these vile acts with both the Mandingo/buck stereotype and the African American right to have governmental representation.

We of the South have never recognized the right of the negro to govern white men, and we never will. We have never believed him to be the equal of the white man, and we will not submit to his gratifying his lust on our wives and daughters without lynching him.[52]

Whether the perpetrators of racist violence believed the African savage stereotype or simply utilized them as an excuse, it should be clear that the character had deadly consequences. A Tuskegee Institute study found that at least 3,446 African Americans were lynched from 1882 to 1968.[53]

In the modern post Civil Rights era, these stereotypes are just as common but some of the most offensive aspects are somewhat muted. The negative effect on how African Americans are viewed is just as potent.

The savage stereotype has truly been in play during the "age of Obama". Some whites have argued that racism in the United States is a thing of the past simply because Barack Obama was elected president. Ironically, white anxiety has certainly peaked due to his presidency. The conservative right-wing group known as the Tea Party has led the charge with repeated demands for the Hawaii-born Obama to show them his birth certificate. Racist signs and t-shirts are a routine sight at their boisterous rallies.

Image 5.14: Racist Signs in the Age of Obama - (Top Left) Racist Tea Party rally sign depicts President Obama as a "witch doctor". (Top Right) Tea Party sign suggests lynching Obama while manipulating the campaign's "Hope and Change" slogan. (Middle Left) Sign on Highway 99 near Lodi, California uses racist play on words. (Bottom Left) Sign misspells "Muslim" while calling President Obama a "half-breed". (Bottom Right) Rally sign calls for the president to be deported to Kenya.

Popular images of the "Black savage" in the media have continued to be prevalent. In April 2008, Vogue magazine seemed to depict popular basketball player, Lebron James, as a "Mandingo" King Kong as he crudely grasped blonde-haired German supermodel, Giselle Bündchen. James was the first African American man to grace Vogue's cover. The cover focuses on Black male physical, primal, and sexual prowess and reinforces the most racist images of African American men. Lebron is not just one of the best athletes to play basketball ... he's dribbling down the court to steal your innocent (white) wives and daughters.

Image 5.15: Basketball superstar Lebron James clutches supermodel Giselle Bündchen in a manner which seems to recall King Kong (African primate). The cover seems to mimic a 1917 World War I poster which implores the reader to "destroy this man brute". Is it possible that the picture's composers were looking to reduce the basketball star whose nickname is "King James" to "King Kong"?

Cable television's highest rated show, *The Walking Dead*, displayed the "noble savage" in full form with its character, Tyrese Williams. Played by muscular actor, Chad Coleman, Tyrese shows displeasure with violent acts.   However, one of the main white female characters was actually exiled because the group leader feared Tyrese would harm her. *The Walking Dead* portrays humans trying to survive during the aftermath of a zombie apocalypse. All of the main characters have become experts in utilizing weapons like small firearms and crossbows, which allow them to defend themselves at a distance.   Conversely, Tyrese gets up close and personal most often with the zombie "walkers" as his choice weapon is a hammer. He is most effective when he is enraged. In one episode he goes berserk, defending himself with his claw hammer on his own from dozens of "walkers" who have surrounded him as the other characters flee. While he is a hero, several of the other characters seemed concerned about his powerfully blind rage. If these racist images were simply misconceptions which were based on old prejudices, the entire issue would be academic at best. However, just as in the Reconstruction Era (post Civil War), these stereotypes have violent consequences.

The issue of police brutality has been a primary concern in the African American community since the end of the Civil War. However, the issue doesn't truly gain national attention until grainy video of the beating of Rodney King was broadcast in 1991. Rodney King was beaten nearly to death by four police officers who struck him 56 times as he lay on the ground. Earlier in the day the officers described another conflict in an African American neighborhood as a scene "right out of 'Gorillas in the Mist' ".[54] As the officers savagely beat Mr. King, the officers commented that they believed that he was either on the PCP, a drug believed to make the user impervious to pain and give them super-human strength, or that he was an ex-convict who had spent his time weightlifting.

This depiction of African American men as having animalistic strength without intellectual ability was also on display in virtually every other police involved killings. When New York Police Department Officer Daniel Pantaleo killed Eric Garner with a chokehold in Staten Island, New York, the police officials often mentioned Garner's size as an explanation for the extreme force used. When Mike Brown was shot and killed by Officer Darren Wilson in Ferguson, Missouri, Wilson exclaimed that when he grabbed Brown he "felt like a 5-year-old holding onto Hulk Hogan".[55] Whenever the issue of police killings of unarmed African Americans is raised, conservative media outlets exclaim that the real issue is "black-on-black" crime. A term which, when wielded by conservatives, seems to describe African American neighborhoods as a wild, uncivilized jungle at the mercy of rampaging Black youth.

It is of critical importance to dismantle the African savage stereotype. As we have seen, it has been used with deadly effect in the 150 years since the Civil War. While the entire world needs to understand the role that Africans have played in human civilization, it is incumbent on people of African descent to become aware of the true history of their people. They must begin to recognize that their historic greatness must serve as a blueprint for a return to the forefront of human civilization. The lives of our children literally hang in the balance.

For Additional Research

BOOKS
1. Robinson, C., Battle, R., and Robinson, E. (1987). The Journey of the Songhai People. Philadelphia: The Pan African Federation Organization.
2. Wiener, L. (1992). Africa and the Discovery of America. Brooklyn: A&B Books Publishers.
3. Davidson, B (1965). A History of West Africa 1000-1800. Harlow, UK: Longman Group.
4. Niane, D.T. (2006). An Epic of Old Mali. Edinburgh Gate, Harlow (UK): Pearson Education Limited.
5. Conrad, D. (1992). Searching for History in the Sunjata Epic: The Case of Fakoli. History in Africa.
6. Van Sertima, I (1976). They Came Before Columbus: The African Presence in Ancient America. New York: Random House Trade Paperbacks.
7. Conrad, D. (2010). Great Empires of the Past: Empires of Medieval West Africa. New York: Chelsea House.
8. Asante, M.K. (2014). The History of Africa: The Quest for Eternal Harmony. London: Routledge.
9. Levtzion, N. (1963). The Thirteenth- and Fourteenth-Century Kings of Mali. The Journal of African History. 4(3). Cambridge: Cambridge University Press.
10. Davidson, B (1965). A History of West Africa 1000-1800. Harlow, UK: Longman Group.
11. Levtzion, N. Ancient Ghana and Mali (1980). London: Holmes & Meier Publishers.
12. Davidson, B (1998). West Africa Before the Colonial Era: A History to 1850. London: Routledge
13. Diop, Cheikh Anta. (1988). Precolonial Black Africa. Chicago, IL: Chicago Review Press

14. Williams, Chancellor. (1992). Destruction of Black Civilization: Great Issues of a Race from 4500 B.C. to 2000 A.D. Chicago, IL: Third World Press.
15. Obenga, T. (1995). Readings in Precolonial Central Africa: Texts & Documents. Lawrenceville, NJ: Red Sea Press.
16. McKissack, P and McKissak, F. (1995). The Royal Kingdoms of Ghana, Mali, and Songhay: Life in Medieval Africa. London: Macmillian

CHAPTER 6:
"COLUMBUS DISCOVERED AMERICA"

Image 6.1: 1519 Portrait of a Man Believed to be Christopher Columbus by Sebastiano del Piombo. The portrait was completed posthumously.

Uncovering the Lie

On a beautiful Sunday in October, a phalanx of high school students marched with militaristic precision past the 20-foot-tall statue of Christopher Columbus hewn in marble on the corner of President Street and Eastern Avenue in Baltimore, MD. The statue of the Italian explorer peers east as he grasps a rolled map in his left hand while placing his right hand on a globe. The high stepping youth clad in maroon, gold-accented blazers with tall fluffy black feathers would soon cede the spotlight to a large wooden float constructed to look like a sailing ship. Emblazoned with the words "Santa Maria", the boat features Donald Castronova in period clothing on the bow. Castronova has portrayed Christopher Columbus in the parade for over 40 years. In fact, this celebration is the 124th year that Baltimore's Italian community has displayed their admiration for Columbus. The commemoration featured more than 40 musical, school, and civic organizations; visits from the mayor and governor; and a ravioli dinner at St. Leo the Great Roman Catholic Church.

An influential member of the Columbus Celebration Committee, Domenic Petrucci, described the importance of the celebration to the local CBS affiliate. "That's why I'm in America, thanks to Columbus. And, I don't know if anybody care (sic), this year is my 45th anniversary in this country."[1]

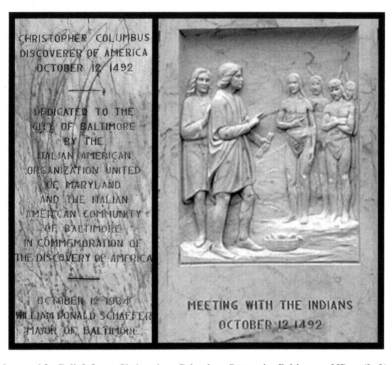

Image 6.2: Relief from Christopher Columbus Statue in Baltimore, MD - (Left) Commemorative engraving recognizes Columbus' "discovery of America". (Right) Relief of Columbus depicting his meeting with Native Americans as equals.

Mr. Petrucci probably didn't mean that he literally immigrated to the United States because of Christopher Columbus' journey in the late 15th century. He was probably referring to a popular bit of folk history in the western world. Virtually every elementary school student learned the following poem:

IN 1492
In fourteen hundred ninety-two
Columbus sailed the ocean blue.

He had three ships and left from Spain;
He sailed through sunshine, wind and rain.

He sailed by night; he sailed by day;
He used the stars to find his way.

A compass also helped him know
How to find the way to go.

Ninety sailors were on board;
Some men worked while others snored.

Then the workers went to sleep;
And others watched the ocean deep.

Day after day they looked for land;
They dreamed of trees and rocks and sand.

October 12 their dream came true,
You never saw a happier crew!

"Indians! Indians!" Columbus cried;
His heart was filled with joyful pride.

But "India" the land was not;
It was the Bahamas, and it was hot.

The Arakawa natives were very nice;
They gave the sailors food and spice.

Columbus sailed on to find some gold
To bring back home, as he'd been told.

He made the trip again and again,
Trading gold to bring to Spain.

The first American? No, not quite.
But Columbus was brave, and he was bright.

- Author Unknown

While most Italian American organizations that convene Columbus Day parades are no longer very clear about why anyone should celebrate the holiday, the Order Sons of Italy in America (OSIA) actually includes a document entitled "Why We Should Celebrate Columbus Day" among its press materials. OSIA describes itself as a national organization of men and women who represent the estimated 26 million Americans of Italian heritage.

> Columbus Day recognizes the achievements of a great Renaissance explorer who founded the first permanent European settlement in the New World. The arrival of Columbus in 1492 marks the beginning of recorded history in America. *Columbus Day celebrates the beginning of cultural exchange between America and Europe.* After Columbus, came millions of European immigrants who brought their art, music, science, medicine, philosophy and religious principles to America. These contributions have helped shape the United States and include Greek democracy, Roman law, Judeo-Christian ethics and *the tenet that all men are created equal.* (Italics added)[2]

One might ask why it would even be necessary to publish this document at all. If Columbus' voyage was so entrepreneurial and brought forth the tenet that all men are created equal to the New World, then wouldn't its merits be obvious? These voyages are one of the most chronicled events in western history. What are the Columbus celebrations and the OSIA publication omitting? Did Columbus "discover America"? Did he meet the "Indians" with "joyful pride"? How did the "Arakawa" respond to meeting Columbus in the Bahamas? Let's explore these issues en route to understanding the actual effect of Christopher Columbus' voyage to the "New World".

The Real Deal

Christoforo Colombo (Latinized Christophorus Columbus) was born in the Republic of Genoa in 1451. The region would later be part of modern-day Italy. Christopher's father, Domenico Columbo, owned a cheese shop which young Christopher assisted in. From a very young age it seems Columbus began working on ships. He journeyed to Greece, Iceland, England, and even Africa. He would eventually learn mapmaking in Portugal.

Through his extensive work in the sailing industry, he realized that identifying a western sea route to Asia would be a lucrative proposition. At the time, the profitable European trade with China and India for gold, ivory, spices and other goods was conducted through Arab and Turkish middle men who charged high fees.

Image 6.3: (1843) *Columbus before the Queen* by Emanuel Leutze

Believing he had properly measured the distances to Asia and had identified the sea winds that would allow him to make the journey, Columbus negotiated sponsorship with several European powers. He and his brother, Bartholomew, unsuccessfully lobbied the king of Portugal twice, the King of England, and also the powerful leaders of Genoa and Venice (both now part of modern-day Italy).

It is now believed that Christopher Columbus and many educated Europeans were likely aware that the earth was round and not flat. However, this knowledge did not ensure the accuracy of Columbus' navigation skills. All of the experts under the employment of the rulers believed that Columbus' calculations of the distance to Asia by sea were largely underestimated. They were correct.

Undeterred, Columbus would next make his case to the rulers of Spain, King Ferdinand II and Queen Isabella I. The monarchs would finally agree to sponsor him after two years of petitions. While the journey was a significant risk, the terms of their sponsorship were quite lucrative. If successful, he would assume the rank of "Admiral of the Ocean Sea" and would be appointed Viceroy and Governor of all lands claimed for Spain. Additionally, Columbus could submit three individuals to hold any office in these lands. Ferdinand and Isabella would appoint the office holder from the three names. Finally, he would forever receive 10 percent revenues from the territories and the option of buying one-eighth stake in the land's commercial ventures. In August of 1492, Christopher Columbus would depart for his first voyage to the New World in the sailing ships known as the Nina, the Pinta, and the Santa Maria.

After stopping for repairs and supplies in the Canary Islands, the flotilla arrived at one of the islands that comprise the modern-day nation of the Bahamas approximately five weeks after departing from Spain. Almost immediately upon their arrival, the natives came out to the men on long canoes. Columbus, still believing he was in Asia, states that the people he met called themselves the Lucayos (often called the Lucayans in English) and that their island was called Gaunahani.[3] They may have been a branch of the Taino people that belonged to the Arawak group. He states that the Lucayans were friendly people that the Spaniards could develop a "great friendship with"[4]. They brought the sailors water and food without it being requested. They gave anything they had on their person freely to his crew including parrots and cotton. The Lucayans seemed to be unfamiliar with metal swords. When handling them, they mistakenly cut themselves.

It must be noted that there are those who still describe Columbus' trip positively. They argue that Columbus brought those aspects of western civilization that they assume are positive to the New World. However, he should be judged by his own words.

They should be good servants and intelligent, for I observed that they quickly took in what was said to them, and I believe that they would easily be made Christians, as it appeared to me that they had no religion. I, our Lord being pleased, will take hence, at the time of my departure, six natives for your Highnesses, that they may learn to speak ... I might be able to give a full account to your Highnesses, and also where a fortress might be established ... though I do not see that it would be necessary, for these people are very simple as regards the use of arms. [Perhaps you] should order them all to be brought to Castille, or to be kept as captives on the same island; for with fifty men they can all be subjugated and made to do what is required of them[5]

The explorer also takes note that some of the Lucayans wore small gold beads in their noses, although they didn't seem anxious to take him to the source. Even though Columbus was almost immediately aware of what the natives called their island, he automatically decided to call it San Salvador, clearly a forceful act of claiming a people's homeland. As soon as he sets foot on this unusual land, he decides that he could enslave its inhabitants, convert them to Christianity, rename their home, and exploit any resources he believed to be of value.

Image 6.3: (1880 CE) A group of Awarak and Carib people assembling to meet with the Dutch Governor in Modern-day Suriname.[6]

On the balance of his first voyage, Columbus visited the modern-day Cuba (which he believed to be China). He also left 39 of his men on the island of Hispanola, which houses modern-day Haiti and the Dominican Republic. He believed this island was Japan. Columbus wanted to send a clear message to the native inhabitants of these islands. When the Santa Maria ran aground on the beach, it was abandoned. He decided to destroy it with the bombardment of his canons in order to instill fear in the native peoples. Columbus took approximately 25 more natives captive, but it seems only around seven returned to Spain alive. Columbus returned to Spain in March of 1493 and he authored a letter from Lisbon, Portugal to King Ferdinand II and Queen Isabella I. The exploits of his journey were widely reported throughout Europe and he received the title "Admiral of the Ocean Sea" due to its perceived success.

Columbus would not forgo the opportunity to enslave native peoples and exploit the natural resources of a region previously unknown to European powers. He returned to the New World three more times, although he *never realized that he hadn't reached Asia*. On these trips he returned better prepared to invoke misery upon millions of native peoples for personal and national gain.

Columbus left for his second trip to the New World in September 1493 with 17 ships and 1,500 colonists. He was prepared to establish permanent colonies in the New World. It also seems that several of these passengers may have actually been Africans as well.[7] One of the permanent planned settlements, named La Isabella for his Spanish patron queen, was established on the northern coast of the Dominican Republic. La Isabella would not last long as it struggled through internal discord, turbulent weather, and disease. The ruins of the settlement were in fairly good condition until the 1950's. An excavation of the church cemetery which commenced in 1983 found the remains of the colonists of La Isabella and another early European settlement known as Campeche. A study of the carbon isotopes in the teeth of these remains seem to show that several of the colonists at both sites were African (based on the carbon chemical signature left in their teeth and bones by their diet). The burials of these Africans seem to have been in equal stature to the other burials. It is likely these free Africans became part of the settlements prior to the enslavement period.

Much of Columbus' route took him through the group of islands in the Caribbean Sea known as the Lesser Antilles. He continued to assign European (Spanish) names for islands that he visited or simply passed from a distance. Eventually the flotilla returned to the island of Hispaniola to inspect the permanent settlement (La Navidad) which was created by the 39 men who were left behind on his first voyage. All that remained were ruins as the Taino people probably destroyed the fort. Columbus would establish a new settlement here during his second trip.

While Columbus' modus operandi with regard to the treatment of the natives of these lands might have been revealed during his first trip, it is on the second voyage that we begin to understand just how evil the explorer's intentions were. Michele da Cuneo was one of the passengers on this journey. An Italian aristocrat and a childhood friend of Columbus, Cuneo authored a letter demonstrating that Columbus sought to forcefully exploit more than just the land of the natives he described as "friendly". Columbus "gifts" Cueno with one of the captured native women.

> While I was in the boat, I captured a very beautiful Carib woman, whom the said Lord Admiral (Columbus) gave to me. When I had taken her to my cabin she was naked—as was their custom. I was filled with a desire to take my pleasure with her and attempted to satisfy my desire. She was unwilling, and so treated me with her nails that I wished I had never begun. But—to cut a long story short—I then took a piece of rope and whipped her soundly, and she let forth such incredible screams that you would not have believed your ears. Eventually we came to such terms, I assure you, that you would have thought that she had been brought up in a school for whores.[8]

Columbus seems to have been personally involved in the rape of native women and even the sale of native children into sexual slavery. In a log written in 1500, he nonchalantly explains that "a hundred castellanoes are as easily obtained for a woman as for a farm, and it is very general and there are plenty of dealers who go about looking for girls; those from nine to ten are now in demand."[9]

Image 6.4: 1817 drawing of an Arawak woman by John Gabriel Stedman for his book Narrative.

The second voyage of Columbus was chiefly about the rape and murder of the largely peaceful peoples that were encountered. Records of this trip demonstrate how brutal sexual aggression was not a byproduct, but an expectation of those who argued their major aim was to bring Christianity to the New World. Cueno also describes how the murder and enslavement of native peoples were also an objective of the trip.

> [W]e came to [an] island of Caribs very beautiful and fertile, and we arrived at a very beautiful harbor. As soon as the Caribs saw us they ran away to the mountains like those of the other island and they emptied their houses, into which we went and took whatever pleased us.

> When our caravels were ready to depart for Spain, aboard which I intended to return home, we gathered at our settlement 1,600 Indians, male and female; we loaded 650

of the best--both men and women--aboard those caravels on 17 February 1495. Regarding the rest, it was declared that whoever wanted some of them could take them as he wished, and so it was ... Among the captives was one of their kings with two principal men; it was decided that they should be executed with arrows the following day. For this purpose they were shackled, but that night they were so adept at gnawing at one another's heels with their teeth that they escaped from the shackles and fled.[10]

During this trip, Columbus and his compatriots would establish gold mines and cotton fields on Hispaniola. They would rain brutality upon the native peoples as they forced them to toil for their profit.

Ironically, it seems there was little challenge to Columbus' violent acts when they were relegated to the native population. However, as a result of his agreement with the Spanish monarchs who sponsored him, he was named governor of the region. It seems he was an aggressively violent administrator. A man accused of stealing corn had his ears and nose cut off before he was sold into enslavement. A female colonist who suggested that Columbus' family was "low class" was stripped naked, forced to walk through town, and finally had her tongue cut out.[11] Columbus even had several of his crew members hanged for disobedience. The colonists eventually took their complaints to the king and queen. He did, however, restrict the most heinous punishments for the native population. To quell a native rebellion, he murdered and dismembered scores of native people. Their body parts were strewn around the town as a deterrent to future insurrections.

By Columbus' third voyage to the New World in 1498, the explorer was falling out of favor with the Spanish crown. This trip was primarily convened to provide supplies for existing settlements. After stopping in modern-day Trinidad to regroup and replenish their fresh water, the flotilla arrived in Hispaniola to find the colonists in revolt against Columbus' rule. Upon returning to Spain in 1500 CE, Columbus was stripped of his governorship and he and his three brothers were imprisoned as the colonist complaints had preceded him to the court of Ferdinand II and Isabella I. Columbus would be freed, but he did not have his governorship reinstated.

Columbus took his fourth and final trip to the New World in 1502. He spent considerable time exploring the coast of Central America. As his crew recognized an intense hurricane in its path, they sought refuge at Hispaniola, but the new governor did not approve giving them sanctuary. Columbus and his crew took shelter in the mouth of a nearby river. As the hurricane intensified, a portion of the Spanish fleet, which included the governor of Hispaniola, was largely destroyed. Bombarded by another storm, Columbus became stranded in modern-day Jamaica as he sought assistance from Hispaniola for over a year. After receiving aide, Columbus returned to Spain with his stature diminished. He would die just two years later in his early 50s.

EARLIER VOYAGES LEAD BY *AFRICAN NATIONS* AND OTHERS

Many are not aware that Columbus was not even the first European to arrive in the New World. That title seems to have gone to the Viking explorer, Leif Ericson. Ericson established a temporary settlement on the northern tip of Newfoundland at around 1000 CE—Nearly 500 years earlier than Columbus' voyage.[12] Columbus never even set foot on or even saw the North American continent. At no time in his life did he even realize that he had not traveled to Asia.

While written evidence of explorers from other lands requires much more research, a very basic logical argument must not be overlooked. Genetic studies have finally proven that humanity has its origins in Africa. Mitochondrial DNA studies instruct us that every single human is the relative of one woman of African descent. So how did these Africans come to populate virtually every corner of the globe?

The accumulated work of dozens of scholars has now established the case for Ancient African explorations to the Americas. In fact, several of these scholars begin their treaties with a very interesting source: Christopher Columbus' third voyage. The poet Washington

Irving recounts Columbus' conversations with the native people about their interactions with people of African descent.

> Columbus expected to find such people more to the south and southeast. He recollected that the natives of Hispaniola had spoken of black men who had once come to their island from the south, the heads of whose javelins were of guanin, or adulterated gold.[13]

Interestingly, few scholars focused on Columbus' reports of Africans traveling to the Americas until Jose Maria Melgar y Serrano made his groundbreaking 1862 discovery in Tres Zapotes, Mexico. Melgar y Serrano, a Mexican explorer, was the first to describe the massive sculptures known today as the "Olmec Heads". He also described their ethnic features as "Ethiopian".[14] These colossal basalt stone carvings, which date to around 900 BCE, continue to serve as a powerful argument for African influence on one of the earliest civilizations of note in the Americas. The most comprehensive argument for ancient African exploration of the Americas was conducted by the well-renowned scholar, Dr. Ivan Van Sertima. Van Sertima's work, *They Came Before Columbus*, not only features the Olmec Heads, but also examines Trans-Atlantic Ocean currents which could have assisted journeys from Africa to the Americas. Van Sertima even notes the presence of plants which seem to have been transported to and from the Americas and the "seaworthiness" of ancient African vessels. Derided or simply ignored by many "mainstream" European scholars, Van Sertima's analysis is as thorough as it is cogent. However, unequivocally identifying which African nations actually sailed successfully to the Americas has not been achieved. Were these intrepid Africans Ancient Kemetic explorers (perhaps under the auspices of King Ramesses III) or were they led by the Malian Mansa Abubakari II (see Chapter 5)? Perhaps future scholars will lay claim to the incontrovertible proof. The first step to empowering these future scholars is to discard the propaganda of Columbus' journey and eradicate the racist belief that Africans were incapable of oceanic travel.

Image 6.5: Olmec Head 1 [15] -This colossal head was discovered by Jose Maria Melgar y Serrano in 1862. Melgar y Serrano notes, "What astonished me was the Ethiopian type represented. I reflected that there had undoubtedly been Negroes in this country, and that this had been in the first epoch of the world." [16] Seventeen of these colossal statues, weighing up to 40 tons, have been unearthed.

THE LASTING EFFECT OF THE VOYAGES OF CHRISTOPHER COLUMBUS

What is the true legacy of Christopher Columbus? Advocates of the Italian explorer routinely defend him by stating that he should be given at least partial credit for the existence of the United States, one of the most powerful countries in human history. They also give Columbus credit for the presence of Judeo-Christian values in the New World. More recently we also hear that the contemporary drive towards globalization is a byproduct of his journeys. These defenses exist without any recognition of the actual historical record.

How could Columbus be given credit for the "discovery of the Americas" when some estimates put the region's inhabitants at anywhere between 50 and 100 million prior to his arrival? [17] Is it possible to discover someone else's home? This position nullifies the presence of the New World's native people. It reduces them to little more than "native wildlife".

Image 6.6: 16th Century illustrations of some of the atrocities committed by the Spanish on the natives of the New World as described by Father Bartolomé de las Casas. (Top) The Spanish cut off the noses and hands of the natives. (Bottom) Spanish conqueror hanging native woman and feeding her babies to his dogs.

Perhaps the most important characteristic of Columbus' voyage to the New World was its unparalleled level of brutality and perverseness. Within a few moments of meeting the indigenous people of the Bahamas on his first voyage, Columbus remarks that they were friendly, peaceful people. He next comments that they could be easily enslaved and that they were adorned with a small amount of gold jewelry. The deadly, torturous atrocities which he committed were both planned and disturbingly effective.

Columbus forced the native people of the island of Hispaniola to either labor in gold mines or to toil on cotton fields. The writings of Father Bartolomé de las Casas provide us with an adequate illustration of the manner in which the native people were abused.

Las Casas journeyed to the New World in 1502 (in fact, his father was on Columbus' second voyage). He had actually owned an *encomienda* (similar to a plantation) and was an exploiter of the native people. In 1515 he gave away his possessions and not only became a Roman Catholic priest, but a "protector" of the natives.

Las Casas describes the brutality of the Spanish occupation of the New World:

From that time onward the Indians began to seek ways to throw the Christians out of their lands. They took up arms, but their weapons were very weak and of little service in offense and still less in defense. And the Christians, with their horses and swords and pikes began to carry out massacres and strange cruelties against them. They attacked the towns and spared neither the children nor the aged nor pregnant women nor women in childbed, not only stabbing them and dismembering them but cutting them to pieces as if dealing with sheep in the slaughter house. They laid bets as to who, with one stroke of the sword, could split a man in two or could cut off his head or spill out his entrails with a single stroke of the pike. They took infants from their mothers' breasts, snatching them by the legs and pitching them headfirst against the crags or snatched them by the arms and threw them into the rivers, roaring with laughter and saying as the babies fell into the water, "Boil there, you offspring of the devil!" Other infants they put to the sword along with their mothers and anyone else who happened to be nearby. They made some low wide gallows on which the hanged victim's feet almost touched the ground, stringing up their victims in lots of thirteen, in memory of Our Redeemer and His twelve Apostles, then set burning wood at their feet and thus burned them alive. To others they attached straw or wrapped their whole bodies in straw and set them afire. With still others, all those they wanted to capture alive, they cut off their hands and hung them round the victim's neck, saying, "Go now, carry the message," meaning, Take the news to the Indians who have fled to the mountains. They usually dealt with the chieftains and nobles in the following way: they made a grid of rods which they placed on forked sticks, then lashed the victims to the grid and lighted a smoldering fire underneath, so that little by little, as those captives screamed in despair and torment, their souls would leave them ...[18]

Las Casas then describes the violent depopulation of the Caribbean.

[On the] Island of Hispaniola, of the above three millions souls that we once saw, today there be no more than two hundred of those native people remaining ... The island of Cuba is almost as long as from Valladolid to Rome; today it is almost devoid of population. On the Isles of the Lucayos [the inhabitants of the Bahamas] . . . where there were once above five hundred thousand souls, today there is not a living creature. (Brackets added)[19]

The truest legacy of Christopher Columbus must be religious intolerance (as he sought to forcibly convert natives peoples), economic exploitation, rape, the sexual trafficking of minors, and genocide.

While Las Casas was a forceful protector of the indigenous people of the New World, he once suggested that one of the best ways to end the brutal forced labor of the people was to substitute them with Africans. He would eventually reverse this position and argue that the enslavement of any group is inhumane. However, this position did assist with the establishment of the Trans-Atlantic enslavement trade. By extension, the brutal voyages of Christopher Columbus are the predecessor of the enslavement of Africans.

Reasons for and effects of the LIE

Most groups who still openly advance Christopher Columbus as a character worthy of respect, often argue that his Italian heritage is a source of pride. Others point to his Christian background, while still others argue Columbus brought Western Civilization to the New World. Virtually none of these positions exist on logical grounds. Just as illogical is the fact that the United States is the nation with the largest number of monuments to Christopher

Columbus, even though he never set foot on the North American continent!

While there are those who would object to the term, it should be clear that the continued focus on the Italian explorer only serves one aim; to advance white supremacy. Why else would anyone elevate an individual who should be described as a practitioner of genocide, an enslaver, a pedophile, and a human trafficker? Emphasis on Columbus occurs because there are those who would like to make European history, language, religion, and culture *primary*.

It is critical for all people to understand the roots of the countries in the New World which are dominated by people of European descent. Understanding how they gained this primary position (through the vilest human rights abuses) will allow citizens to recognize their fundamental relationship to society.

For Additional Research

BOOKS
1. Williams, E. (1984). From Columbus to Castro: The History of the Caribbean. New York: Vintage Books.
2. Carew, J. (1994). Rape of Paradise: Columbus and the Birth of Racism in the Americas. Brooklyn, New York: A&B Publishers.
3. Van Sertima, I. (1976). They Came Before Columbus: The African Presence in Ancient America. New York: Random House Trade Paperbacks.
4. Van Sertima, I. (1992). African Presence in Early America. New Brunswick, New Jersey: Transaction.
5. Imhotep, D. (2011). The First Americans Were Africans: Documented Evidence. Bloomington, Indiana: AuthorHouse.
6. Clarke, J.H. (1992). Christopher Columbus and the Afrikan Holocaust: Slavery and the Rise of European Capitalism. Brooklyn, New York: A&B Books.
7. Thacher, J.B. (1903). Christopher Columbus: His Life, His Works, His Remains: As Revealed by Original Printed and Manuscript Records, Together with an Essay on Peter Martyr of Anghera and Bartolomé de Las Casas, the First Historians of America, Volume 2.

8. Columbus, C. (1893). Journal of Christopher Columbus During His First Voyage 1492-93. (C.R. Markham, Trans.). London: Hakluyut Society.

9. Cueno, M. (1963). Michele de Cuneo's Letter on the Second Voyage, 28 October 1495. In S.E. Morison (Ed.). *Journals and Other Documents on the Life and Voyages of Christopher Columbus.* New York: Heritage Press.

10. Las Casas, B. (2007). A Brief Account of the Destruction of the Indies. (Original work 1552). Project Gutenburg. Retrieved from http://www-personal.umich.edu/~twod/latam-s2010/read/las_casasb2032120321-8.pdf

CHAPTER 7:
"ABRAHAM LINCOLN FREED THE SLAVES"

Image 7.1: This popular lithograph commemorated an early version of the Emancipation Proclamation. The imagery recalls an admonition by Lincoln for the freed Africans to thank only God—not him. Notice the African's position of subservience and indebtedness, not anger or frustration. This depiction may have been crafted to reassure whites that Africans would be thankful, and not seek retribution for hundreds of years of brutal enslavement.

Uncovering the Lie

The date was Tuesday, January 20, 2009. It was a brisk winter day in Washington, D.C., but the electricity in the air was due to so much more than the weather. The National Mall in Washington, D.C. has been the site of historic gatherings including the 1963 March on Washington, the 1969 Vietnam War Memoriam Rally and the 1995 Million Man March. However, the crowd for this historic event was the largest ever recorded. The theme of the event, "A New Birth of Freedom", was a phrase from Abraham Lincoln's Gettysburg Address. President Lincoln delivered the speech hoping to shift the focus of the Civil War from simply a struggle to save the United States to creating "equality" for all by ending enslavement. 2009 was the 200th anniversary of Lincoln's year of birth.

Image 7.2: Barack Hussein Obama is sworn in as President of the United States. His right hand rests on a bible which belonged to President Abraham Lincoln

As the main character of this historic event stepped to the stage, he placed his right hand on a bible used by President Lincoln. While similar acts have occurred on this location every four years, this event had even more historical significance. This event was the inauguration of President Barack Hussein Obama, the first African American president of the United States.

To further symbolically connect his first inauguration with President Lincoln, President Obama took a ceremonial train journey from Philadelphia, Pennsylvania to Washington, D.C. to mimic the last leg of the train trip taken by President Lincoln to his 1861 inauguration. The president would also utilize carefully crafted themes related to Lincoln's address.

While it seems Lincoln has been popular for quite some time, his presidency might have reached new heights in recent years. Lincoln was ranked the second most popular president among scholars in a 2000 survey[1] and also in a public Gallup survey in 2011[2]. He tops the list in a 2014 survey of 162 members of the American Political Science Association's Presidents & Executive Politics section.[3] No other president has been captured as much in popular depictions. The blockbuster biopic, *Lincoln*, garnered the actor Daniel Day Lewis the Academy Award for Best Actor the same year that the fictional action film *Abraham Lincoln, Vampire Hunter* hit the big screen (2012).

When President Obama invokes Lincoln, however, it is probably not because they are both thin lawyers from Illinois who had to contend with costly unpopular wars. When the first African American president invokes Lincoln, most people—especially African Americans—recognize that he is also paying homage to Lincoln as the "Great Emancipator". Throughout his presidency Obama has continued to reference Lincoln and even quote from him directly. When asked about his affection for the 16th president, President Obama explained, "There is a wisdom there and a humility about his approach to government, even before he was president, that I just find very helpful."[4]

Lincoln has been long endeared by African Americans. When historian Carter G. Woodson and the Association for the Study of Negro Life and History selected the second week in February for Negro History Week, Woodson explained that the week was selected because African Americans were already celebrating the birthdays of Abraham Lincoln (February 12) and Frederick Douglass (February 14). By the 1970's, Negro History Week would be expanded into Black History Month. When the Daughters of the American Revolution would not allow world-class African

American contralto Marian Anderson to sing at Constitution Hall in 1939, First Lady Eleanor Roosevelt resigned from the group. Roosevelt was instrumental in providing Anderson a much grander location to showcase her amazing voice ... the Lincoln Memorial on Easter Sunday. Perhaps the most famous gathering of African Americans (and others) at the Lincoln Memorial would occur nearly a quarter century later. The historic 1963 March on Washington for Jobs and Freedom was organized by civil rights leader A. Philip Randolph and provided a global stage for the ascension of the Reverend Dr. Martin Luther King, Jr. Dr. King references Lincoln at the very beginning of his historic speech.

> Five score years ago, a great American, in whose symbolic shadow we stand today, signed the Emancipation Proclamation. This momentous decree came as a great beacon light of hope to millions of Negro slaves who had been seared in the flames of withering injustice. It came as a joyous daybreak to end the long night of their captivity.[5]
>
> - Rev. Dr. Martin Luther King
> 1963 March on Washington for Jobs and Freedom

While Americans of all backgrounds feel Lincoln was one of the country's best presidents, these feelings are even more intense for African Americans. For some of the descendants of enslaved Africans, Lincoln became an almost messianic figure; reinforced by his struggle to end slavery and his eventual death at the hand of a racist fanatic. It is understandable that African Americans would have a special connection to Abraham Lincoln more than any other president (besides perhaps Barack Obama).

Image 7.3: African Americans at the Lincoln Memorial - (Top) Civil rights leaders gather for the 1963 March on Washington for Jobs and Freedom. (Bottom Left) President Barack Obama delivers a speech at the opening inaugural event in 2013. (Bottom Right). Marian Anderson sings on Easter Sunday 1939 after being refused the stage at Constitution Hall by the Daughters of the Revolution.

It is true that Lincoln played an important role in ending African American enslavement, but the common phrase "Lincoln freed the slaves" implies much more. It implies the 16th president's role in the abolition of enslavement was altruistic or moral; that he was a friend to the African. To better understand this assertion, we must ask several important questions:

- Was it Lincoln's expressed intent to free enslaved Africans or was he forced to?
- What were his feelings/beliefs about African people?
- Most people believe that enslaved Africans were freed by the signing of the Emancipation Proclamation. What role does it actually play in the freedom of African Americans?
- What was Lincoln's plan for newly freed Africans?

In this chapter, we will explore these issues en route to refuting the common lie that "Lincoln Freed the Slaves".

The Real Deal

MAJOR FACTORS LEADING TO THE END OF ENSLAVEMENT
The period immediately preceding the Civil War was particularly focused on the struggle between the "free states" and the "slave states". While all of the thirteen colonies initially enslaved Africans, the increasing progression toward the end of enslavement was created by three primary factors: the continual resistance of enslaved Africans, the contradictions of the nation's "equality rhetoric" (like the Declaration of Independence), and the organized abolitionist movement. As these factors became more prevalent, the costs of continuing to enslave Africans became more difficult to bear. It has long been said that "the business of the United States is business".[6] Without as much economic benefit, the institution of enslavement eventually came to an end. Let's briefly explore the three factors in order to truly understand how "the slaves were freed".

Table 7.1: Major Factors Leading to the End of Enslavement

1. Continual Resistance of Enslaved Africans
2. "All Men are Created Equal" Rhetoric
3. The Organized Abolitionist Movement

Contrary to the popular depictions of African enslavement, Africans resisted their enslavement in every manner imaginable from the very beginning of the inhumane trade. Often this resistance was violent and deadly. In fact, almost no one remembers the fate of the very first European settlement on the North American continent,

San Miguel de Gualdape. The site, which may have been located within the modern-day state of Georgia, was settled by Spanish explorer, Lucas Vázquez de Ayllón, in around 1526.[7] Within three months it would be completely razed by the enslaved Africans who Ayllón brought with him to settle the location. The explorer was killed and it is believed that the Africans simply went to live with the indigenous people of the area, the Guale.

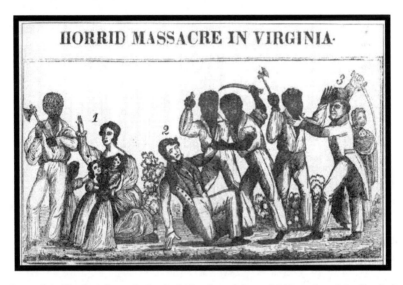

Image 7.4: Woodcut from the book *Authentic and Impartial Narrative of the Tragical Scene Which Was Witnessed in Southampton Count.* The image purports to describe some of the events which took place during the 1831 Nat Turner Rebellion.

The events of this revolt and many others were not lost on the Europeans who enslaved Africans in the New World. Africans never stopped resisting. Large revolts such as the New York Slave Revolt of 1712 led by an African named Kofi, the Stono Rebellion led by Jemmy (South Carolina, 1739), and the Nat Turner Rebellion of 1831 (Virginia) were widely reported. These revolts sometimes destroyed large swaths of valuable property and even killed whites. The mechanisms used to try to prevent these insurrections were costly. Slaveholders would need to hire more overseers, tamp down reports of revolts, and even construct settlements with uprising in mind. None of these would purchase peace of mind for those involved. It seems that whites were in continual fear of violent reprisal. Wealthy Virginia slaver, William Byrd, expressed this fear in 1736:

> We have already at least 10,000 men of these descendants of Ham, fit to bear arms, and these numbers increase every day, as well by birth as by importation. And in case there should arise a man of desperate fortune, he might with more advantage than Cataline kindle a servile war... and tinge our rivers wide as they are with blood (Cataline was a Roman senator who attempted to overthrow the government) (Parentheses Added).[8]

Byrd's concerns were not unfounded. Africans never relented in their struggle for freedom. While quantifying the cost and extent of African armed resistance to enslavement is challenging due to sparse documentation across at least a dozen countries, several contemporary scholars have scoured available sources in an attempt to provide an appropriate analysis. In the monumental work, *American Negro Slave Revolts*, Herbert Aptheker outlines at least 250 rebellions which include at least ten or more enslaved Africans in North America from 1526 to 1860. A comprehensive database of revolts aboard "slave ships" that forcibly transported Africans during the Trans-Atlantic trade was first released in 1999. Directed by David Eltis of Emory University, the Trans-Atlantic Slave Trade Database currently lists 470 shipboard revolts from 1509 to 1865. African armed resistance was certainly common.

The financial costs of the Jamaican enslaved African revolt which commenced on December 27, 1831 have been well documented. Organized by a charismatic, literate, Baptist preacher named Samuel "Daddy" Sharpe, the event has also been called the Christmas Rebellion or the Baptist War. Sharpe and his compatriots had initially planned the action as an act of civil disobedience, but when the planters refused their demands of freedom and payment for work they turned to full rebellion.

When the militia put down the rebellion after a week of battles, over 200 Africans and 25 whites had been killed. In the aftermath over 300 Africans were executed. The heroic leader of the rebellion, "Daddy" Sharpe, was captured and was hanged in righteous fashion.

His last words were, "I would rather die upon yonder gallows than to live in slavery."[9]

Image 7.5: Depiction of Samuel "Daddy" Sharpe on Jamaica's fifty dollar bill. The rebellion leader has continued to symbolize dogged determination to liberty and justice.

Historians agree that the cost of the rebellion were part of the rationale used to abolish African enslavement under the British crown. The military costs were upwards of $11,502,645 while the cost in damaged property and lost labor was approximately $75,900,000.[10] Another major factor in the drive towards the end of African enslavement was the very rhetoric which was used in the establishment of the United States. The contradiction of Judeo-Christian values being espoused by powerful plantation owners who enslaved Africans was always a problem. This brutally racist hypocrisy became even more obvious as the thirteen colonies began their struggle for independence from Great Brittan.

Image 7.6: (Left) Lithograph of the Boston Massacre with escaped enslaved African Crispus Attucks as the first casualty. (Right) Portrait of Crispus Attucks.

One of the greatest of cruel ironies is that one of the emblems of the American Revolutionary movement was Boston sailor and ropemaker, Crispus Attucks. Attucks was an escaped enslaved African (historians believe he might have also been half Native American).[11] When a British soldier struck a young white colonist during a simple disagreement, a mob of colonists vociferously protested the boy's treatment. Confronted with a growing, angry mob that surrounded them, the soldiers fired on the gathering. The first casualty and symbol of the colonist's fight for "freedom" from British rule would be Crispus Attucks, an escaped enslaved man who could have been *legally* recaptured and re-enslaved.

The white colonists would wage an armed insurrection against the British in what could be described as a disagreement on taxation. They accused the British of "tyranny" and of fostering "injustice". They argued that they were fighting for liberty and freedom while raping and brutalizing people they enslaved. This contradiction was not lost on enslaved Africans or others who opposed enslavement.

During the summer of 1775, representatives of the powerful, white, land-owning men who controlled the colonies gathered for the Second Continental Congress in Philadelphia, Pennsylvania. The result of the meeting was the document which supposedly set forward the governing principles of the colonies during their war with the British, the Declaration of Independence.

Early drafts of the Declaration were authored by Thomas Jefferson, who owned enslaved Africans and did not see fit to free all of them even upon his death. Jefferson included language which stated that the British king had forced enslavement on the colonies, but the Congress removed this passage under his disagreement. The final Declaration exclaimed that "all men are created equal, that they are endowed by their Creator with certain unalienable Rights, that among these are Life, Liberty and the pursuit of Happiness."[12] In fact it seems at least 41 of the 56 signers of the document had enslaved Africans.[13]

Image 7.7: The cover of the book, *American Declaration of Independence Illustrated* (c 1861) displays two African Americans, one with broken chains, being held aloft by an American eagle, American flags and the words "All men are created equal" and "Stand by the Declaration".

The racist hypocrisy of the Declaration's egalitarian language did not deter groups from attempting to make its language truthful, however. It actually emboldened many. Enslaved Africans not only directly petitioned state legislatures for their freedom based on the Declaration's language, but they also fought on both the side of the British and of the colonies in search of their freedom.[14] The British made several decrees, like Dunmore's Proclamation[15], which granted freedom to Africans who escaped their patriot masters to enlist in the British army. They were critical of the Declaration of Independence on the grounds of its hypocrisy towards enslaved Africans. Even some of the signers of the Declaration were later struck with the duplicity of their words. Several signers emancipated the Africans they enslaved. William Whipple, the representative to the Second Continental Congress from New Hampshire, decided to emancipate, Prince, the young African man who he enslaved after he aided him in the Revolutionary War. Whipple wrote that he hoped his colleagues in a southern state, South Carolina, would be moved to emancipate the Africans enslaved within its borders after they fought side-by-side with African American soldiers during the war.

> The last accounts from South Carolina were favorable. A recommendation is gone thither for raising some regiments of Blacks. This, I suppose will lay a foundation for the emancipation of those wretches in that country. I hope it will be the means of dispensing the blessings of Freedom to all the human race in America.[16]

The rhetoric of the Declaration of Independence and the Revolutionary War furthered the goal of ending African enslavement. This language even helped to strengthen the third major factor leading to the end of enslavement, the organized Abolitionist Movement. One of the leaders of the Abolitionist Movement, the powerful rhetorician and formerly enslaved Frederick Douglass, was asked to deliver a speech in commemoration of the signing of the Declaration of Independence:

> Fellow citizens, pardon me, and allow me to ask, why am I called upon to speak here today? What have I or those I represent to do with your national independence? Are the great principles of political freedom and of natural justice, embodied in that Declaration of Independence, extended to us? And am I, therefore, called upon to bring our humble offering to the national altar, and to confess the benefits, and express devout gratitude for the blessings resulting from your independence to us? ...
>
> I say it with a sad sense of disparity between us. I am not included within the pale of this glorious anniversary! Your high independence only reveals the immeasurable distance between us. The blessings in which you this day rejoice are not enjoyed in common. The rich inheritance of justice,

liberty, prosperity, and independence bequeathed by your fathers is shared by you, not by me. The sunlight that brought life and healing to you has brought stripes and death to me. This Fourth of July is yours, not mine. You may rejoice, I must mourn. To drag a man in fetters into the grand illuminated temple of liberty, and call upon him to join you in joyous anthems, were inhuman mockery and sacrilegious irony. Do you mean, citizens, to mock me, by asking me to speak today?

> - *What to the American Slave Is Your 4th of July?*
> Frederick Douglass; July 4, 1852[17]

The Abolitionist Movement played an important role in shifting popular American views on enslavement. Ironically, European Americans are usually depicted as the founders of the movement. It is certainly true that whites played an important role, but the roots of the Abolitionist Movement are unarguably Black. In fact, most conductors along the Underground Railroad were free northern African Americans.[18] Frederick Douglass sets the record straight:

> Without the initiative of the Afro-American people, without their illumination of the nature of slavery, without their persistent struggle to be free, there would have been no national Abolitionist movement. And when the movement did appear, the participation of Black people in every aspect was indispensable to its functioning and its eventual success.[19]

A major aspect of the Abolitionist Movement was its public drive to recruit members of "anti-slavery societies" and its work to share the horrors of enslavement. These mostly anecdotal narratives began as escapees described their lives. The public myth of a genteel, comfortable life for enslaved Africans was shattered by the actual words of these escapees. This served to slowly change popular white sentiment.

Image 7.8: (Top Left) William Lloyd Garrison was the editor of the important abolitionist newspaper *The Liberator* and frequent collaborator of (Top Right) Frederick Douglass until they parted ways. Formerly enslaved, Douglass would become a master orator and editor of The North Star newspaper. (Bottom) Flyer for an abolitionist meeting convened to discuss the scheduled execution of enslaved African rebellion leader John Brown.

One of the most important organs of the Abolitionist movement was the weekly newspaper, *The Liberator*. The Liberator was founded by white Massachusetts printer William Lloyd Garrison. Garrison had initially believed that the solution to the conundrum of African enslavement in the United States was the repatriation of freed African Americans to West Africa until his African American friends convinced him otherwise.[20] He would then become a radical anti-enslavement activist. He founded the New England Anti-Slavery Society in 1831 and *The Liberator* served as its official publication.

It is clear that Garrison played a very important role in organizing the abolitionist groups throughout the nation. Within a year of founding the New England Anti-Slavery Society, it boasted several thousand diverse members and a dozen local affiliates. Nearly fifty groups from Maine to Ohio used the New England Anti-Slavery

Society as their model.[21] By 1833, Garrison and others founded a national organization called the American Anti-Slavery Society, which would eventually feature approximately 2,000 auxiliary groups and at least 150,000 members including Susan B. Anthony, Elizabeth Cady Stanton, and Henry Highland Garnet. Garrison published its weekly newsletter, the *National Anti-Slavery Standard.*

William Lloyd Garrison's anti-enslavement agitation also made him a target for the violent aims of pro-enslavement advocates. One southern paper offered "an adequate reward to any person who will deliver him [Garrison] dead or alive into the hands of the authorities of any state south of the Potomac".[22] There were also dangers associated with organizing in the north. Garrison was confronted by an angry mob during an 1835 meeting of the Boston Female Anti-Slavery Society. The group dragged him through the streets of Boston for what might have been a tar and feathering until he was saved by the city's mayor. Garrison was briefly held in the Leverett Street Jail for his own protection.

The Abolitionist Movement was often galvanized by the burgeoning struggle between the industrial economy of the northern "free states" and the agrarian economy of the southern "slave states". These factions made compromises ever since the founding of the country which allowed enslavement to continue in order to ensure the integrity of the union. Essentially the very cohesion of the union was contingent upon the continued brutal oppression of the African.

In the period immediately preceding the Civil War, these compromises were even more controversial as both factions attempted to dominate the other by controlling whether territories entering the union would enter as free or slave states. Having an imbalance could allow either side to have dominance over the other. For example, the Missouri Compromise of 1820 regulated enslavement in the western territories by prohibiting it in the former Louisiana Territory north of the parallel 36°30′, except within the boundaries of the proposed state of Missouri. The controversial decision made plain the tenuousness of the union and even led Thomas Jefferson to question whether it could be held together in a letter to American ambassador, William Short.

> The [Missouri] question aroused and filled me with alarm ... But the coincidence of a marked principle, moral & political with a geographical line, once conceived, I feared would never more be obliterated from the mind; that it would be recurring on every occasion & renewing irritations until it would kindle such mutual & mortal hatred, as to render separation preferable to eternal discord. I have been among the most sanguine in believing that our Union would be of long duration. I now doubt it much ...[23]

Abolitionists would be truly enraged by two other political events which sought to ensure the viability of enslavement in the U.S. In the 1840's pro-slavery president James Polk waged war with Mexico for the expressed purpose of obtaining new territory in the west which could be brought into the union under enslavement. In 1850, The United States Congress passes the Fugitive Slave Act which mandates that northern states return escaped enslaved Africans to their southern enslavers. It is in this context that a Republican centrist candidate came to prominence. The Republican Party was most aligned with northern, abolitionist interests but they did not put forth a candidate with clear abolitionist positions. They put forth a candidate, who was against enslavement, but was not closely aligned with either movement. Abraham Lincoln would serve a tumultuous term as the sixteenth President of the United States.

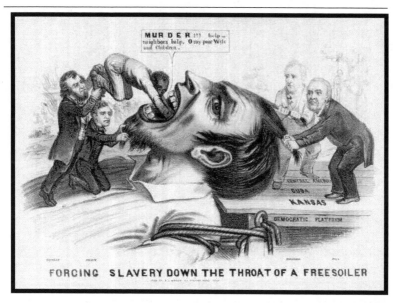

Image 7.9: This 1856 political cartoon blames the Democratic Party for the violence which was visited upon Kansas "freesoil" settlers. It also references areas that might have been considered fertile ground for enslavement as they were made parts of the U.S. Two of the Democratic politicians depicted are presidential candidate James Buchanan and Senator Stephen A. Douglas.

ABRAHAM LINCOLN: SAVIOR OF THE UNION ... FRIEND TO THE AFRICAN?

When Illinois lawyer Abraham Lincoln enters national consciousness, he does so in the arms of the contentious struggle between the free and slave states. Once a member of the Whig Party, Lincoln later helped establish the Republican Party. Lincoln would become one of the faces of the movement to limit the expansion of enslavement into the new territories as he engaged in seven highly publicized debates. Commonly known as the Lincoln-Douglas Debates, Lincoln debated Democratic incumbent Stephen A. Douglas for the United States Senate seat from Illinois. Lincoln was opposed to the institution of enslavement and was quoted very frequently on the matter.

> We think slavery a great moral wrong, and while we do not claim the right to touch it where it exists, we wish to treat it as a wrong in the territories, where our votes will reach it.[24]

> I think slavery is wrong, morally, and politically. I desire
> that it should be no further spread in these United States,
> and I should not object if it should gradually terminate in
> the whole Union.[25]

Douglas had served two terms in the senate and supported a concept
similar to the "states rights" position which would be used during
the later Jim Crow Era called "popular sovereignty". Advocates of
popular sovereignty argued that whether a territory allowed
enslavement when they joined the Union should be decided by its
residents. The federal government, under this paradigm, would not
dictate the territory's enslavement status. Douglas also held more
strident racist views. He rebuked Lincoln as an abolitionist; he
warned that his "black Republican Party" was seeking to alter the
founders' concept of unequal races.[26] Douglas was strongly in favor
of the 1857 Dred Scott Supreme Court decision. Chief Justice
Roger B. Taney wrote in his decision that the African Americans
belonged to an "inferior order" with "no rights that a white man was
bound to respect".[27] Douglas chided Lincoln on his opposition to
the decision.

> Mr. Lincoln said in his first remarks that he was not in favor
> of the social and political equality of the negro with the
> white man. Every where up north he has declared that he
> was not in favor of the social and political equality of the
> negro, but he would not say whether or not he was opposed
> to negroes voting and negro citizenship. I want to know
> whether he is for or against negro citizenship? He declared
> his utter opposition to the Dred Scott decision, and
> advanced as a reason that the court had decided that it was
> not possible for a negro to be a citizen under the
> Constitution of the United States. If he is opposed to the
> Dred Scott decision for that reason, he must be in favor of
> conferring the right and privilege of citizenship upon the
> negro! ,,, I say that this Government was established on the
> white basis. It was made by white men, for the benefit of
> white men and their posterity forever, and never should be
> administered by any except white men. I declare that a
> negro ought not to be a citizen, whether his parents were
> imported into this country as slaves or not, or whether or

not he was born here. It does not depend upon the place a negro's parents were born, or whether they were slaves or not, but upon the fact that he is a negro, belonging to a race incapable of self-government, and for that reason ought not to be on an equality with white men.[28]

Image 7.10: Portrait of Dred Scott - The plaintiff in Dred Scott v. Stanford, Scott sued his enslaver for his and his family's freedom since they had been taken to a "free" state. In 1857, the United State Supreme Court ruled that Scott was not even eligible to bring his case to trial as African Americans had no right to petition the courts. Chief Justice Roger Taney stated that Africans had "no rights that a white man was bound to respect" in his decision. The court also ruled that the federal government had the right to regulate enslavement in the territories after the initial creation of the United States.

It is true that Lincoln was opposed to the expansion of enslavement and, in fact, to the institution of enslavement itself. However, Lincoln goes to great lengths in his response to Douglas's claims to explain that he *is not in favor of African American equality* and believes *whites are superior to Africans.*

I will say then that I am not, nor ever have been, in favor of bringing about in any way the social and political equality of the white and black races, [applause]-that I am not nor ever have been in favor of making voters or jurors of negroes, nor of qualifying them to hold office, nor to intermarry with white people; and I will say in addition to this that there is a physical difference between the white and black races which I believe will forever forbid the two races living together on terms of social and political equality. *And inasmuch as they cannot so live, while they do remain together there must be the position of superior and inferior, and I as much as any other man am in favor of having the superior position assigned to the white race.* I say upon this occasion I do not perceive that because the white man is to have the superior position the negro should be denied every thing. I do not understand that because I do not want a negro woman for a slave I must necessarily want her for a wife. My understanding is that I can just let her alone. I am now in my fiftieth year, and I certainly never have had a black woman for either a slave or a wife. So it seems to me quite possible for us to get along without making either slaves or wives of negroes. I will add to this that I have never seen, to my knowledge, a man, woman or child who was in favor of producing a perfect equality, social and political, between negroes and white men. (Italics added)[29]

It is indisputable that Lincoln sought to end enslavement. He believed that the legal infrastructure that was created to ensure white supremacy was morally wrong. However, just as he believed that there was a middle ground between dismantling these racist laws and acknowledging full equality for enslaved Africans. Similarly, it is clear that there is also a middle ground between Lincoln's quest to end white supremacist laws and viewing him as a friend to the enslaved African.

Prior to being elected the 16th president, waging the Civil War, and signing the Emancipation Proclamation, Lincoln was absolutely clear about his beliefs on two topics: interracial mixing was abhorrent and Africans were inferior.

There is a *natural disgust* in the minds of nearly all white people, to the idea of an indiscriminate amalgamation of the white and black races ... In some respects she (the negro woman) *certainly is not my equal*; but in her natural right to eat the bread she earns with her own hands without asking

leave of any one else, she is my equal, and the equal of all others (Italics and parenthesis added).[30]
- Abraham Lincoln, Speech on the Dred Scott Decision
Springfield, Illinois; June 26, 1857

I have no purpose to introduce political and social equality between the white and black races. There is a physical difference between the two, which, in my judgment, will probably forever forbid their living together upon the [footing] of perfect equality, and inasmuch as it becomes a necessity that there must be a difference, *I, as well as Judge Douglas, am in favor of the race to which I belong having the superior position.* I have never said anything to the contrary (Italics ad brackets added).[31]
- Abraham Lincoln; September, 1858

While Abraham Lincoln would lose his attempt to unseat incumbent Senator Stephen A. Douglas, he was eventually tapped as a presidential candidate in 1860. Lincoln was a moderate politician with national recognition from Illinois—a swing state. He was elected president with very little support from the southern states on a platform which focused on restricting the expansion of enslavement. Lincoln's election was polarizing to the seven southern states that featured economies which were dependent on the labor of enslaved Africans. The states decided to secede from the Union prior to him taking office. South Carolina would lead the secessionist movement as it left the Union in December of 1860.

In an attempt to bring these seven southern states, now the Confederate States of America, back into the fold before his inauguration, Abraham Lincoln seems to have worked behind the scenes. His partners in the creation of what would be known as the "Corwin Amendment" were Democratic President James Buchanan and Republican members of the House of Representatives, Thomas Corwin and William Seward.[32] The controversial proposed provision stated that "no amendment shall be made to the Constitution, which will authorize or give to Congress the power to abolish, or interfere within any State, with the domestic institutions thereof, including that of persons held to labor or service by the laws of said State."[33] In other words, while Lincoln ran on a platform focused on preventing the expansion of enslavement, he was prepared to continue to allow its existence in order to bring seceded states back into the fold. The Corwin Amendment failed on a technicality, but it must be made clear that it seems Lincoln's motivation was not to free enslaved Africans but instead to maintain the integrity of the Union.

The attempts to placate the confederate states were unsuccessful. The Confederate Army began to attack and take control of several U.S. military installations located within their states. A garrison of Union troops located at Fort Sumter in Charleston Harbor, South Carolina was running dangerously low on supplies by April of 1861. A Confederate blockade of the sea fort prevented its resupply; instead demanding surrender. President Lincoln ordered a fleet of ships to enter the harbor to resupply Sumter. However the Confederate Army would begin their bombardment of the fort on April 12, 1861. With this action, the Civil War had begun.

The war most often called the Civil War today has actually been known by many names, the War Between the States, the War of the Rebellion, and even the War of Northern Aggression. Among the African American population, this war commanded by President Abraham Lincoln, has often been called the Freedom War. Ironically, during the early stages of conflict, Lincoln and his troops seemed to have had an ambivalent position towards the institution of enslavement. In March of 1861, three Africans in Pensacola, Florida fled their enslavers reaching an installation of U.S. troops.[34] They were incredulously returned to their enslavers by the Union troops. The Union military understood that Lincoln did not want to deal with the issue of escaped Africans. There was no clear policy so uneven responses were at first common. By June 1861, Col. Harry Brown was commanding Fort Pickens in Pensacola, Florida. He took a very clear stance which demanded a response from his commanding officer.

> I shall not send the negroes back as I will never be voluntarily instrumental in returning a poor wretch to slavery but will hold them subject to orders.[35]

DOCTOR LINCOLN'S NEW ELIXIR OF LIFE—FOR THE SOUTHERN STATES.

Image 7.11: This 1862 political cartoon by Thomas Nast depicts President Lincoln as a compassionate doctor with African emancipation as the cure for the southern Confederate states. Was the emancipation of enslaved Africans proof of Lincoln's morality and anti-racist motivations? Or was it necessitated by something else?

Conversely, General George B. McClellan sought to reassure Virginia plantation owners that he would certainly not side with escaping enslaved Africans.

> Your homes, your family and your property are safe under our protection. All your rights shall be religiously respected ... not only will we abstain from all such interference but we will on the contrary with an iron hand crush any attempt at insurrection on [the slaves'] part.[36]

Without clear direction otherwise, many of the Union Army commanders enforced the Fugitive Slave Act of 1850. They returned enslaved Africans to the Confederates that they escaped from. However, enslaved Africans continued to escape towards Union troops and the states that remained in the Union. As the flow of enslaved Africans from Virginia increased in the District of Columbia, Lincoln became concerned about white Virginians who remained loyal to the Union even though the state had seceded. In

July of 1861, Lincoln asked the region's military commander whether it might be appropriate to "allow owners to bring back [enslaved Africans] which crossed the Potomac" with Union soldiers.[37] As a result, the Department of Washington Commander, General Joseph Mansfield directed his troops to "take stringent measures to prevent fugitive slaves from passing over the river particularly as servants with the regiments."[38]

Image 7.12: This Civil War Era cartoon depicts enslaved Africans escaping the plantation to Fort Monroe, Virginia. Virginia was part of the Confederacy, but since Fort Monroe remained in Union control, it became a symbol of freedom.

The African American intellectual and activist Frederick Douglass articulates the contradiction of African subjugation by the "slave-holding" south and betrayal of the "slave-freeing" north. In his speech entitled "What the Black Man Wants", Douglass opines that "the South was fighting to take slavery out of the Union, and the North was fighting to keep it in the Union ... both despising the Negro, both insulting the Negro."[39]

While many might be surprised that President Lincoln routinely sent escaped enslaved Africans back into the arms of their brutal enslavers, those who are familiar with his speeches would find this behavior characteristic. In response to the secession of the

Confederate states, Lincoln clearly outlines his views in his first inauguration.

> I have no purpose, directly or indirectly, to interfere with the institution of slavery in the States where it exists. I believe I have no lawful right to do so, and I have no inclination to do so.[40]

Ironically, the "Great Emancipator" would continue to espouse a similar view just as he considered issuing an early version of the Emancipation Proclamation. Lincoln's primary concern was to save the Union, not to contend with the United States' "original sin" of enslavement. Lincoln was challenged on these views by Horace Greeley, an influential editor of the New York Tribune, prominent Republican, and abolitionist. Greeley questioned Lincoln on his ambivalent treatment of escaped enslaved Africans in his paper. With Congress' passage of the Second Confiscation Act, enslaved Africans owned by enslavers who were in rebellion were considered freed. Lincoln was reluctant to utilize these Africans in the Union Army based on public opinion in the four border states who remained in the Union. He even backed a proposal to compensate slavers in these states for the federal government emancipating the enslaved Africans they continued to hold.[41] Attempting to clarify this precise opinion, Lincoln penned a letter in response to Greeley.

> I would save the Union. ... If there be those who would not save the Union, unless they could at the same time save slavery, I do not agree with them. If there be those who would not save the Union unless they could at the same time destroy slavery, I do not agree with them. My paramount object in this struggle is to save the Union, and it is not either to save or to destroy slavery. If I could save the Union without freeing any slave I would do it, and if I could save the Union by freeing all the slaves then I would do it; and if I could save it by freeing some and leaving others alone I would also do that. *What I do about slavery, and the colored race, I do because I believe it helps to save the Union*; and what I forbear, I forbear because I do not believe it would save the Union. (Italics added)[42]

On September 22, 1862—precisely one month later—Lincoln would issue his preliminary Emancipation Proclamation. What precipitated this seemingly contradictory action? We have seen Lincoln proclaim the supremacy of whites (and by extension the inferiority of African people) while expressing that his primary concern was not to end enslavement, but to save the Union. What factors motivated this change in tact?

	The Union Northern States	The Confederacy Southern States
Population	**Advantage** 21 Million	**Disadvantage** 9 Million (Including 3.5 million enslaved Africans)
Industrial Capacity	**Advantage** 90% (North made 97% of firearms, 96% of trains, 94 % of the cloth, 93% of the iron, and over 90% of the boots and shoes; Twice the density of railroads)	**Disadvantage** 10%
Military Size in 1861	**Equal** Almost Equal	**Equal** Almost Equal
Military Approach	**Disadvantage** Offense (Forced primarily to attack to retake ground)	**Advantage** Defense (Retain sites within boundaries of the Confederacy)
Military Leadership	**Disadvantage** Overwhelming majority of military schools located in South	**Advantage** Advantage (7 of 8 military colleges in the South)
Public Military Motivation	**Disadvantage** Save the Union (prior to Emancipation Proclamation)	**Advantage** Save our homes, maintain "way of life", protect "our constitutional rights"

Table 7.2: Relative Advantages of the Union versus the Confederate States during the Beginning of the Civil War[43]

It seems that even though the Union had military and numerical advantages in nearly every major military category, they were either losing the war or at best fighting to a stalemate. To its benefit, the Confederacy actually utilized their few advantages very well. The Union needed to be on the offense as it was looking to retake ground which had been lost to secession, but taking control of such a vast area proved difficult. The Confederacy was spread over more than 750,000 square miles with over 3,000 miles of coastline; a very difficult area to enact an effective blockade.[44] Perhaps most importantly, Confederate public propaganda gave them a regional recruitment advantage. Initially Lincoln was not comfortable connecting the goal of the war to ending enslavement. Instead the North fought to "save the Union". Clearly this is a much more cerebral purpose than the rallying cry of the Southern secessionist. They were fighting to protect their homes, to ensure their way of life, and even "to preserve their constitutional rights" (a euphemism for continuing enslavement). These reasons prompted the Southern army to fight tirelessly.

From late summer to early fall of 1862, the Union Army hadn't won any decisive victories. Lincoln was faced with a trio of challenges which forced his hand: challenges from the left on his policy on the critical issue of the war—the emancipation of enslaved Africans; concerns about the possibility of the entrance of the British into the conflict on the side of the Confederacy; and declining military enrollments juxtaposed with the exploding numbers of African escapees to the Union. Lincoln was still committed to uphold the Constitution, even though the South could have been considered a foreign entity after leaving the Union. He crafted a military solution, which by definition would not affect enslavement in the states which remained in the Union (Delaware, Kentucky, Maryland, and Missouri). The preliminary Emancipation Proclamation served as a warning to the Confederate states. All of the enslaved Africans in the states involved in the rebellion would be freed if the state did not return to the Union by January 1, 1863. As none of the Confederate states returned to the Union, Lincoln issued the final order on January 1. Roughly 3 of the 4 million enslaved Africans in the United States were instantly freed.

Image 7.13: Illustration commemorating Lincoln's signing of the Emancipation Proclamation. The scene features an African American family in center and Lincoln in the bottom center. Surrounding these images are the inhumane realities of enslavement.

The Proclamation was truly a military document. It did not outlaw the institution of enslavement or grant citizenship to the enslaved. It did, however, allow for the formerly enslaved to be enrolled into the Union military and for the military to protect the ex-enslaved. It would be hard to view the Emancipation Proclamation as a moral document, even though it ended one of the most inhumane institutions for the overwhelming majority of enslaved Africans in the United States. The Emancipation Proclamation entirely conforms with Lincoln's edict of only freeing the enslaved if it would save the Union. The North's military campaign was floundering and now, more than ever, the Southern enslavers would be looking behind their backs. Either they would need to deal with an exploding number of escapees or, as many feared, violent insurrection amongst those they had brutally enslaved. With the signing of the Emancipation Proclamation, the North had also gained motivational impetus. No longer were they fighting for the overly cerebral goal of "saving the Union", they would now be motivated by fighting for liberation. With the motion of a pen, Lincoln would be seen (perhaps incorrectly) as the "Great

Emancipator" and the momentum of the Civil War clearly shifted in his direction.

Some historians describe Abraham Lincoln as a changed man after encountering the crucible of the Civil War. While Lincoln seemed to always believe enslavement was wrong, he also viewed Africans as inferior and believed that Europeans and Africans could not live side-by-side before the war. Did his views change by being a major character in one of the most transformational moments in history? The answer must be emphatically no. While most credit Lincoln with signing the Emancipation Proclamation, few actually ask, "What was Lincoln's plan for newly freed Africans?" We find the little-known answer to this question at a curious meeting between free-African leaders and President Lincoln during the Civil War.

On August 14, 1862, Lincoln met with a delegation of free-Africans from African American churches in the Washington, D.C. area. The delegation consisted of 5 members from 5 churches including the pastor of each church. The delegates were undoubtedly honored to have an audience with the President in the Presidential Mansion. However, it should be understood that much of Lincoln's message was greatly offensive to the attendees.

> You and we are different races. We have between us a broader difference than exists between almost any other two races. Whether it is right or wrong I need not discuss, but *this physical difference is a great disadvantage to us both, as I think your race suffer very greatly, many of them by living among us, while ours suffer from your presence.* In a word we suffer on each side. If this is admitted, it affords a reason at least why we should be separated.

> See our present condition—the country engaged in war!— *our white men cutting one another's throats*, none knowing how far it will extend; and then consider what we know to be the truth. But for your race among us there could not be war, although many men engaged on either side do not care for you one way or the other. *Nevertheless, I repeat, without the institution of Slavery and the colored race as a basis, the war could not have an existence.*

I suppose one of the principal difficulties in the way of colonization is that the free colored man cannot see that his comfort would be advanced by it. You may believe you can live in Washington or elsewhere in the United States the remainder of your life [as easily], perhaps more so than you can in any foreign country, and hence you may come to the conclusion that you have nothing to do with the idea of going to a foreign country. This is (I speak in no unkind sense) an extremely selfish view of the case ... you ought to do something to help those who are not so fortunate as yourselves (Italics added).[45]

A little more than a month before he signed his preliminary Emancipation Proclamation, President Abraham Lincoln had the gall to issue several insults to the descendants of those brought forcibly to the United States under the most heinous conditions. First, he begins by telling this assembly of free, probably educated Africans, that they are undoubtedly inferior. Then he blames them for the whites who had died during the Civil War. Finally he argues that it would be best for all Africans to be sent to establish a colony in an unidentified country in Central America. If one includes some of the military aspects of the Emancipation Proclamation, then we understand that Lincoln believed that Africans should fight and die in a war which would result in our freedom, but then we should immediately leave the United States as what would likely be subjugated colonist. The racist, entitled ideas of the man who would be commonly known as the "Great Emancipator" were nearly unfathomable. This historical analysis of the words and deeds of this man are rarely discussed popularly. If this occurred, it is unlikely that he would be viewed favorably.

It should be noted that African American soldiers from all over the country, fought in the Civil War with valor unparalleled. During the war approximately 175 regiments of more the 178,000 free-Africans and freedmen served, comprising at one point nearly one-tenth of all of the Union enlisted. They served in all theaters of the war and took heavy casualties. Nearly 37,000 of the men, known as the United States Colored Troops, were killed.[46] After blaming enslaved Africans for the war itself, President Lincoln was forced to acknowledge the critical role that they played. Lincoln stated in 1865 that "without the military help of the black freedmen, the war against the South could not have been won."[47]

Image 7.14: Gordon Triumphant - The subject of one of the most reprinted images displaying the barbarity of enslavement, Gordon walked 40 miles barefoot to escape to his freedom. (Top right) Gordon immediately upon his escape to Union lines. (Bottom right) Gordon displays his badly welted, whipped back. (Left) Engraving of Gordon as a soldier fighting to end enslavement in the Union Army.

By the beginning of 1864, it seemed that the tide had actually turned. The Union had benefited from the infusion of African American troops who fought quite literally for the freedom of their people. Even the reinvigorated white soldier could argue that he fought for a loftier goal. Lincoln would next install Ulysses S. Grant as Commander of all the Union forces. Grant's strategy was to force an increasingly decimated Confederate Army to fight to protect major cities. This strategy had the effect of centering the fight on a more confined battlefield. Grant also began to focus on taking supplies and destroying plantations and even railroads. These resources, Grant reasoned, would be used to further the Southern war effort. Major victories in hard fought, high casualty battles in Richmond and Atlanta would also work to thin the Confederate Army to death and desertion. As the arc of justice would have it, the Confederate capital would be conquered by Union XXV Troops which were comprised of African American soldiers. On April 9, 1865, General Robert E. Lee would surrender at the McLean Court House in Appomattox, Virginia. The Union has finally won the Civil War. Without truly seeing the conclusion and aftermath of the entire conflict, President Abraham Lincoln would be killed by John Wilkes Booth, Confederate spy and vehement racist, at Ford's Theater in Washington D.C.

Prior to his death Lincoln had pushed for the passage of the Thirteenth Amendment to the constitution. The Amendment would end enslavement in the United States except as punishment for a crime. The final ratification of the Amendment would not occur until December 18, 1865. While it is likely Lincoln never discarded his views on African inferiority or his belief the Africans should leave the United States, it is likely that he sought passage of the Amendment to ensure that the institution of enslavement would never imperil the Union or its economic advancement again. It is also likely that benefit to the African by the Thirteenth Amendment was to Lincoln a byproduct of United States' (meaning white) self-interest.

Reasons for and effects of the LIE

The fallacious rhetoric that is used to describe Abraham Lincoln is both puzzling and dangerous. The implications of the statement "Lincoln freed the slaves" are easily disproved by his own well-documented words. Few presidents have received as much scrutiny as Lincoln, but much of that scrutiny has been conducted by and projected by those who do not align with the interests of people of African descent or have general reverence for early American presidents. The people who are most connected to Lincoln's legacy—African Americans— have not spent much time analyzing him.

Image 7.15: The bronze statue of "Lincoln and a Boy" in the middle of the President Abraham Lincoln Houses in Harlem, New York depicts Lincoln in a caring pose with a young African American boy. The naming of the New York City owned, low-income housing complex conveys a very common message: "African Americans owe everything to the genuine morality of this president." This idea is both damaging and untrue. Is the boy in the statue a metaphor for a dependent, immature people?

There are many who probably believe that misunderstanding the legacy of Lincoln is a small thing; a trivial matter which does little harm to African Americans today. In actuality, the unwarranted deference which is paid to the 16th president is one of the earliest and best instances of the "white savior" myth.

The white savior is a common fixture in popular culture. In films like Michelle Pfeiffer's "Dangerous Minds", Kevin Bacon's "The Air Up There" and Sandra Bullocks's "The Blind Side", the main character is a white person in a position of authority who enters into violent, chaotic, and/or uncivilized environment and through their general goodness (which the character must often find) they selflessly enhance the lives of the people of color around them. The character serves different purposes for different audiences. It placates white liberal guilt while reassuring a general white audience of their superiority. These portrayals display African American social pathology and focuses on the white character in a story which should rightfully focus on the characters of color. Ironically, the causes of the deficient environment that the white character descends into are seldom traced back to the larger white community who should be blamed for it. For African Americans and other people of color, the myth serves to vent the righteous anger which they feel for being forced into environments which are deprived of resources. Uncritical African American viewers end up misled on the true nature of their subjugation. They say to themselves: "I shouldn't be upset about my condition. There is no one, no group that has created this environment. I just need to treat everyone appropriately. The white savior is out there!" Truthfully their condition is deficient because other individuals/groups have taken a larger share of resources than they deserve. Small acts of kindness by member of that group do not alter the environment's fundamental unfairness.

When African Americans treat Abraham Lincoln as "one of the 'good' presidents", we are not recognizing that his actions were: 1) minor in comparison to the scale of the injustice; 2) primarily based on selfish goals; 3) miniscule compared to other actors. This focus on an individual who did not think very highly of us also ignores our own role in the drama. It ignores the risks that African American actors took as conductors on the Underground Railroad, participants in revolts of the enslaved, abolitionist leaders, and even soldiers in the Army. Ignoring or discounting our role in ending one of the most lucrative AND barbaric institutions destroys our individual and communal agency. Perhaps if we truly understood the magnitude of our role, we would understand just how *powerful* we truly are. We would recognize that we are the saviors we are waiting for. This understanding would obliterate African American apathy, and reassure us of our fundamental humanity and nobility.

African American agency in the face of oppression is not an overlooked historical narrative, but rather a powerful solution to our continued subjugation. Aren't views of those African Americans as inferior still alive and well today? Did the Civil War or its aftermath create equal access to resources for all people, and most importantly, for Africans? Absolutely not! Understanding that people of African descent have been, and will continue to need to be their own redeemers is critically important. An accurate depiction of our role in the end of our own enslavement would jolt us forward toward this goal. Abraham Lincoln did not "free the slaves". Directly and Indirectly, Africans in the United States forced this president, so wrought with racist ideas and white entitlement, to do so.

For Additional Research

BOOKS
1. Bennett, Jr., L. (2007). *Forced into Glory: Abraham Lincoln's White Dream.* Chicago, Illinois: Johnson Publishing Company.
2. Foner, E. (2011). *The Fiery Trial: Abraham Lincoln and American Slavery.* New York, NY: W.W. Norton & Company.
3. Cornish, D.T. (1965). *The Sable Arm: Black Troops in the Union Army, 1861-1865.* New York, NY: W.W. Norton. & Company.
4. Dobak, W. (2011). *Freedom by the Sword: The U.S. Colored Troops, 1862-1867.* Washington, D.C.: Center for Military History.
5. Smith, J.D. (2002). *Black Soldiers in Blue: African American Troops in the Civil War Era.* Chapel Hill, North Carolina: The University of North Carolina Press.
6. Lawrence, M. (2000). *Against Slavery: An Abolitionist Reader.* London, UK: Penguin Classics.
7. Douglass, F. (1845). *Narrative of the Life of Frederick Douglass, an American Slave.* Boston, MA: Anti-Slavery Office.

CONCLUSION: A BLUEPRINT FOR THE REHABILITATION OF THE BLACK IMAGE

The 7 Little White Lies
1. Caucasians are the Original People
2. Ancient Africa Contributed Nothing to Civilization
3. The Ancient Egyptians were 'Caucasian'
4. Hebrew Slaves Built the Pyramids
5. Africans Were Savages When the Europeans Enslaved Them
6. Columbus Discovered America
7. Abraham Lincoln Freed the Slaves

So what does this all mean? What is the effect of living for hundreds of years under the accumulated weight of these lies? What happens to the child who is raised to believe that they are not among the flock of humans first endowed by the creator? What if those supposed original people were the people who were most characteristically different from them? What if that child was also socialized to believe that they played no important role in the advancement of humanity?

Imagine if the child was forced to believe that while their people had been oppressed, the conditions that they were taken from were actually more barbarous than those they were forced into. Furthermore, their subjugation was ended due to the charity of those who perpetrated the act. Wouldn't these "facts" fundamentally affect the manner in which the child viewed themselves? These facts alter the child's self-worth and their faith in their personal and group control. Even with physical shackles removed, the child's potential would be stunted. He or she would treat those like them without regard. They would ridicule the few among them that were able to achieve anything as alien. The child would automatically believe that they were less desirable, less intelligent, and less capable.

What if the entire society also believed these "facts" as well? Wouldn't everyone believe that the child deserved, perhaps even caused, every problem and every calamity that plagued them? Would that child's *life matter*? These lies may seem inconsequential, but they could not be more damaging, more nefarious. It is much more dangerous for victims of oppression to believe that they deserved their mistreatment.

> If you can control a man's thinking you do not have to worry about his action. When you determine what a man shall think you do not have to concern yourself about what he will do. If you make a man feel that he is inferior, you do not have to compel him to accept an inferior status, for he will seek it himself. If you make a man think that he is justly an outcast, you do not have to order him to the back door. He will go without being told; and if there is no back door, his very nature will demand one.[1]

\- Dr. Carter G. Woodson
The Mis-Education of the Negro, 1933

Image 8.1: This 1884 Pears Soap Ad which was published in the *Graphic* plays on the damage Black self-esteem has withstood through hundreds of years of subjugation in order to sell soap.

Some will disagree with the central thesis of this work. While they may take issue with the fallacies that we have described in great detail, they will most likely argue that the effect on people of African descent is negligible. These detractors will probably cite the body of studies which actually argue that African American self-esteem tends to be equal to or even *higher than* that of their European American peers.[2,3, and 4]

What these studies fail to capture is the curious manner that self-esteem occurs in African Americans. A series of studies conducted in the 1990s by renowned African American psychologist Dr. Claude Steele uncovered a major contradiction as it focused on the differences in self-esteem among a variety of ethnic/racial groups.[5, 6] As in other studies, Steele found relatively high self-esteem for African American students, but he also found lower relative academic achievement for Black students. Steele argued that high academic achievement is decoupled from high self-esteem. Essentially, African American students internalize the racist stereotypes regarding the intellectual inferiority of people of African descent. This manifests itself in the painful admonition that Black students who excel in school are "acting white". What do these students conceive of what it means to "be Black"?

A number of other studies describe relatively higher self-esteem but a relatively lower sense of efficacy (the perceived ability to positively alter one's environment).[7] At this point it must be asked: If a higher self-esteem doesn't improve one's ability to perform on intellectual tasks or even enhance whether they feel they can control their environment, then why is it even useful? The Black self-image has devised these convolutions to attempt to protect itself from a system which despises it, which seeks to continue its subjugation. It is impossible to have high self-esteem when one's race-esteem has been violated. How can you truly feel good about yourself and about your abilities when you have been socialized to believe that your entire lineage and all those like you are inferior? This contradiction is more difficult in a society which was built upon racial dichotomies. Dismantling the lies which have been intentionally crafted to destroy Black/African race-esteem must be the most urgent objective. While this book has identified and dismantled the most dangerous fallacies which damage the Black self-image, how can we correct the damage which has been done?

THE ROAD AHEAD: SEVEN STEPS FOR RECLAIMING THE BLACK-IMAGE

1. Form Community-Based Study Groups

While many might believe confronting the false information delivered in school settings should be the first area to address, this approach will be resource intensive and time-consuming. A more immediate strategy can be the creation of book clubs and afternoon or Saturday schools (similar to the African Genesis Institute). These can be very effective in countering this false narrative. We should not allow racist or even misleading propaganda to continue to be forced into the mind of our youth uncontested for another day! In some ways, this approach is similar to the Hebrew School movement which has been popular in the United States since the 1800s.[8] Jewish students are often educated in secular environments like most other children in the U.S., however, Jewish community members ensure that their children receive a comprehensive education in Jewish religion, language, and culture. They understand that this task is far too important to leave to anyone else.

While corrective history programs for youth are of preeminent importance, adult groups should also be created. Often "conscious" individuals who are attempting to learn their history engage in this process on their own. We should, however, attempt to establish groups in order to create critical mass for action and support. Advancements in communication technology such a videoconferencing sites on the internet has also made the formation of study groups much easier. Study group members no longer need to be in the same geographic location. In fact, groups could take a page from cable television and utilize internet-based teleconferencing sites to discuss topics with book authors and experts.

2. Form Educational Advocacy Groups

Most people learn history while still in school. The average adult rarely engages in learning history. Many don't recognize the connection between their everyday lives and the manner that people of African descent are viewed and view themselves. It is critical for Africans to address the damage that is done to the most vulnerable, our children, in both public and private school settings. Educational Advocacy Groups must be established to confront the misinformation taught in schools. While obviously racist messages such as referring to Africa as the "Dark Continent" in history text books is no longer routine, more subtle messages can be almost as damaging. Subtle racist messages are allowed into the psyche with much less resistance.

In October of 2015, a mother expressed her outrage at the depiction of enslaved Africans as "workers" in a Texas text book. Her widely viewed posts on Facebook and Twitter eventually led to articles in major newspapers like the New

York Times.[9] A milquetoast correction in the form of a sticker using the term "forced migration" was the publisher's (McGraw-Hill Education) inadequate fix to an utterly inappropriate book. Most parents of African descent who viewed the book probably didn't even notice the racist inference. It stands to reason that many more students read the textbook without their parents. Of greater concern is how these lies will be addressed throughout history text books and other materials used in other subjects on a more permanent basis. We must form educational advocacy groups while supporting and expanding existing groups which challenge the fallacious narrative described in this book.

3. **Obtain Advanced Expertise and Specialized Skills in Order to Challenge Racism in Academic Settings**
One of the major difficulties that African centered scholars and independent researchers confront is that they often have difficulty accessing historical sites and artifacts in order to do primary research. The scholars often have to rely on the research of biased Eurocentric scholars to make their case. The key to furthering the accurate historical record of the African is to assist African scholars with obtaining advanced degrees in fields where they can more readily confront Eurocentric or "orthodox" scholars.

For example, while African centered scholars have been arguing the African ethnic/"racial" heritage of the ancient Kemites (misnomered Ancient Egyptians), none have actually had access to Kemetic mummies. With a lack of African centered geneticists, it is difficult to even push for appropriate genetic analyses or even to have direct access to the genetic studies that sit in the basement of the Egyptian Museum in Cairo. After disrespectfully deriding those who advanced Kemet's African heritage, Egypt's Minister of Antiquities, Zahi Hawass, would later bury curious results in a report on the genetic haplogroup of King Rameses III. The powerful king's Y chromosomal haplogroup (E1b1a), or ethnic/regional family, is the most common group found in sub-Saharan African men (for more see Chapter 3). This fact has gotten virtually no coverage while popular depictions of the Kemites are still dominated by people of European or Arabic descent. With more scholars in areas such as history, chemistry, genetics, linguistics, and archeology; the type of primary research which can shift this false narrative can be conducted. We will not have to wait for our detractors, like Hawass. Our research will be primary.

4. **Utilize Traditional and New Media to Advance Corrective History and the Positive Black-Image**
In order to counter the negative image of African people, we will need to use all of the available tools. We cannot simply look to print media (such as books and journals) or wait to amass budgets which would allow us to create major motion pictures. We must take advantage of social media and streaming video sites which could allow us to reach large numbers of people with smaller budgets and engage them in critically important dialogues.

5. **Create Historical Dramas with Accurate Depictions**
One of the most effective ways to advance concepts to a popular audience is through fictional dramatic productions on television and in movies. Many more people will visit their local theatre for a single major summer blockbuster than will take a history course. The images are enduring. They greatly affect the manner that we view the role of groups in history, even though these depictions are fictional.

For example, while many think of simple huts when they think of buildings in ancient Africa, they would probably conceive of castles as an ancient European structure. In fact, the model of the fortress of Buhen in Ancient Kemet reveals that similar structures existed in Africa approximately 2,000 years earlier. This misnomer is due to film franchises like Harry Potter and Lord of the Rings. Where are the dramatic depictions of ancient Africa?

Image 8.2: Model of the Fortress of Buhen - The fortress was constructed during the reign of King Senusret III around 1860 BCE. Notice the common features which this structure shares with the European castle including the moat, battlements, and curtain wall. The earliest castles in Europe would be built over 2,000 years later!

6. Support Productions with Redeeming Characters of African Descent

One of the best ways to ensure corrective images of people of African descent is to vote with our dollars. We must support complex, positive depictions of Black folk. This will ensure that those who are attempting to set the record straight in all forms of media will be able to obtain appropriate financial support for their projects. *Black Enterprise* estimates African American purchasing power to be approximately $1.1 trillion in 2015.[10] There are few projects which could not be successful without our support. While many can rightfully critique the Fox Network show, *Empire*, it has become one of the highest rated shows on television and a cultural dynamo. African American viewership is quite valuable to advertisers and networks. We must strategically capitalize on this potential strength.

7. Confront Our Adversaries (Including Poorly Socialized Africans)

Powerful groups defend their interests. People of African descent must act quickly to punish those who continue to portray us in an inappropriate manner. Unfortunately, many of us are excited by the conflict which is featured on shows like

Real Housewives. Therefore we must ensure that depictions which portray us appropriately are also created. This may also mean that we will need to confront those of us who have not begun to undo their socialization which is based on self-hatred and denial. However, we should remember that they are also victims. Instead of having protracted disagreements in the media, we should simply not financially support their endeavors.

While this book has clearly assigned blame, we cannot expect those who benefit (consciously or unconsciously) from our continued subjugation to relinquish their relative advantage. We cannot entrust the futures of our children to anyone including well-intentioned whites who cannot possibly understand the burdens of Africans in a European dominated world. The stakes are far too high not to work to alter this condition ourselves. Hopefully this treatise has provided an understanding of how damaging widely-held beliefs can actually be. It is precisely this "oppression by acquiescence through common false beliefs" which we must work tirelessly to defeat.

REFERENCES AND NOTES

Introduction

[1]Merriam-Webster Learner's Dictionary. Website. Retrieved from: http://www.learnersdictionary.com/definition/lie

[2]The Free Dictionary. Website. Retrieved from: http://idioms.thefreedictionary.com/little+white+lie

[3]Merriam-Webster Learner's Dictionary. Website. Retrieved from: http://www.learnersdictionary.com/definition/white%20lie

[4]Conley, M. (May 30, 2012). *More TV, Less Self-Esteem, Except for White Boys.* ABC News. Retrieved from: http://abcnews.go.com/blogs/health/2012/05/30/more-tv-less-self-esteem-except-for-white-boys/.

[5]Rideout, V, Lauricella, A. and Wartella, E. (June 2011). *Children, Media, and Race Media Use Among White, Black, Hispanic, and Asian American Children.* Northwestern University. Center on Media and Human Development School of Communication Northwestern University.

[6]Fletcher, M. (October 8, 2014). *Whites think discrimination against whites is a bigger problem than bias against blacks.* The Washington Post. Retrieved from: https://www.washingtonpost.com/news/wonk/wp/2014/10/08/white-people-think-racial-discrimination-in-america-is-basically-over/.

[7]Barrows, Jr., R. (2001). *James H. Cone and Black Liberation Theology.* Jefferson, North Carolina: McFarland. pp. 21.

[8]Whittaker, K.D., Author's personal notes from public lecture convened August 5, 2006 in Accra, Ghana.

Chapter 1: "CAUCASIANS ARE THE ORIGINAL PEOPLE"

[1] This story comes from Plato's *Timaues* Dialogue written circa 360 BCE.

[2] Diodorus Siculus, The Library of History, Books II.35 - IV.58, Translated by C.H. Oldfather, Harvard University Press, 2000.

[3] In this instance it is not clear whether Ethiopia refers to a Northern African area or simply dark-skinned people. "Ethiopia" is derived from the Greek term "burnt-face". Either way, these royal ladies were of African descent.

[4] If the indigenous people of each of the world's countries controlled their respective natural resources, Europeans would be among the poorest groups on the planet. The European land mass is relatively deficient of natural resources. An April 2014 analysis of the top ten natural resource wealthy nations did not include even one European nation (unless one included Russia)! In fact, Russia is the only nation on the list which has indigenous 'white' people. Source: http://247wallst.com/special-report/2012/04/18/the-worlds-most-resource-rich-countries/3/. Retrieved: 12/5/14.

[5]Zinn, Howard. (2005) *The People's History of the United States*. New York, NY: Harper Perennial.

[6]Smedley, Audrey. (2007). History of the Idea of Race ... And Why It Matters. American Anthropological Association. Conference: Race, Human Variation and Disease: Consensus and Frontiers

[7] Wertenbaker, Thomas J. (2009). Bacon's Rebellion, 1676. Williamsburg, VA: Virginia 350th Anniversary Celebration Corporation. pps. 21-22.

[8] Smedley. (2007). p. 2.

[9]Liggio, Leonard P. (1976). "English Origins of Early American Racism." Radical History Review 3. pg. 31.

[10] Virtual Jamestown. *Laws on Slavery*. Retrieved from http://www.virtualjamestown.org/laws1.html#2

[11] ibid.

[12] ibid.

[13]Africans in the Americas. *Virginia's Slave Codes 1705*. Retrieved from: http://www.pbs.org/wgbh/aia/part1/1p268.html.

[14]Stuurman, Siep. (Autumn, 2000). Francois Bernier and the Invention of Racial Classification. History Workshop Journal. pps. 1-21. Oxford University.

[15]Smith, Justin E. H. (MAY 27, 2008). The Invention of Race. Retrieved from: http://www.jehsmith.com/1/2008/05/the-invention-o.html

[16]Graves, Joseph L (2001). *The Emperor's New Clothes: Biological Theories of Race at the Millennium*. Rutgers University Press

[17]Jefferson, Thomas. (1784). Notes on the State of Virginia, Queries 14 and 18, 137--43, 162--63

[18]There are some who would challenge whether Thomas Jefferson raped Sally Hemings. They forget to mention that not only was she only 14 when the "relationship" began, she was an enslaved African who was "owned" by Jefferson. She could not give consent. Jefferson did not even see fit to free Hemings upon his death.

[19]Gould, Stephen Jay. (1998). *On Mental and Visual Geometry*. Isis. University of Chicago Press. pp. 502-504

[20]Bhopal, Raj; Usher, Bruce and Usher, John. (Dec 22, 2007). *The beautiful skull and Blumenbach's errors: the birth of the scientific concept of race*. British Medical Journal. Retrieved from: http://www.ncbi.nlm.nih.gov/pmc/articles/PMC2151154/

[21]Voltaire *Les Lettres d'Amabed* (1769), Septième Lettre d'Amabed

[22]Gould, Stephen Jay. (1980). The Panda's Thumb. New York, NY: W. W. Norton & Company, Inc. p. 117.

[23]Marks, J. (2010). Anthropology and the Bell Curve. In P. Erickson & L. Murphy (Eds.), *Readings for a History of Anthropological Theory*, (3rd ed., pp.

587). Toronto, Canada: University of Toronto Press, Higher Education Division.

[24]Australopithecus afarensis ('Lucy'). Natural History Museum. Retrieved from http://www.nhm.ac.uk/nature-online/life/human-origins/early-human-family/australopithecus-afarensis/

[25]Tierny, J. (January 11, 1988). The Search for Adam and Eve. Newsweek.

[26] Modern humans and Neanderthals 'interbred in Europe'. (June 22, 2015). BBC News. Retrieved from: http://www.bbc.com/news/science-environment-33226416

[27]Roach, J. (June 11, 2003). Oldest *Homo Sapiens* Fossils Found, Experts Say. National Geographic News. Retrieved from http://news.nationalgeographic.com/news/2003/06/0611_030611_earliesthuman.html

Chapter 2: "ANCIENT AFRICA CONTRIBUTED NOTHING TO CIVILIZATION"

[1] Image taken by Nelson Minar 10/5/05. Retrieved from http://flickr.com/photos/62218395@N00/89867366

[2] Narrative on the early life of Afro-Puerto Rican, Arturo Schomburg based on Knight, R. (1995) Arthur "Afroborinqueño" Schomburg. Civil Rights Journal. U.S. Commission on Civil Rights. Retrieved from: http://intelligent-designs.biz/wbai/Earthwatch/www/schombrg.html

[3] Dr. John Henrik Clarke recalls a similar story with regard to an authority figure telling him that African had no history. As he sought to find something interesting to contribute in his classroom the next day, he asked a lawyer than he worked for after school for a book on African in early world history, the white attorney told him, "I'm sorry John, you came from a people who have no history." Dr. Clarke would not accept this proclamation either. He would study with Arturo Schomburg as a teenager. Source: Wesley Snipes (Executive Producer) and St. Claire Bourne (Director). (1996). *Dr. John Henrik Clarke: A Great and Might Walk* [Motion Picture]. United States: Black Dot Production.

[4] Kant, I. (2004). Prolegomena to Any Future Metaphysics. Cambridge: Cambridge University Press. pp. XXVI.

[5] Boswell, J. (1776). Boswell in Extremes. New York: Mcgraw-Hill

[6] McArthur, N., Falkenstein, L. (eds) (2013). Essays and Treatises on Philosophical Subjects. Ontario:Broadview Press. p. 548.

[7] Garrett, A. (April 2000). Hume's Revised Racism Revisited. Hume Studies, Volume XXVI, Number 1. pp. 171-172.

[8] Hegel, G. (1956). The Philosophy of History. New York: Dover.

[9] Hegel, G. pp 99. Quoted from a lecture circa 1830.

[10] Seligman, C.S. Races of Africa (1930). Quoted from Saunders, E. (1969). The Hamitic Hypothesis; Its Origin and Functions in Time Perspective. Journal of African History, X, 4. Cambridge: Cambridge University Press. pp. 521.

[11] Actually the story of Noah, his ark, and his family comes to us first in the Judaic tradition and is also present in all of the other Abrahamic faiths (Christianity, Islam, and Baha'i).

[12] Ironically, C.F. Volney was not born with this name. He assumed it in part in recognition of the philosopher Voltaire. As we described earlier, Voltaire harbored pernicious racist notions, Volney is an abolitionist who acknowledges the African origin of civilization.

[13] Volney, C.F. (1890). The Ruins. New York: Twentieth Century Pub. Co.

[14] McCabe, J. (1927). Life Among the Many Peoples of the Earth: The Story of the Races of Mankind and Their Relationship. Haldeman-Julius Publications. pp. 26.

[15] Saggs, H.W.F., (1991) Civilization Before Greece and Rome. Yale University Press. pp. 240

[16] Wilson, W.; Grande, C.; and Hoyt, D (Eds). (2007). Trauma: Emergency Resuscitation, Perioperative Anesthesia, Surgical Management, Volume I. London: CRC Press. pp 2.

[17] Breasted, J. (1991). The Edwin Smith Surgical Papyrus: published in facsimile and hieroglyphic transliteration with translation and commentary in two volumes. Chicago: University of Chicago Press.

[18] Rodney, C. (2004). Scientific American Inventions and Discoveries, Hoboken: John Wiley & Songs, Inc. pp. 393. The first scientific medical experiment is usually considered the British Military Surgeon James Lind's study on scurvy.

[19] Nunn, J. (2002). Ancient Egyptian Medicine. Norman, Oklahoma: University of Oklahoma Press.

[20] A Timeline of Pregnancy Testing. a thin blue line: The History of the Pregnancy Test Kit. Office of NIH History. Retrieved from http://history.nih.gov/exhibits/thinblueline/timeline.html

[21] Blake, J. (1952).. The Inoculation Controversy in Boston: 1721–1722. Boston: The New England Quarterly 25:4

[22] National Institutes of Health. U.S. National Library of Medicine. (April 27, 1998). *Cesarean Section - A Brief History Part 2*. Retrieved from https://www.nlm.nih.gov/exhibition/cesarean/part2.html

[23] Francesco d'Errico et al. (2012) Early Evidence of San Material Culture Represented by Organic Artifacts from Border Cave, South Africa. Proceedings of the National Academy of Sciences. Vol. 109, No. 33

[24] Darling, D. (2004). The Universal Book of Mathematics: from Abracadabra to Zeno's Pardoxes. Hoboken, New Jersey: John Wiley & Songs, Inc. pp. 184.

[25] Brooks, A.S. and Smith, C.C. (1987): "Ishango revisited: new age determinations and cultural interpretations", *The African Archaeological Review*, 5 : 65-78

[26] Darling, D. pp 167.

[27] While not from Kemet's golden era, the discovery of nine papyri as old as 2,000 years old in the personal papers of a deceased Luther College professor and administrator demonstrates how there documents were simply sold like booty by antiquity dealers in modern day Egypt. Luther College is a small Lutheran college in Iowa. Ancient Egyptian papyri discovered at Luther College. (February 21, 2014). Luther College. Retrieved from: https://www.luther.edu/headlines/?story_id=533743.

[28] Clagett, Ml. (1999). Ancient Egyptian Science: A Source Book. Volume 3: Ancient Egyptian Mathematics. Memoirs of the American Philosophical Society 232. Philadelphia: American Philosophical Society

[29] The Rhind Mathematical Papyrus. Department of Mathematics. University of Washington. Retrieved from: https://www.math.washington.edu/~greenber/Rhind.html

[30] Belluck, P. (December 7, 2010). "Math Puzzles' Oldest Ancestors Took Form on Egyptian Papyrus". New York Times. pp. D3

[31] Doh, Emmanuel Fru. (2009). Stereotyping Africa: Surprising Answers to Surprising Questions. Bamenda, Cameroon: Langaa Pcig. pp. 110.

[32] Consider the folklore around Abraham Lincoln building a log cabin and juxtapose it with the negative connotation attached to African huts. Are they both not locally source simple homes?

[33] Clayton, P. (2002). The Seven Wonders of the Ancient World. New York: Routledge.

[34] Iker, G and Correa, A. "Race to Build." Mas Context. Retrieved from http://www.mascontext.com/issues/11-speed-fall-11/race-to-build/

[35] E. Haldeman-Julius quote from: Jackson, J. (1939). Ethiopia and the Origin of Civilization. Retrieved from: https://archive.org/stream/EthiopiaAndTheOriginOfCivilization/EOC_djvu.txt

[36] Shaw, Ian, (ed.) (2000). The Oxford History of Ancient Egypt. Oxford University Press. p. 480.

[37] Diagram of per djet taken from Wikipedia Commons. Image author: Oesermaatra0069 (http://commons.wikimedia.org/wiki/File:Mastaba.jpg)

[38] Clayton, P. (1994). The Chronicle of the Pharaohs. London: Thames and Hudson, Ltd. pp. 46.

[39] A Brief History of the World's Tallest Buildings. Time Magazine Online. Retrieved from: http://content.time.com/time/photogallery/0,29307,1950812_2018361,00.html

[40]Whitman, E. (Jul/ August 1975). An Obelisk for Central Park. Saudi Aramco World. Volume 26, Number 4. pp 4-9. Retrieved from: http://www.saudiaramcoworld.com/issue/197504/an.obelisk.for.central.park.htm

[41] The Khedive is a role similar to a viceroy, an responsible for a colony or country for a monarch. The Khedive ran Egypt for the Ottoman Turks.

[42] Images of tekhen in Central Park taken from Wikipedia Commons. Top image author: Ingfbruno (http://commons.wikimedia.org/wiki/File:USA-NYC-Central_Park-Cleopatra%27s_Needle5.jpg)
Bottom image author: Captain-tucker
(http://commons.wikimedia.org/wiki/File:Cleopatra%27s_Needle-2.jpg).
Cropped to bottom of image

[43] Tyson, P. (August 27, 1999). The Third Attempt. Mysteries of the Nile. PBS Online: Nova Online Adventures. Retrieved from: http://www.pbs.org/wgbh/nova/egypt/dispatches/990827.html

[44]Baldridge, C. (2012). Prisoners of Prester John: The Portuguese Mission to Ethiopia in Search of the Mythical King, 1520-1526. Jefferson, NC: Mcfarland pp 252.

[45]Marcus, H. (1994). A History of Ethiopia. Berkeley: University of California Press. pp 12.

[46]McCord, D. (Ed.) (1840). The Statutes at Large of South Carolina. Vol. 7, Containing the Acts Relating to Charleston, Courts, Slaves, and Rivers. Columbia, SC: A.S. Johnston. pp. 397.

[47]Ibid.

[48]Smith, M. (2005). Stono: Documenting and Interpreting a Southern Slave. Columbia, South Carolina: University of South Carolina Press.

[49] The Palette of Narmer is called "humanity's oldest document of an event". Brier, B and Hobbs, Hoyt. (2008). Daily Life of the Ancient Egyptians. Westport, Connecticut: Greenwood. pp. 2.

[50] Hilliard III, A, Williams, L, and Dimali, N (Eds). (2012). The Teachings of Ptahhotep: The Oldest Book in the World Paperback. Grand Forks, North Dakota: Blackwood Press.

[51] Overland, P. (1996). "Structure in The Wisdom of Amenemope and Proverbs," in J. E. Coleson and V. H. Matthews (Eds.). Go to the Land I Will Show You: Studies in Honor of Dwight W. Young. Winona Lake, Indiana: Eisenbrauns. pp. 275-291

[52] Quote taken from: Asante, M. (July 2004). *An African Origin of Philosophy: Myth or Reality?* City Press

[53]Lloyd, N and Thompson, A. (April 7, 2011). "Is Britain to blame for many of the world's problems?" BBC News Magazine. Retrieved from: http://www.bbc.com/news/magazine-12992540

[54]Bradley, M. (Oct 5, 2012). *Republican extremists, in their own words.* Arkansas Blog. Arkansas Times. Retrieved from: http://www.arktimes.com/ArkansasBlog/archives/2012/10/05/republican-extremists-in-their-own-words

[55]Griffin, E. (1997). Voodoo Child. Transcribed by author from: https://www.youtube.com/watch?v=y7tyAOlZqaM

[56]Collins, E. (March 11, 2011). *Hannity Buddy Thanks God For Slavery.* NewsHounds (Website). Retrieved from: http://www.newshounds.us/hannity_buddy_thanks_god_for_slavery_03112012

Chapter 3: "THE ANCIENT EGYPTIANS WERE 'CAUCASIAN'"

[1]Hamilton, Lynn. Tell Ridley Scott to Stop Racist Casting! Care2 Petitions (Website). Retrieved from: http://www.thepetitionsite.com/664/448/866/tell-ridley-scott-to-stop-racist-casting/?z00m=21437422. 25,601 signature on 1/9/15.

[2] Edwards, Breanna. (Dec. 12 2014). *Exodus: Gods and Kings: Flooded With Race Problems (and White People).* The Root (website). Retrieved from: http://www.theroot.com/articles/culture/2014/12/exodus_gods_and_kings_flooded_with_race_problems_and_white_people.html

[3]Fincher, Russ. (November 26, 2014). *Ridley Scott Says Whitewashing was the Only Way to Finance 'Exodus: Gods and Kings'.* Film: blogging the reel world (Website). Retrieved from: http://www.slashfilm.com/exodus-whitewashing/#more-265584

[4]Gajewski, Ryan. (November 29, 2014). *Rupert Murdock Defends 'Exodus' Cast: "Since when are Egyptians Not White?".* The Hollywood Reporter (website). Retrieved from: http://www.hollywoodreporter.com/news/rupert-murdoch-defends-exodus-cast-752805

[5]Mendelson, Scott. (November 27, 2015). Lionsgate Responds to 'Gods of Egypt' Whitewashing Controversy. Forbes (website). Retrieved from: http://www.forbes.com/sites/scottmendelson/2015/11/27/exclusive-lionsgate-responds-to-gods-of-egypt-whitewashing-controversy/#1164d54031f4.

[6]While most sources credit Champollion for the initial decipherment of the Medu Neter, many also credit the British scholar Thomas Young for important contributions to the process. Some even give him primary credit.

[7] Quoted from Diop, C. A. (1989). The African Origin of Civilization: Myth or Reality. Chicago, IL: Chicago Review Press. pp 47.

[8]Bryant, M. and Eaverly, M.A. (September 2007). Egypto-Modernism: James Henry Breasted, H.D., and the New Past. Modernism/modernity. Volume 14, Number 3. pp. 435-45. Retrieved from: https://muse.jhu.edu/login?auth=0&type=summary&url=/journals/modernism-modernity/v014/14.3bryant.pdf

[9] Breasted's reckoning with the realities of World War I and his quest to secure the field of Egyptology in the United States are described masterfully in an article by Lindsay Ambridge: Ambridge, L. (2012) *Imperialism and Racial Geography in James Henry* Breasted's *Ancient Times, a History of the Early World.* Journal of Egyptian History 5. pp. 12 - 33.

[10] Breasted, J. H. (1926). The Conquest of Civilization. New York, NY: Harper and Brothers. pp. 112.

[11] Pietrie, W.M.F. (1939). The Making of Egypt. New York, NY: Macmillian.

[12]Wicker, F.D.P. (July 1998). *The Road to Punt*. The Geographic Journal. Vol. 164, No. 2. pp. 155-167.

[13]Pankhurst, R. (2001). The Ethiopians: A History. Hoboken, NJ: Wiley-Blackwell.

[14]Jarus, O. (April 26, 2010). Baboon mummy analysis reveals Eritrea and Ethiopia as location of land of Punt. The Independent. (website). Retrieved from: http://www.independent.co.uk/life-style/history/baboon-mummy-analysis-reveals-eritrea-and-ethiopia-as-location-of-land-of-punt-1954547.html.

[15]Biographical and Bibliographical Milestones. cheikhantadiop.net (website). Translated with Google Chrome. Retrieved from http://www.cheikhantadiop.net/cheikh_anta_diop_biograph.htm

[16]Nagel, R. (1993) Diop, Cheikh Anta 1923–1986 Contemporary Black Biography. Encyclopedia.com (website). Retrieved from: http://www.encyclopedia.com/topic/Cheikh_Anta_Diop.aspx

[17] "Albarello MUMIA 18Jh" by Bullenwächter. Retrieved from http://commons.wikimedia.org/wiki/File:Albarello_MUMIA_18Jh.jpg#mediaviewer/File:Albarello_MUMIA_18Jh.jpg

[18] The table reflecting the analysis of the 42 films is included in the appendix.

[19]"Nones" on the Rise. Pew Research Religion and Public Life Project (website). Retrieved from: http://www.pewforum.org/2012/10/09/nones-on-the-rise/

[20] The Roman historian Cassius Dio is quoted in Tyldesley, J. (2011). Cleopatra: Last Queen of Egypt. London: Profile Books. pp. 64.

[21] Scholars today acknowledge that Cleopatra was probably of Greek and Persia background. This image is probably very different than the Elizabeth Taylor version. Furthermore, Austrian archeologist Hilke Theur was able to examine the skull of Cleopatra's sister, Arsinoe. Hilke argues that their mother (if, in fact, they shared a mother) must have been of African descent. Another

European scholar also questions the commonly held ethnicity of the queen. Egyptologist Dr. Sally-Ann Ashton created a three dimensional image of Cleopatra based on composites of several ancient depictions of the queen. Her rendering is clearly of a woman who would be considered "Black" today. Sources: *Elizabeth Taylor's Cleopatra 'Nowhere Near Reality'.* (December 16, 2008). The Telegraph (newspaper website). Retrieved from: http://www.telegraph.co.uk/news/science/science-news/3792872/Elizabeth-Taylors-Cleopatra-nowhere-near-reality.html
Cleopatra's Mother 'was African'. (March 16, 2009). BBC News (website). Retrieved from: http://news.bbc.co.uk/2/hi/also_in_the_news/7945333.stm.

[22] Herodotus, T. and Eliot, C (Ed.). (2010). Voyages and Travels: Ancient and Modern. New York: Cosimo, Inc. pp. 51.

[23] Aristotle. (September 1, 2014). Complete works of Aristotle, volume 1: the revised Oxford translation. Princeton: Princeton University Press. pp. 1247.

[24] Tutankhamun 'was not black'. (September 26, 2007). News24 Archives. (website on behalf of Agence France-Presse). Retrieved from: http://www.news24.com/Africa/News/Tutankhamun-was-not-black-20070925.

[25] Tutankhamun Facial Reconstruction. (May 7, 2005). National Geographic Press Room (Website). Retrieved from: http://press.nationalgeographic.com/2005/05/07/tutankhamun-facial-reconstruction/

[26] Gugliotta, G. (May 11, 2005). *A New Look at King Tut.* Washington Post. Retrieved from: http://www.washingtonpost.com/wp-dyn/content/article/2005/05/10/AR2005051001522.html

[27] Handwerk, B. (May 11, 2005). *King Tut's New Face: Behind the Forensic Reconstruction.* National Geographic News (Website). Retrieved from: http://news.nationalgeographic.com/news/2005/05/0511_050511_kingtutface.html

[28] Hawass, Z., Ismail, S. and others. (December 17, 2012). Revisiting the harem conspiracy and death of Ramesses III: anthropological, forensic, radiological, and genetic study. BMJ. BMJ 2012;345:e8268.

[29] ibid., p 2.

[30] Haplogroup E-V38. Wikipedia page. Retrieved from http://en.wikipedia.org/wiki/Haplogroup_E-V38

[31] Gates, Jr., H.L. (Mar. 15, 2001). A debate on activism in black studies. In Manning, M (Ed.), Dispatches from the ebony tower: Intellectuals confront the African American experience. (pp. 186 - 187). New York: Columbia University Press.

[32] Fryer, R. (Winter 2006). "Acting white": Paying the social price for getting good grades. Education Next. (6)1.

[33] Ibid.

Chapter 4: "HEBREW SLAVES BUILT THE PYRAMIDS"

[1]Professor Amihai Mazar is reported to state that the myth of Jews building the Egyptian pyramids stems from a claim by Menachem Begin. Deitch, I. (January 12, 2010). *Egypt: New Find Shows Slaves Didn't Build Pyramids.* U.S. News & World Report. Retrieved from http://www.usnews.com/science/articles/2010/01/12/egypt-new-find-shows-slaves-didnt-build-pyramids?page=2

[2] Perry, S. (February, 27, 2007). Israelites didn't build the pyramids. ynetnews.com. Retrieved from: http://www.ynetnews.com/articles/0,7340,L-3370258,00.html.

[3]Herodotus. (Translated by Macaulay, G.C.). (Reprinted January 25, 2013). An Account of Egypt. Project Gutenberg. Retrieved from: http://www.gutenberg.org/files/2131/2131-h/2131-h.htm.

[4]Josephus, T. F. (Translated by Whiston, W.). (Reprinted January 4, 2009). The Antiquities of the Jews, Book II. Chapter 9. Project Gutenberg. Retrieved from: http://www.gutenberg.org/files/2848/2848-h/2848-h.htm

[5]Exodus 1:6-13. King James Version.

[6]Top 100 Films of All-Time (Domestic Gross Adjusted for Inflation). AMC Filmsite (Website). Retrieved on February 7, 2015from: http://www.filmsite.org/boxoffice3.html.

[7]de Morales, L. (April 10, 2012). 'The Ten Commandments' pulls off a ratings miracle for ABC. The TV Column. The Washington Post (Website). Retrieved from: http://www.washingtonpost.com/blogs/tv-column/post/the-ten-commandments-pulls-off-a-ratings-miracle-for-abc/2012/04/10/gIQAUhf18S_blog.html .

[8]Gladstone, R. (December 26, 2014). *Egypt Reported to Ban Latest U.S. 'Exodus' Film.* New York Times. pp. A7.

[9]The Prince of Egypt Awards. IMDB (Website). Retrieved from: http://www.imdb.com/title/tt0120794/awards.

[10] Clayton, P. (1994). The Chronicle of the Pharaohs. London: Thames and Hudson, Ltd. pp. 46.

[11] Dash, G. (Spring 2013). How the pyramid builders found their true north. AERAGRAM. (14)1. pp. 8-14

[12] A Brief History of the World's Tallest Buildings. Time Magazine Online. Retrieved from: http://content.time.com/time/photogallery/0,29307,1950812_2018361,00.html

[13]Mooney, M. (July 20, 1997). Slaves worked to death. New York Daily News. Retrieved from: http://www.nydailynews.com/archives/news/slaves-worked-death-article-1.773557

[14] Ibid.

[15]Mack, M. and Blakey, M. (2004). The New York African Burial Ground project: past biases, current dilemmas, and future research opportunities. Society for Historical Archaeology. 38, 1 pp. 10 -17.

[16]Hawass, Z. (Jan. 12, 2010). The discovery of the tombs of the pyramid builders at Giza. Guardians.net (Website). Retrieved from http://www.guardians.net/hawass/buildtomb.htm.

[17]Kratovic. K. (Jan. 12, 2010). Egypt: New Find Shows Slaves Didn't Build Pyramids. *US News and World Reports (Website)*. Retrieved from http://www.usnews.com/science/articles/2010/01/12/egypt-new-find-shows-slaves-didnt-build-pyramids

[18] Mintz, J. (March 26, 2012). *Were Jews ever really slaves in Egypt, or is Passover a myth*. Haaretz (Digital edition).

[19] David, A.R., (1986). The pyramid builders of Ancient Egypt: a modern investigation of pharaoh's workforce. London: Routledge

[20]*A planned town of the Middle Kingdom: Kahun*. (January 1, 2005). Arts and Humanities Through the Eras. Gale. Retrieved from: http://www.highbeam.com/doc/1G2-3427400025.html

[21]Exodus 1:11. King James Version.

[22] Ibid #17.

[23]Marcus, J. (June 1974). The larger task. The Jacob Rader Marcus Center. American Jewish Archives. pp. 2. Retrieved from: http://americanjewisharchives.org/media/docs/marcus/largerTask.pdf

[24]Pithom. Jewish Encyclopedia.com (Website). Retrieved from: http://www.jewishencyclopedia.com/articles/12192-pithom

[25]Naville, E. (1885). Egypt exploration fund: the store-city of Pithom and the route of the exodus. London: Messrs. Trubner & Co. pp. 11.

[26]Seters, J. The geography of the exodus. cited in Dearman, J and Graham, M (Eds.). (2002). The land that I will show you: essays on the history and archaeology of the Ancient Near East in honor of J. Maxwell Miller. London: A&C Black.

[27]Ibid. pp. 256.

[28]Ibid. pp. 255-256

[29]Exodus 12:35, 37, and 38. King James Version.

[30]Moore, M. and Kelle, B. (2011). Biblical history and Israel's past: the changing study of the bible and history. Grand Rapids: Wm. B. Eerdmans Publishing Co. pp. 81.

[31]Mission taken from Society of Biblical Literature website page entitled About SBL. Retrieved from: http://www.sbl-site.org/aboutus.aspx.

[32]Killebrew, A. (2005). Biblical peoples and ethnicity: an archaeological study of Egyptians, Canaanites, Philistines, and early Israel 1300-1100 B.C.E. Atlanta: Society of Biblical Literature. pp. 152.

[33]Proten, B. (2011). The Elephantine papyri in English: three millennia of cross-cultural continuity and change. Atlanta: Society of Biblical Literature.

[34]Josephus, T.F. (1737). Against apion. (Whiston, W, trans.). Retrieved from: http://www.utom.org/library/books/Josephus.pdf. Book 1, section 14.

[35]Clayton, P. (1994). Chronicles of the pharaohs: the reign-by-reign record of the rulers and dynasties of Ancient Egypt. London: Thames and Hudson, Ltd.

[36]Ibid. # 31.

[37]McGowan, J.A. and Kashatus, W.C. (2011). Harriet Tubman: a biography. Santa Barbara: ABC-Clio. pp. xix.

[38]Harriet Tubman. National Park Service (Website). Retrieved from http://www.nps.gov/resources/person.htm?id=175.

[39]Exodusters. Homestead: National Monument of America Nebraska. National Park Service (Website). Retrieved from: http://www.nps.gov/home/learn/historyculture/exodusters.htm.

[40]King, Jr., M.L. (April 3, 1968). I've been to the mountaintop. Retrieved from: http://www.americanrhetoric.com/speeches/mlkivebeentothemountaintop.htm

[41]El Shabazz, H. M. (November 20, 1963). Malcolm X at Columbia University. Malcolm X Files (Website). Retrieved from: http://malcolmxfiles.blogspot.com/2013/06/columbia-university-november-20-1963.html

[42]King, Dr., M.L. (May 17, 1956). The Death of Evil upon the Seashore. The Martin Luther King, Jr. Papers Project. Retrieved from: http://mlk-kpp01.stanford.edu/primarydocuments/Vol3/17-May-1956_DeathOfEvil.pdf.

Chapter 5: "AFRICANS WERE SAVAGES WHEN THE EUROPEANS ENSLAVED THEM"

[1]Clarkson, T. (1839). The history of the rise, progress, and accomplishment of the abolition of the African slave-trade by the British parliament. London: John W. Parker, West Strand. pp. 304.

[2]Ibid. pp. 305.

[3] This tension is well described in a 1976 article by Tyrone Tillery. Tillery, T. (1976). The Inevitability of the Douglass-Garrison Conflict. Phylon. 37(2). 137-149.

[4]Anonymous Author. (1788). An address, to the inhabitants in general of Great Britain, and Ireland: relating to a few of the consequences which must naturally result from the abolition of the slave trade. London: Mrs. Egerton Smith. pp. 7.

[5]Sheffield is a city in South Yorkshire, England.

[6]Holroyd, J.B. (1791). Observations on the project for abolishing the slave trade, and on the reasonableness of attempting some practicable mode of relieving the Negroes. London: Printed by J. Cooper for J. Debrett, pp. 34.

[7]It is that over 95% of all enslaved Africans were taken from West Africa. Lovejoy, P. (2011). Transformations in Slavery: A History of Slavery in Africa. London: Cambridge University Press. pp. 19.

[8] Map based on original version "Map of the Ghana Empire (German Version)". Uploaded by Luxo as BlankMap-World gray.svg. https://en.wikipedia.org/wiki/Ghana_Empire#/media/File:Ghana_empire_map. png

[9]LaPierre, Y (2004). Ghana in Pictures. Minneapolis: Lerner Publications Group. pp. 20.

[10]Davidson, B (1965). A History of West Africa 1000-1800. Harlow, UK: Longman Group. pp. 35.

[11]Image taken by Holger Reineccius. Salzkarawane auf dem Weg von Agadez nach Bilma in Niger (Salt caravan en route from Agadez to Bilma in Niger). Retrieved from: https://commons.wikimedia.org/wiki/File:Bilma-Salzkarawane1.jpg

[12]al-Bakri, A.U. (1068), A Description of 11th Century Ghana. In Crandall-Bear, D (2001). Exploring the Global Past: Original Sources in World History, Volume 1. Dubuque, LA: Kendall/Hunt. pp. 150-153.

[13]Levtzion, N. Ancient Ghana and Mali (1980). London: Holmes & Meier Publishers, Ltd. pp. 4.

[14]Ibid. pp. 4.

[15]Mauny, R. The question of Ghana (1954). *Journal of the International African Institute, 24*(3) pp. 204

[16]Schomburg General Research and Reference Division, The New York Public Library. (1890). *Guerriers Sarrakholais.* Retrieved from http://digitalcollections.nypl.org/items/510d47e0-2216-a3d9-e040-e00a18064a99

[17]Levtzion. pp. 4.

[18]al-Bili, U (2008). Some Aspects of Islam in Africa. Ithaca: Ithaca Press. pp. 11.

[19]Waines, D (2010). The Odyssey of Ibn Battuta: Uncommon Tales of a Medieval Adventurer. London: I.B. Tauris & Co. Ltd.

[20]Wolny, P (2014). Discovering the Empire of Mali. New York: The Rosen Publishing Group, Inc. pp. 4.

[21]The griot or jeli are West African storytellers who maintain the collective knowledge of their people through their historic epics.

[22]Niane, D.T. (2006). An Epic of Old Mali. Edinburgh Gate, Harlow (UK): Pearson Education Limited. pp. 41-42.

[23]Conrad, D. (1992). Searching for History in the Sunjata Epic: The Case of Fakoli. *History in Africa. 19.* pp. 147-200.

[24]Most aspect of the Epic of Sundiata taken from Niane, D.T. (2006).

[25]United Nations Educational', Scientific and Cultural Organization. Website: Manden Charter, proclaimed in Kurukan Fuga. Retrieved from: http://www.unesco.org/culture/ich/index.php?lg=en&pg=00011&RL=00290.

[26] Hamdani, A (1994). An Islamic Background to the Voyages of Discovery. Language and Literature" in Jayyusi, S. K.and Marín, M. The Legacy of Muslim Spain. Leiden, Netherlands: Brill Academic Publishers. pp. 276.

[27]The work of Ivan Van Sertima (Van Sertima, I (1976). They Came Before Columbus: The African Presence in Ancient America. New York: Random House Trade Paperbacks.) was also influenced by the work of Harvard professor, Leo Weiner (Weiner, L (1922). Africa and the Discovery of America: Vols 1-3. Philadelphia: Innes & Son.)

[28]Ibid. Niane, D.T. (2006).

[29]While Mansa Kankan Musa's servants have usually been called "slaves", this term is very misleading. Particularly after the enslavement of Africans in the West, the term "slave" is usually believed to imply that an entire race/class of people are held in chattel bondage. Their children would also be held in bondage with no opportunity to alter their social condition. This circumstance doesn't actually describe the position that is generally called "slavery" in early Africa.

[30]Goodwin, A.J.H. (1957). The Medieval Empire of Ghana in *The South African Archaeological Bulletin. 12*(47). pp 110.

[31]Conrad, D. (2010). Great Empires of the Past: Empires of Medieval West Africa. New York: Chelsea House. pp. 47.

[32]Ibid. Goodwin. pp. 110.

[33]Ham, Anthony (2009). West Africa. Melbourne, Australia: Lonely Planet. pp. 28.

[34]Mansa Musa I's wealth is estimated at around an inflation adjusted $400 billion. The second wealthiest people according to the website Celebrity Net Worth were the Rothschild Family ($350 billion) and John D. Rockefeller ($340 billion). Warner, B. (April 14, 2014). The 25 Richest People Who Ever Lived - Inflation Adjusted. Website: Celebrity Net Worth. Retrieved from http://www.celebritynetworth.com/articles/entertainment-articles/25-richest-people-lived-inflation-adjusted/

[35]Ibid. Davidson, B. (1965).

[36]Rainer, C. (May 27, 2003). Reclaiming the Ancient Manuscripts of Timbuktu. National Geographic News. Website: National Geographic. Retrieved from: http://news.nationalgeographic.com/news/2003/05/0522_030527_timbuktu.html.

[37]Ibid. Rainer, C. (2003)

[38]While many believe large numbers of manuscripts were destroyed by the Ansar Dine rebels, it appears only a few hundred were torched. Most of the documents were secreted away prior to the burning. The situation still highlights the dangerous position that the texts are in. Harding, L. (January 28, 2013). Timbuktu mayor: Mali rebels torched library of historic manuscripts. Website: The Guardian. Retrieved from: http://www.theguardian.com/world/2013/jan/28/mali-timbuktu-library-ancient-manuscripts
Kottoor, N. (June 4, 2013). How Timbuktu's manuscripts were smuggled to safety. Website: BBC News. Retrieved from: http://www.bbc.com/news/magazine-22704960.

[39]Ibid. Conrad, D. (2010). pp. 61.

[40]Asante, M.K. (2014). The History of Africa: The Quest for Eternal Harmony. London: Routledge.

[41]Levtzion, N. (1963). The Thirteenth- and Fourteenth-Century Kings of Mali. The Journal of African History. 4(3). Cambridge: Cambridge University Press. pp. 350.

[42] Davidson, B (1965). A History of West Africa 1000-1800. Harlow, UK: Longman Group. pp. 53.

[43]Levtzion, N. Ancient Ghana and Mali (1980). London: Holmes & Meier Publishers, Ltd. pp. 83.

[44]Davidson, B (1998). West Africa Before the Colonial Era: A History to 1850. London: Routledge. pp 44.

[45]Davidson, B (1965). A History of West Africa 1000-1800. Harlow, UK: Longman Group.

[46]Cissoko, S.M. (1984). The Songhai from the 12th to the 16th Century in Niane, D.T. (ed). General History of Africa IV: Africa from the Twelfth to the Sixteenth Century. Paris: United Nations Educational, Scientific, Cultural Organization.

[47]Es-Sadi, A. (1656). History of the Sudan. quoted in Walker, R. and Millar, S. (1999). The West African Empire of Songhai in 10 Easy Lessons: Introduction to Black History. South Lanarkshire, UK: Concept Learning, Ltd.

[48]Picture credit: "Djenne great mud mosque" by Ruud Zwart - Photo taken by Ruud Zwart. Licensed under CC BY-SA 3.0 via Commons - https://commons.wikimedia.org/wiki/File:Djenne_great_mud_mosque.jpg#/media/File:Djenne_great_mud_mosque.jpg

[49]McKissack, P and McKissak, F. (1995). The Royal Kingdoms of Ghana, Mali, and Songhay: Life in Medieval Africa. London: Macmillian. pp. 96.

[50]Africanus, L. (c. 1492). The History and Description of Africa. Translated by Pory, J. (1550) London: Hakluyt Society. pp 4.2. Retrieved from: http://www.learnnc.org/lp/editions/nchist-colonial/1982

[51]Wells-Barnett, I. (1895). The Red Record: Tabulated Statistics and Alleged Causes of Lynching in the United States. Retrieved from: http://www.gutenberg.org/files/14977/14977-h/14977-h.htm#chap6

[52]Herbert, B. (2008, January 22). The Blight that is Still with Us. *New York Times*. Retrieved from http://www.nytimes.com/2008/01/22/opinion/22herbert.html?_r=0.

[53]Lynchings: By State and Race, 1882–1968. University of Missouri-Kansas City School of Law. Retrieved from http://law2.umkc.edu/faculty/projects/ftrials/shipp/lynchingsstate.html

[54]Judge Says Remarks on 'Gorillas' May Be Cited in Trial on Beating. (1991, June 12). *New York Times*. Retrieved from http://www.nytimes.com/1991/06/12/us/judge-says-remarks-on-gorillas-may-be-cited-in-trial-on-beating.html

[55]Bouie, J. (2014, November 26). Michael Brown wasn't a Superhuman Demon: But Darren Wilson's Racial Prejudice Told Him Otherwise. *Slate*. Retrieved from http://www.slate.com/articles/news_and_politics/politics/2014/11/darren_wilson_s_racial_portrayal_of_michael_brown_as_a_superhuman_demon.single.html

Chapter 6: "COLUMBUS DISCOVERED AMERICA"

[1]Matz, R. (Reporter). (2014, October 4). *Little Italy Welcomes the 124th Annual Christopher Columbus Celebration This Sunday*. CBS Baltimore. Retrieved from: http://baltimore.cbslocal.com/2014/10/03/little-italy-welcomes-the-124th-annual-christopher-columbus-celebration-this-sunday/

[2]The Order Sons of Italy in America in Washington, D.C. *Why We Should Celebrate Columbus Day. Retrieved from: https://www.osia.org/documents/Celebrate_Col_Day.pdf*

[3]Columbus, C. (1893). Journal of Christopher Columbus During His First Voyage 1492-93. (C.R. Markham, Trans.). London: Hakluyut Society. pp. 36.

[4]Ibid. pp. 37.

[5]Ibid. pp. 38, 41.

[6]Picture credit: Tropenmuseum Royal Tropical Institute Object Number 60008905 A group of Arawak and Carib in fe.jpg. Retrieved from https://en.wikipedia.org/wiki/Arawak#/media/File:Tropenmuseum_Royal_Tropical_Institute_Objectnumber_60008905_Een_groep_Arowakken_en_Karaiben_in_fe.jpg

[7]Lydersen, K. Dental Studies Give Clues About Christopher Columbus's Crew (2009, May 18). *The Washington Post*. Retrieved from http://www.washingtonpost.com/wp-dyn/content/article/2009/05/17/AR2009051701885.html

[8]Wood, S. (2001) Sexual Violation in the Conquest of the Americas. In M.D. Smith (Ed.), *Sex Without Consent: Rape and Sexual Coercion in America.* New York: NYU Press. pp. 11

[9]Thacher, J.B. (1903). Christopher Columbus: His Life, His Works, His Remains: As Revealed by Original Printed and Manuscript Records, Together with an Essay on Peter Martyr of Anghera and Bartolomé de Las Casas, the First Historians of America, Volume 2. New York: G.P. Putnam's Sons. pp. 435.

[10]Cueno, M. (1963). Michele de Cuneo's Letter on the Second Voyage, 28 October 1495. In S.E. Morison (Ed.). *Journals and Other Documents on the Life and Voyages of Christopher Columbus.* New York: Heritage Press. pp 209-28.

[11]Tremlett, G. (2006, August 7). Lost document reveals Columbus as tyrant of the Caribbean. *The Guardian.* Retrieved from http://www.theguardian.com/world/2006/aug/07/books.spain

[12]Springer, K. (1999). The Fact and Fiction of Vikings in America. Nebraska Anthropologist. Paper 124. Retrieved from http://digitalcommons.unl.edu/cgi/viewcontent.cgi?article=1123&context=nebanthro

[13]Irving, W. (1896). *Columbus, His Life and Voyages.* New Rochelle, New York: The Knickerbocker Press. pp. 216.

[14]Shujaa, M.J. and Shujaa, K (2015). The Sage Encyclopedia of African Cultural Heritage in North America. Thousand Oaks, California: Sage Publications.

[15]Picture taken by Wikimedia user Mesoamerican. Retrieved from: https://commons.wikimedia.org/wiki/File:Olmec_Head_No._1.jpg

[16]Ibid, pp. 664.

[17]Jacobs, W. (1974, Jan). The Tip of an Iceberg: Pre-Columbian Indian Demography and Some Implications for Revisionism. The William and Mary Quarterly, 3rd Scr. (31)1. pp. 123-132.

[18]Las Casas, B. (2007). A Brief Account of the Destruction of the Indies. (Original work 1552). Project Gutenburg. Retrieved from http://www-personal.umich.edu/~twod/latam-s2010/read/las_casasb2032120321-8.pdf

[19] Las Casas, B. (2007). A Brief Account of the Destruction of the Indies. (Original work 1552). Project Gutenburg. Retrieved from http://www-personal.umich.edu/~twod/latam-s2010/read/las_casasb2032120321-8.pdf

Chapter 7: "LINCOLN FREED THE SLAVES"

[1]Lindgren, J. Ranking Our Presidents: How did 78 Scholars Decided (sic) How to Rank the presidents from Washington to Clinton?. Retrieved from http://history-world.org/pres.pdf.

[2]Newport, F. (2011). Americans Say Reagan is the Greatest U.S. President. Gallup. Retrieved from http://www.gallup.com/poll/146183/Americans-Say-Reagan-Greatest-President.aspx.

[3]Rottinghaus, B. and Vaughn, J. (February 16, 2015). New Ranking of U.S. Presidents puts Lincoln at No. 1, Obama at 18; Kennedy Judged Most Overrated. The Washington Post.

[4]Hornick, E. (January 18, 2009). For Obama, Lincoln was Model President. CNN. Retrieved from http://www.cnn.com/2009/POLITICS/01/17/lincoln.obsession/index.html?eref=onion

[5]King, Jr., M.L., (August 28, 1963). I Have a Dream. Delivered at Lincoln Memorial, Washington, D.C. American Rhetoric: Top 100 Speeches. Retrieved from http://www.americanrhetoric.com/speeches/mlkihaveadream.htm

[6]The quote "the business of the United States is business" is actually a common misquote of a 1925 statement of President Calvin Coolidge. Coolidge actually said "the chief business of the American people is business". Retrieved from http://www.thisdayinquotes.com/2010/01/business-of-america-is-business.html

[7]Hudson, C. and Tesser, C.C. (eds.). (1994). The Forgotten Centuries: Indians and Europeans in the American South 1521-1704. Athens, GA: University of Georgia Press.

[8]Zinn, H. (2005) *The People's History of the United States.* New York, NY: Harper Perennial. Retrieved from http://www.historyisaweapon.com/defcon1/zinncolorline.html

[9]The Emancipation Wars. National Library of Jamaica. Retrieved from http://www.nlj.gov.jm/history-notes/The%20Emancipation%20Wars.pdf

[10]Ibid. pp. 19.

[11]Alexander, L. and Rucker, W. (Ed.) (2010). *Encyclopedia of African American History.* Santa Barbara, California: ABC-CLIO.

[12]*Declaration of Independence.* (1776, reprinted 1910) Washington, D.C.: Department of State. Retrieved from https://books.google.com/books?id=TNRCAAAAIAAJ&printsec=frontcover&source=gbs_ge_summary_r&cad=0#v=onepage&q&f=false

[13]A study which found that 41 of the 56 signers enslaved Africans at some point was conducted by the 8th Grade students at Chardon Middle School in Chardon, Ohio during October, 2014. Results were retrieved from http://www.mrheintz.com/how-many-signers-of-the-declaration-of-independence-owned-slaves.html

[14] *Slave Petition for Freedom to the Massachusetts Legislature. (January 13, 1777).* Heritage Foundation. Retrieved from http://www.heritage.org/initiatives/first-principles/primary-sources/slave-petition-for-freedom-to-the-massachusetts-legislature

[15]Johnson, R. (Contributor). *Lord Dunmore's Proclamation on Slave Emancipation (1775).* Retrieved from http://www.upa.pdx.edu/IMS/currentprojects/TAHv3/Content/PDFs/Dunmore_Proclamation_1775.pdf

[16]Vaughan, D.M. (February 24, 1964). *This Was a Man: A Biography of General William Whipple.* Read at a Meeting of The National Society of The Colonial Dames in the State of New Hampshire. Retrieved from http://www.whipple.org/william/thiswasaman.html

[17]Douglass, F. (July 4, 1852). *What To The American Slave Is Your 4th Of July?* Retrieved from https://brainmass.com/file/1385559/Douglass_July_4_1852.pdf.

[18]Gates, Jr, H.L. (March 25, 2013). *Who Really Ran the Underground Railroad?* Website: The Root. Retrieved from: http://www.theroot.com/articles/history/2013/03/who_really_ran_the_underground_railroad.html

[19]Maass, A. (April 12, 2011). The Struggle that Set the Stage for a Civil War. Website: Socialistworker.org. Retrieved from: http://socialistworker.org/2011/04/12/struggle-before-the-civil-war.

[20]Ibid.

[21]Roberts, T. (2003). *New England Antislavery Society.* Dictionary of American History. Retrieved from http://www.encyclopedia.com/doc/1G2-3401802935.html

[22]Swift, L. (1911). *William Lloyd Garrison.* Philadelphia: George W. Jacobs & Company. pp. 85.

[23]Jefferson, T. (April 13, 1820). Thomas Jefferson to William Short, April 13, 1820. The Thomas Jefferson Papers at the Library of Congress. Retrieved from: http://www.loc.gov/item/mtjbib023789/

[24]Basler, R.P. (1953). *The Collected Works of Abraham Lincoln, Volume IV.* New Brunswick, NJ: Rutgers University Press. pp. 16.

[25]Basler, R.P. (1953). *The Collected Works of Abraham Lincoln, Volume III.* New Brunswick, NJ: Rutgers University Press. pp. 440.

[26]Stevenson, J. (Spring 1994). Lincoln vs. Douglas Over the Republican Ideal. American Studies Journal. (35) 1. pp. 73.

[27]Taney, R. (1857). The Dred Scott Decision. Website: Digital History. Retrieved from http://www.digitalhistory.uh.edu/disp_textbook.cfm?smtID=3&psid=293

[28]Lincoln, A and Douglas, S.A. (September 18, 1858). Fourth Debate: Charleston, Illinois. Website: National Park Service. Retrieved from http://www.nps.gov/liho/learn/historyculture/debate4.htm.

[29]Ibid.

[30]Lincoln, A. (June 26, 1857). *Speech on the Dred Scott Decision.* Website: TeachingAmericanHistory.org. Retrieved from http://teachingamericanhistory.org/library/document/speech-on-the-dred-scott-decision/

[31]*Mr. Lincoln and Negro Equality.* (December 28, 1860). New York Times. Website: The New York Times. Retrieved from http://www.nytimes.com/1860/12/28/news/mr-lincoln-and-negro-equality.html?pagewanted=all

[32]The recent discovery of a form letter authored by Lincoln to present the amendment which would have restricted the federal government's ability to "end" enslavement may demonstrate his support for continuing enslavement with the purpose of bring the confederate state back into the union. Lupton, John. *Abraham Lincoln and the Corwin Amendment.* Website: Illinois Periodicals Online. Retrieved from http://www.lib.niu.edu/2006/ih060934.html

[33]Ibid

[34]Dobak, W. (2011). *Freedom by the Sword: The U.S. Colored Troops, 1862-1867.* Washington, D.C.: Center for Military History. pp. 3.

[35]Holzer, H., Medford, E.G., and Williams, F.J. (2006). *The Emancipation Proclamation: Three Views.* Baton Rouge, Louisiana: LSU Press. pp. 7.

[36]Ibid, pp. 7

[37]War Department of the United States. (1894).*The War of the Rebellion: A Compilation of the Official Records of the Union and Confederate Armies.* Washington, D.C.: U.S. Government Printing Office. pp. 760.

[38]Ibid, pp. 760.

[39]Douglass, F. (April 1865). *What the Black Man Wants.* Delivered at the Annual Meeting of the Massachusetts Anti-Slavery Society at Boston Reprinted in Bascom, L. (2009). *What the Black Man Wants.* Voices of the African American Experience. Santa Barbara, California: ABC-CLIO. pp. 213.

[40]Lincoln, A. (March 4, 1861*). First Inaugural Address.* Website: Bartleby.com. Retrieved from http://www.bartleby.com/124/pres31.html

[41]Rodriguez, J. (1997). *The Historical Encyclopedia of World Slavery* Santa Barbara, California: ABC-CLIO. pp. 181

[42]Lincoln, A. (August 22, 1862). *Letter to Horace Greeley.* Website: Abraham Lincoln Online. Retrieved from: http://www.abrahamlincolnonline.org/lincoln/speeches/greeley.htm

[43]Most of the information taken from *33b. Strengths and Weaknesses: North vs. South.* Website: U.S. History.org. Retrieved from http://www.ushistory.org/us/33b.asp

[44]Sheehan-Dean, A. (January 25, 2012). *Causes of Confederate Defeat in the Civil War.* Website: Encyclopedia Virginia.org Retrieved from http://www.encyclopediavirginia.org/causes_of_confederate_defeat_in_the_civil_war.

[45]Lincoln, A. (August 14, 1862). *Address on Colonization to a Committee of Colored Men.* Reprinted in Hammond, S.J., Hardwick, K.R. and Lubert, H.L. (2007). *Classics of American Political and Constitutional Thought: Origins through the Civil War.* Indianapolis, Indiana: Hackett Publishing. pp. 1100-1101.

[46]Cornish, D.T. (1965). *The Sable Arm: Black Troops in the Union Army, 1861-1865.* New York, NY: W.W. Norton. & Company

[47]Friedheim, W. and Jackson, R. (1996). *Freedom's Unfinished Revolution: An Inquiry Into the Civil War and Reconstruction*
New York, NY: The New Press. pp. 8.

Conclusion: A Blueprint for the Rehabilitation of the Black Image

[1]Woodson, C.G. (1933). *The Mis-education of the Negro.* Washington, D.C.: The Associated Publishers, Inc. pp. 71.

[2]Twenge, J.M. and Crocker, J. (May 2002). Race and self-esteem: Meta-analyses Comparing Whites, Blacks, Hispanics, Asians, and American Indians and Comment on Gray-Little and Hafdahl. *Psychological Bulletin*, 128(3), pp. 371-408. http://dx.doi.org/10.1037/0033-2909.128.3.371

[3]Richman, C. L., Clark, M.L., and Brown, K.P. (1989). General and Specific Self-esteem in late adolescent students: Race×Gender×SES effects. Adolescence, 20(79), pp. 555-566.

[4]Bachman, J.G. and O'Malley, P.M. (November 1984). Black-White Differences in Self-Esteem: Are They Affected by Response Styles? *American Journal of Sociology*, 90(3), pp. 624-639.

[5]Steele, C. (1992). Race and the schooling of Black Americans. *The Atlantic Monthly*, 269(4).

[6] Steele, C. (1997). A threat in the air: How stereotypes shape intellectual identity and performance. *American Psychologist*, 52

[7] Hunt, L and Hunt, J. (October 1975). Race and the Father-Son Connection: The Conditional Relevance of Father Absence for the Orientations and Identities of Adolescent Boys. Social Problems, 23(1). pp. 35-52. DOI: 10.1525/sp.1975.23.1.03a00040

[8]Abrahams, I. and Montefiore, C.G.(eds.) (July 1900). The Jewish Sunday School Movement in the United States. *Jewish Quarterly Review*, 12(48). pp. 563-601.

[9]Fernandez, M and Hauser, C. (October 5, 2015). Texas Mother Teaches Textbook Company a Lesson on Accuracy. The New York Times. Retrieved from: http://www.nytimes.com/2015/10/06/us/publisher-promises-revisions-after-textbook-refers-to-african-slaves-as-workers.html?_r=0

[10] Baker, C.D. (December 23, 2015). African-American's Buying Power Projected to be $1.1 Trillion By 2015. Black Enterprise. Retrieved from: http://www.blackenterprise.com/small-business/african-american-buying-power-projected-trillions/1

INDEX

ABOUT THE

AFRICAN GENESIS INSTITUTE

African Genesis Institute Founders
Helen and Ali Salahuddin

The African Genesis Institute is a 501c-3, nonprofit, "school without walls". Its focus is to teach African American and Latino youth, ages 7 - 14, the correct history of their ancestors and ancestral home. The mission of the African Genesis Institute is to raise the race and self-esteem of the students, improve their academic and financial literacy, promote a healthy lifestyle and encourage entrepreneurship. The

Institute's slogan, "It is better to build a child than repair an adult", aptly describes the importance it places on our youth.

The aims of the institute are accomplished through a 27-month study program focused on teaching students ancient African history utilizing curricula designed by Dr. Edward Robinson, Chike Akua and Jabari Osaze. The program consists of educational workshops, reading assignments, oral presentations, and study tours to important historic sites in the United States and Canada. Upon graduation, the students and their adult group leader take free trip to Egypt (Kemet).

The Institute was founded in 1993 by the husband and wife team of Helen and Ali Salahuddin in their native Philadelphia. Initially it named the d'Zert Club and featured afternoon dance parties for teenagers and cultural events such as Kwanzaa and Juneteenth celebrations. After drawing inspiration from the Million Man March, the Institute's mission became educational. The current program was created after the founders traveled to Africa in 1996. The first graduating class traveled to Senegal in 1998. Over 3,000 diasporan Africans have sojourned to their African motherland since the program's inception. Perhaps most remarkable about this milestone is that it has been accomplished primarily through internal fundraising within the African American and Latino communities. The institute has never received donations from large, European controlled corporations.

For more information about the African Genesis Institute, visit AfricanGenesis2.org, email AfricanGenesis@aol.com, or call 215-247-1545.

ABOUT THE AUTHOR
JABARI OSAZE
HISTORIAN • MEDIA CRITIC • KEMETIC PRIEST • EDUCATOR

Jabari Osaze leading a tour of the Holy of Holies in Karnak Temple in Kemet. Osaze has been facilitating tours in Africa since 2002.

Jabari Osaze has studied ancient Africa for over 25 years, focusing primarily on Ancient Kemetic (Egyptian) history and spirituality. Brother Osaze has led annual study tours to Egypt since 2002 in partnership with the African Genesis Institute. More than 3,000 people seeking to uncover the wisdom and accomplishments of ancient Africans have taken these epic journeys. He has also led monthly tours of the world-renowned Egyptian collections of the Metropolitan Museum of Art, the Brooklyn Museum, the University of Pennsylvania Museum of Archaeology and Anthropology, the Oriental Institute of the University of Chicago, and the Museum of Fine Arts in Boston.

Brother Osaze obtained his Bachelor of Science degree in Human Services and Africana Studies from Cornell University. He began focusing on the *practice* of the Ancient Egyptian (Kemetic) ideal. He currently serves as the Chief Priest of the Shrine of Ma'at. Mr. Osaze obtained his Master of Science in Administration from the Metropolitan College of New York and is a doctoral candidate at the University of Metaphysical Sciences. In 2006, He and his wife Anika Daniels-Osaze co-founded the Center for the Restoration of Ma'at; an institution devoted to the application of the Ancient African ethical paradigm in our daily lives. He is the executive producer and co-host of the weekly television show, Kemetic Legacy Today—the journal of Ancient Kemetic and Ancient African history and spirituality. The consummate historian/priest, Brother Osaze teaches a variety of courses on ancient African history, and lectures on a wide variety of historical and motivational topics. He is a proud resident of the village of Harlem, NY.

Made in the USA
Middletown, DE
10 March 2016